PRAISE FOR *REAL M...*

Thank you Grace and Mark for your extraordinary transparency and spot-on biblical insights. Whether engaged, newlywed, or veteran, *Real Marriage* will serve as an invaluable resource. I highly recommend this book.

ANDY STANLEY, AUTHOR OF *THE GRACE OF GOD* AND
SENIOR PASTOR, NORTH POINT COMMUNITY CHURCH

With more and more couples living more like business partners rather than friends, we don't need another safe, sterile marriage book. We need a direct, compassionate and realistic view of what marriage is, what it can be, and how we can lovingly befriend our spouse for a lifetime. Mark and Grace have helped all of us who have vowed "I do" to wildly enjoy our spouses.

DARRIN PATRICK, LEAD PASTOR,
THE JOURNEY, ST. LOUIS, MISSOURI

Real Marriage is brutally and sometimes painfully honest. Further, it is frank and direct in addressing a number of important marital issues. Sometimes you probably will feel uncomfortable. And, you may not agree with everything Grace and Mark Driscoll say. We didn't. However, this is a book we will gladly use and recommend to others who care about healthy, biblical marriages. We believe both husbands and wives will be blessed by and benefit from its content. Grace and Mark are to be commended for writing a book that bares their souls and, more importantly, points to the redeeming power of the gospel in the sacred covenant called marriage.

CHARLOTTE AND DANIEL AKIN,
SOUTHEASTERN BAPTIST THEOLOGICAL SEMINARY

Real Marriage is a powerfully transparent perspective on marriage for all couples, both single and married.

MILES MCPHERSON,
SR. PASTOR, ROCK CHURCH

Wow! This is the most vulnerable marriage book we've ever read. Its honesty will take your breath away. Mark and Grace expose their relationship—its pain and passion—for all who care to learn the rudiments of real marriage. They don't dance around the tough issues. They don't tip-toe over dicey topics. The Driscolls jump in with wild abandon, and the result is a book that is frank but not crass, practical but not pedantic. If you're married or plan to be someday, do yourself a favor and read every page of this book.

DRS. LES & LESLIE PARROTT,
FOUNDERS OF *REALRELATIONSHIPS.COM* AND AUTHORS OF *LOVE TALK*

At last . . . a marriage book that balances pastoral compassion with prophetic courage! The taboo questions every couple secretly wants to ask are courageously confronted without compromising God's Word or will for couples. Mark and Grace have taken the subject of marriage to an unprecedented place of true transparency, profound practicality, and scriptural solidity . . . which is a place every marriage needs to be.

BOB COY, SENIOR PASTOR,
CALVARY CHAPEL FORT LAUDERDALE

Mark and Grace have written an extraordinary book characterized by compassion for a bewildered generation that has failed to grasp the significance of marriage and covenant love, conviction that God's grace and truth provide healing and guidance, and courage to go where few would dare to go as they display a costly and selfless transparency.

TERRY AND WENDY VIRGO,
NEW FRONTIERS AND CHURCH OF CHRIST THE KING,
BRIGHTON, ENGLAND

One of my greatest concerns is that culture is going to continually define and redefine what marriage is and is not, and the church is going to simply sit on the sidelines and react rather than seeking to actually become proactive by confidently teaching what the Bible has to say about it. That is why I am so thankful that Mark and Grace Driscoll wrote this book. Their approach to marriage, its benefits and challenges, is transparent and challenging, and I honestly believe that every married couple who will work through what they lead us through in this book will not just merely have a marriage that survives in this world bur rather thrives in it.

PERRY NOBLE, SENIOR PASTOR,
NEWSPRING CHURCH

While some sections will be controversial, this book as a whole is a wise, insightful, biblical, and startlingly honest guide to a happy marriage. Mark and Grace Driscoll rightly warn about the long-lasting consequences of sexual sin, point the way to a very happy marriage in obedience to God, and bravely address questions that are rarely brought up in a church setting. We are happy to recommend it.

WAYNE AND MARGARET GRUDEM,
PHOENIX SEMINARY, PHOENIX, ARIZONA

Our thanks to Mark and Grace Driscoll, who have served this generation well by tastefully but boldly addressing the real issues facing real marriages. Taking the unchanging truth of God's word and sprinkling in the story of God's mercy in their own marriage, they have filled every chapter with real helpfulness. This book is powerful, biblical, practical and healing for marriages that hurt. My wife and our adult children read it to great profit.

DR. JAMES MACDONALD,
SENIOR PASTOR, HARVEST BIBLE CHAPEL AND
BIBLE TEACHER FOR WALK IN THE WORD

REAL
MARRIAGE

REAL
MARRIAGE

THE TRUTH ABOUT
SEX, FRIENDSHIP
& LIFE TOGETHER

MARK  GRACE
DRISCOLL

THOMAS NELSON
Since 1798

NASHVILLE   DALLAS   MEXICO CITY   RIO DE JANEIRO

© 2012 by On Mission, LLC

All rights reserved. No portion of this book may be reproduced, stored in a retrieval system, or transmitted in any form or by any means—electronic, mechanical, photocopy, recording, scanning, or other—except for brief quotations in critical reviews or articles, without the prior written permission of the publisher.

Published in Nashville, Tennessee, by Thomas Nelson. Thomas Nelson is a registered trademark of Thomas Nelson, Inc.

Published in association with Yates & Yates, LLP, www.yates2.com.

Thomas Nelson, Inc., titles may be purchased in bulk for educational, business, fund-raising, or sales promotional use. For information, please e-mail SpecialMarkets@ThomasNelson.com.

Unless otherwise noted, Scripture is taken from the NEW KING JAMES VERSION®. © 1982 by Thomas Nelson, Inc. Used by permission. All rights reserved.

Scripture quotations marked NIV are taken from the Holy Bible, New International Version®, NIV®. © 1973, 1978, 1984, 2011 by Biblica, Inc.™ Used by permission of Zondervan. All rights reserved worldwide. www.zondervan.com

ISBN 978-1-4002-0538-7 (TP)

The Library of Congress has cataloged the hardcover edition as follows:

Driscoll, Mark, 1970-
    Real marriage : the truth about sex, friendship, and life together / Mark and Grace Driscoll.
        p. cm.
    Includes bibliographical references and index.
    ISBN 978-1-4002-0383-3 (alk. paper)
    1. Spouses--Religious life. 2. Marriage--Religious aspects--Christianity. 3. Sex in marriage--Religious aspects--Christianity. I. Driscoll, Grace. II. Title.
    BV4596.M3D75 2012
    248.8'44--dc23

                                                                    2011028613

Printed in the United States of America

13 14 15 16 17 QG 5 4 3 2 1

CONTENTS

PREFACE

How *Not* to Read This Book

This is a costly book.

It cost many couples a lot to learn the hard lessons they have shared with us so that we can share them with you. It cost us a lot to learn from our mistakes and sins so that we could have something to share. It cost Jesus His life, as He died to forgive our sin and give us a new life together, which includes our family and ministry. And it will cost you as well. It will cost you time to read it, emotion to consider it, and energy to discuss and implement it.

Because we are a pastor and his wife, we really do want this book to be used of God to help people. It's the kind of book we wished we could have read earlier in our marriage, and wish we could have given to those we served in ministry. So we wrote what we hope is a book that is biblically faithful, emotionally hopeful, practically helpful, sociologically viable, and personally vulnerable.

Before you read our book, there are some ways *not* to read it:

Don't read as a voyeur trying to figure out our sex life. Grace and I are honest throughout the book, hoping you will be able to trust us and also be honest with your spouse and others you trust. Our desire is to help you focus on *yourself* and *your marriage* rather than us and our marriage.

Don't read as a critic trying to find where you think we might be wrong. Although we seek to be faithful to the Bible, this book is not the Bible, and, like you, we are imperfect, so there will be mistakes. Take whatever gifts you find in this book, and feel free to leave the rest.

Don't read sections of the book and tell your spouse, "I told you so." This book is not meant to be a pile of rocks for you to throw at each other in bitterness.

Don't say, "I [we] tried that, and it did not work." If it's rooted in biblical wisdom, keep trying until it works or you die. Try to do it better, more consistently, or differently.

Don't keep thinking about all the other people who need to read this book. Read it for yourself first, and don't fall into the religious trap of ignoring your own spiritual growth by always reading for others and not yourself.

Don't be lazy and unwilling to put in the work that this book requires. We did not write to give you just another book on marriage to add to your stack, but rather to provide an opportunity for the Holy Spirit to give you some things to work hard at in your life and marriage.

Do not read this book seeing your spouse's shortcomings and sins as planks and yours as specks. The small specks are in their eye; the planks are in yours.

Do not fool yourself that you are the exception because of some extenuating life circumstances.

Do not read this book trying to find a way to have a "good enough" (but not great) marriage. Yes, if you really get into the issues in your marriage, you will likely have seasons of crisis and chaos to overcome before you get to a better place. But that is far better than faking it, as too many couples do. The good times do not come despite the bad times; they come after them, if you deal with them.

Do not just read this book, but also talk about it often with your spouse, chapter by chapter. As you do, don't let your tongue get beyond your control. Proverbs 18:21 says, "Death and life are in the power of the tongue." Proverbs 12:18 says, "There is one who speaks like the piercings of a sword." Simply, speak the truth in love and pray for your heart and words so you don't attack, instigate, or lie.

Don't copy our methods. The principles in this book are more important than the methods. Principles are timeless and unchanging. Methods vary from marriage to marriage and person to person. Many marriage books focus too heavily on methods that worked for one couple's marriage, but because you and your spouse are unique, those methods may not work for you and your marriage. So, please do not confuse principles and methods. Hold fast to biblical principles and remain flexible and teachable with methods for your marriage.

In closing, thank you for taking the time to read our book. As a ministry couple, it honestly means the world to us that we might be able to serve you in some way.

Pastor Mark and Grace Driscoll

INTRODUCTION

The couple were devout Christians and virgins when they first met. Forty years later, the pain of their marriage showed on their faces. As they spoke to me of their troubles during our pastoral counseling session in my office, they each hung their heads in loneliness and grief.

There had been no adultery. There had been no divorce. But there had been no friendship. Although they did a lot of work together, they hadn't had much fun. With their children grown and home empty, the glue that once held them together was gone, and they were reduced to life as nearly sexless roommates.

In the most painfully awkward moment of the conversation, I asked the wife what she wanted from her husband. She said that every evening for forty years she had sat on the couch just wanting him to sit and visit with her for twenty to thirty minutes. But he rarely did. Indeed, twenty to thirty minutes is not a lot of time. But when it is missed nearly every day for forty years, a debt of roughly five thousand to seven thousand hours has accrued.

The husband tried to defend himself, talking about the quality times they had, in an effort to excuse the lack of quantity time. But she would have none of it as her bitterness and loneliness seeped out. What wisdom could touch the pain caused by a dying marriage? I struggled with that question as I counseled this couple, and it became obvious to me that they had missed out on God's true design for marriage and sex. And they were far from alone in their struggles.

When my wife, Grace, and I speak at marriage conferences, an overwhelming number of people of all ages come up to us with the most heartbreaking stories of loneliness, marital infidelity, childhood abuse, and extremely detailed "can we do this or that?" sex questions. Often their shame and embarrassment keep them from getting the help they need in their marriages. Also, our church, Mars Hill in Seattle, has people from all ages and life stages but is a young congregation, with lots of twenties and thirties, many singles, and a higher-than-usual percentage of guys. Subsequently, we have spent more than fifteen years counseling people before they were married about how to live as a Christian in such a sexualized culture, what's okay—from a biblical perspective—to do in bed once you are married, and how to deal with intimacy issues all throughout married life.

Grace and I weren't strangers to those issues ourselves. As a young couple we had to deal with the fallout from sexual sin before our marriage, and we hadn't had anyone we could turn to for help. The ramifications would play out in some painful and frustrating ways over the years, as you'll read later in this book, but by the grace of God, we've been able to work through the mess and have emerged as best friends and lovers in the way God intended.

For such a big issue, most teaching on sex inside the church is inadequate, and most teaching on it outside the church is perverted. Fortunately, God has a lot to say to us on the topic of sex and marriage. He planned both, and He gave them to us as wonderful gifts to be enjoyed. In this book we share biblical truths about some of the marital issues you may face, including how to be your spouse's best friend, dealing with porn addiction, overcoming sexual assault, how to avoid being a selfish lover, and yes, even those sex questions you'd be too embarrassed to ask anyone, especially your pastor. We pray this book will be a blessing to your marriage

Part 1
MARRIAGE

1

NEW MARRIAGE,
SAME SPOUSE

Behold, I make all things new.

—REVELATION 21:5

How is your love life?

Are you single, hoping to meet someone and live happily ever after? Seeing someone and contemplating marriage? Maybe you're newly married and still filled with wedded bliss, or a married couple so exhausted from the constant demands of work and parenting that your marriage is slipping. You may be reeling from a devastating sin in your marriage. Or the two of you are still in love and doing pretty well, but you want to avoid ending up like other couples you know who are not getting along and possibly even getting divorced. Perhaps you are empty nesters who have realized that the kids largely held together your family, and you don't have a close friendship now that they're out of the house. Are you a parent or grandparent concerned for the marriage of your child or grandchild? Divorced and trying to figure out what went wrong and how not to endure that pain again? A leader who seeks to help people struggling with relationship issues?

Whether you or someone you know has a problem in marriage—or are trying to avoid one—my wife, Grace, and I hope to help. We want to serve you in this book. So we will be honest about our own failures, sins, mistakes, and griefs. Even a pastor and his wife come into marriage with baggage and a few carry-ons. But God has been faithful to us, and we trust Him to be faithful to you as well. To get started, we thought it would be helpful for us to share our story in hopes that you would get to know us a bit, thereby providing some context for what we write in this book and hopefully earning your trust.

———

Can you imagine being onstage in front of thousands of people, answering the most intimate questions about sex and relationships? That's where I (Grace) found myself a couple of years ago when my husband was preaching the Song of Solomon to our church. At the end of his teaching, I would join Mark onstage, where we'd sit as members of the congregation texted us their questions, which would appear on a big screen next to us. We took turns answering everything from "How long should I wait for my boyfriend to commit to me?" to "Why should I stop sleeping with my girlfriend when we've been together for five years?"

I had prayed for months about whether I should join Mark onstage for this. *What if someone asks me something too embarrassing to answer? What if I say something that sounds foolish? Will people think Mark and I are claiming to know all the answers?* In the end, I made the decision to step out in faith. No, we don't know all the answers, but we have studied for years what God says on the subjects of sex and marriage. And we have certainly learned a lot the hard way. Like many, we entered marriage with a load of habits, secrets, and preconceptions that could have killed our marriage.

For me, the seeds for the potential destruction of my marriage were planted as a child. As a pastor's kid, I gave in to the pressure to pretend that everything was perfect and avoided looking sinful. Unfortunately, it is common for pastors' kids to believe they can't be themselves for fear of ruining the ministry of the church somehow. We often practiced the "silent treatment" when we were upset, rather than dealing with sin issues kindly and honestly, so I learned to hide my sin from my parents and others. I was also afraid of the conflict and exposure it would take to resolve it. I had the misconception that Christianity was just having good values and acting right on the "outside," but I didn't understand true heart-changing repentance. I often felt shame when I sinned but didn't know how to get past it by confessing the sin, asking God and the other person I sinned against to forgive me, receiving that forgiveness, and asking Jesus to help me turn from that sin by the power of the Holy Spirit.

My oldest sister and I had a rough relationship growing up, and I remember often saying I was sorry, but don't recall really feeling bad that I had hurt her. It was more like a script I read to move on or get out of my bedroom "time-out."

Now when I sin I actually feel the impact of sinning against a holy God and whoever else might be involved, which is prompted by the Holy Spirit. If I had understood the gospel more deeply, I would have known that repentance keeps shame from condemning us because Jesus died and scorned the shame.[a]

Though repentance is humbling, there is such a freedom in allowing Jesus to replace sin with His free gift of righteousness. Sadly, I became great at lying and pretending I was a good person. I didn't fully understand my sin nature and need for Jesus to die for my sins. Upon entering junior high, I still lacked confidence and went through two very awkward years believing I had no value. Even though I was a Christian, I still didn't realize my identity needed to be founded on God creating me in His image and Jesus gifting me with His righteousness. I did well in school and started to make friends, thinking I was doing better, but not giving credit to God for giving me those abilities. That's when I met a handsome young man named Mark.

———

I (Mark) was raised in a very rough neighborhood near the airport in Seattle before it was incorporated as a city. Without a local police force, it resembled the Wild West. There were multiple strip clubs, seedy massage parlors, and hourly rate motels down the street from my home. The prostitutes walked the streets openly and were brazen enough to even walk up and knock on my car window, seeking "business," as I waited for the light to turn green. Some of these young women attended my high school; and serial killers murdered some of them. Ted Bundy and the Green River Killer picked up many of their victims in my neighborhood, even dumping at least two of their bodies at my Little League field.

The men on my father's side include uneducated alcoholics, mental patients, and women beaters. This includes an uncle who died of gangrene and his sons, roughly my age, who have been in prison for beating women and were supposedly on the television show *Cops*. One of the main reasons my parents moved from North Dakota to Seattle was to get away from some family members when I was a very young boy.

———

a Heb. 12:2.

Growing up, my goal was to get out of my neighborhood and enjoy a new and better life. I remember building forts as a young boy and treating them as my own home. I did not want to get trapped by gangs, drugs, alcohol, crime, or manipulative women. I wanted to get an education; make some money; live in a better neighborhood; marry a nice, beautiful woman; and be a father. This was my vision from a very young age.

I did not drink, and to this day have never done any drugs or taken a puff of a cigarette. I did well in sports and school. By fifteen I had lied about my age, falsified my birth certificate, bought a car, and drove myself to work at a 7-Eleven (near the strip clubs), where I sold liquor, condoms, porn, and rubbing alcohol for freebasing drug addicts who lived in the low-income apartments next door. Around this time I also started having sex with a girlfriend.

I was the "good guy" in my high school. I graduated high school "Most Likely to Succeed," student body president, Man of the Year, editor of the school newspaper, and a four-year letterman in baseball. I was part of a bond campaign to renovate our school and was active in a state political campaign. I was a moral, religious boy from a Catholic home who, for the most part, stayed out of trouble despite a short wick, foul mouth, and bad temper that resulted in doling out more than a few beatings to various guys—usually for what they were doing to women and children. In short, I was a good guy and a tough guy, so I thought.

At seventeen I became smitten with a cute girl named Grace who was a grade older in school. A friend in common introduced us, and before long we were going out on our first date. Grace was a pastor's daughter, and although she was a Christian, she had fallen into drinking and partying. Underneath the "fun girl" image, though, she was hurting. It was a lonely place for a young woman to be. She was the youngest of three girls and was very shy and naive, not understanding the world around her.

Innocence in a child is normal and healthy, but naivety is when you believe things or trust people without ever questioning them, and it leads to a lack of discernment. Innocence is when a child trusts her parents, as she should be able to, and is free to grow and mature in wisdom with their guidance. Naivety, on the other hand, can be harmful to the person if, as a regular way of thinking, she is unaware of the dangers around her. For example, in college Grace used to walk alone at night around a dark and dangerous campus and would unknowingly put herself in dangerous positions with guys.

Neither Grace nor I was a virgin when we met, and before long we were dating and sleeping together, which continued even after she went off to college while I was finishing high school.

Upon graduation from high school, I was given a free senior trip to Mexico. The company representative said I would receive "VIP treatment" that included lots of alcohol and young women to sleep with. A few weeks before the trip, I declined the offer because I loved Grace and did not want to ruin my relationship with her.

Off to college I went, and—as an unbelieving freshman in college a few hundred miles away from Grace—I joined a fraternity. Our frat party was the first weekend, and while I was not planning on drinking, I was planning on attending the party and was tempted to see what might happen with the young women. Our frat filled the basement with music, beer, and black lights. Soon a parade of young women flooded the hot basement to dance and hand out variously colored highlighter pens, inviting the guys to draw on their white tank tops and T-shirts to glow in the dark. As I was walking into the basement room, I had a strong, strange sense that I should not enter, and I did not know why. I was not a Christian, but it seemed to me that if I walked through that door, my life course would change, and I knew I was supposed to turn and walk away. So I did, and only later came to realize it was God saving me from myself.

The next morning I awoke before anyone else, because I was not hung over. (I was possibly the only guy in the frat who did not drink.) Downstairs I encountered a sorority girl who was still drunk, confused, and crying. She was nearly naked, wrapped in a blanket, unsure of what happened to her, whom she woke up with, or where her clothes were. I gave her a pair of my sweats and walked her home. She cried the entire way, and that morning I decided to leave the frat, without having touched any young woman. And I missed Grace.

My pledge class ended up getting arrested. They spent evenings and weekends in jail or doing community service. I got out just in time by the grace of God.

Not long after, God saved me while I was sitting in my dorm, reading the Bible Grace had given me. Back in high school, once she suspected that I was probably not a Christian, she did not break up with me as she should have. Instead, she bought me a nice leather Bible with my name on it. I had not really read it up until that point, but kept it around as a sort of good-luck charm. That day I finally picked it up. I was not going to church, had not heard a gospel presentation or read the Bible, and no one led me to Christ. In Romans 1:6, I read, "You also are among those . . . who are called to belong to Jesus Christ" (NIV). God highlighted that statement in my soul, and it seemed evident to me from that moment forward that my life was not my own. I belonged to Jesus Christ like a tool in His hand for whatever He wanted.

I soon went searching for a church, unclear of what I was even looking for and afraid that I might end up in a cult. By God's grace, I ended up in a solid Bible-teaching church, where I was taught about Jesus, marriage, sex, and family. I absolutely loved my first church; the people were invaluable in teaching me about life as God intended, without pretention or legalistic rules. I often thank God that my first church was a wonderful church and one of the highlights of my entire life.

In the spring I attended my first men's retreat with the church. The pastor told us to spend some time in prayer with God. I went for a walk and asked God what He wanted me to do with the rest of my life. Uncertain of what would happen, I was basically just walking along a river in the Idaho woods, talking aloud to God, when He spoke to me. I had never experienced anything like that moment. God told me to devote my life to four things. He told me to marry Grace, preach the Bible, train men, and plant churches. Since that day in 1990, that's what I have been pursuing by God's grace.

When I got home, I called Grace to let her know what God had said. She was genuinely thrilled at my conversion and asked a number of questions about what God was teaching me through the Bible. We talked for what seemed like hours; she wanted to know about what church I had chosen as well as the multiple Bible study groups I had signed up for. She had returned to a growing relationship with Jesus after wandering for a few years drinking and partying with friends. Meanwhile, God was transforming me. As soon as she could, Grace transferred to my college and we began attending church together.

It was there I began learning about sex and marriage from the Bible. The pastor seemed to really love his wife, and they had a faithful and fun marriage. The previous church I had attended was Catholic, with a priest who seemed to be a gay alcoholic. He was the last person on earth I wanted to be like. To a young man, a life of poverty, celibacy, living at the church, and wearing a dress was more frightful than going to hell, so I stopped going to church somewhere around junior high. But this pastor was different. He had been in the military, had earned a few advanced degrees, and was smart. He was humble. He bow hunted. He had sex with his wife. He knew the Bible. He was not religious.

In that church I met other men who were very godly and masculine. There were farmers who loved Jesus, hunters who loved Jesus, and even one guy who was on his way to having eleven daughters and two sons with one wife. They had a beautiful family and sometimes invited Grace and me over for dinner. I had never seen a family pray the way they did, sing together, and pretty much just laugh and have fun. Watching that family, I learned about the importance of a dad praying and playing with his kids, reading the Bible to them, and teaching them to repent of their sin to one another and forgive others when sinned against. It was incredible. Before long, Grace and I were volunteering our Friday nights to babysit for free so they could get a date night.

Also, in this season we stopped sleeping together, which was a bummer for me. At a collegiate Bible study, a pastor taught from the Bible about the sin of fornication. To be honest, that f-word was new to me. It sounded as if he was saying that sex with a girlfriend you loved and planned to marry was wrong. I immediately thought, *Of course he doesn't mean that.* So I called that pastor on the phone and told him I had a "friend" I was afraid might be fornicating and wanted to double-check what fornication was. He took me to the Bible, where I realized I was a sinful fornicator.

To be honest, fornicating was fun. I liked fornicating. To stop fornicating was not fun. But eventually Grace and I stopped fornicating, got engaged, and were married between our junior and senior years of college.

I assumed that once we were married we would simply pick up where we left off sexually and make up for lost time. After all, we were committed Christians with a relationship done God's way.

But God's way was a total bummer. My previously free and fun girlfriend was suddenly my frigid and fearful wife. She did not undress in front of me, required the lights to be off on the rare occasions we were intimate, checked out during sex, and experienced a lot of physical discomfort because she was tense.

Before long I was bitter against God and Grace. It seemed to me as if they had conspired to trap me. I had always been the "good guy" who turned down women for sex. In my twisted logic, since I had only slept with a couple of women I was in relationships with, I had been holy enough, and God owed me. I felt God had conned me by telling me to marry Grace, and allowed Grace to rule over me since she was controlling our sex life. I loved Grace, but in the bedroom I did not enjoy her and wondered how many years I could white-knuckle fidelity. Grace was so full of shame and hurt from previous relationships that she didn't trust that I loved her, no matter how many times I said it. She became afraid of me and felt used as I tried to explain how she frustrated me sexually, which added to her feeling less valuable. We desperately needed help but didn't know where to turn. Bitterness and condemnation worsened.

Upon graduation we packed up our old Chevy truck and moved back to our hometown of Seattle, weeping as we drove away from our college town and beloved church. In Seattle we worked simple jobs to pay the bills, house-sat for some months, saving up enough money to rent an apartment, and finally settled in at a multiethnic suburban megachurch half an hour away, volunteering in the college ministry. Before long we were running the college ministry and moved into a rental home in the city near the colleges. We served there for a few years before starting our own new church.

As we both prayed about where to start the church, we felt called to pursue the seemingly impossible. Seattle was the least-churched city in the nation, and the least likely person to attend church there was a college-educated single person, especially a man. So, after fasting and praying over the decision, we decided to plant a church where the need was greatest, although the work was hardest and resourcing was least. We began gathering the core group of maybe a dozen people for our church plant in our home. From the outside, our marriage looked okay. We were still having weekly date nights and were faithful to each other, but in reality we were more life partners than lovers and friends, working jobs and hosting Bible studies to serve others. All our conversations revolved around other people and how to serve and help them. It seemed to be the "right" way to do ministry, but neglect of your own marriage is never the right way.

Making issues even worse, I (Grace) realized I hadn't really followed the Genesis command to leave my family and cleave to Mark as my new family. I still called my mom daily and complained when Mark and I were fighting;

we spent all our holidays, birthdays, and vacations with my side of the family, rather than starting some of our own family traditions. My parents had keys to the house and would stop by at any time unannounced, so we lacked privacy and I didn't see it as a problem. I called them "my family," which made Mark feel as if he and I weren't family. I had to learn to pray and work through our conflict differently, plan some of our own traditions and memories, set healthy boundaries of privacy, and refer to Mark as "my family" and others as our "extended family."

We did ministry nearly every night of the week, with a few thousand people in total passing through our home in a given year, and many even living with us at various times. I (Mark) am an introvert who prefers home to be a refuge, which meant the lack of distinction between ministry and home was killing me. All the while, though, our sex life was still less than stellar, and it became increasingly frustrating in the next few years as we taught premarital counseling to a few hundred couples. Every quarter a new class would pack into our home to hear, among other things, my detailed teaching from the Bible on the freedoms and joys of married sex, after which I would go to bed without enjoying much of it. My bitterness grew.

Our marriage was functional but not much fun. As we approached the launch of the church, Grace was pregnant with our first child and suffering from painful stress-related issues caused by her public relations job, which culminated in me apologizing for not bearing the entire financial burden for our family. She gladly came home from work, and we lived on a very small income from outside jobs and support, because the church plant could not afford to pay me during the first few years.

In this season we shifted into ministry-and-family mode, neglecting our intimacy and failing to work through our issues. This became apparent to me when my pregnant wife came home from a hair appointment with her previously long hair (that I loved) chopped off and replaced with a short, mommish haircut. She asked what I thought, and could tell from the look on my face. She had put a mom's need for convenience before being a wife. She wept.

One night, as we approached the birth of our first child, Ashley, and the launch of our church, I had a dream in which I saw some things that shook me to my core. I saw in painful detail Grace sinning sexually during a senior trip she took after high school when we had just started dating. It was so clear it was like watching a film—something I cannot really explain but the kind of revelation I sometimes receive. I awoke, threw up, and spent the rest of the night sitting on our couch, praying, hoping it was untrue, and waiting for her to wake up so I could ask her. I asked her if it was true, fearing the answer. Yes, she confessed, it was. Grace started weeping and trying to apologize for lying to me, but I honestly don't remember the details of the conversation, as I was shell-shocked. Had I known about this sin, I would not have married her. But God told me to marry Grace, I loved her, I had married her as a Christian, we were pregnant, and I was a pastor with a church plant filled with young people who were depending on me.

———

Grace: Mark had righteous anger and felt totally betrayed. He wondered who I really was and felt trapped, confused, and at a loss to know what in the world he would do now. A bomb had just dropped, and shrapnel was everywhere! *Dear Lord, how could I have done this to You and my husband? How could I have acted like such a good person with such darkness in my heart? How can I ever make up for what I have done?* Mark wished he hadn't married me; I wished I hadn't ever lied. I was pregnant and he felt trapped. I begged forgiveness but told him he had every right to leave. He felt completely stuck; I felt total shame. How could we ever get through this? Mark tried to get counsel from other men, but they didn't know what to say or do. I didn't think we should tell anyone since we were just planting the church, but that decision only made the pain go on longer for both of us. We should have sought counsel from someone, but we just both felt alone.

Where was the freedom I was supposed to feel after finally telling the truth? Why didn't we get closer in our marriage after exposing what seemed to be the deepest sin? God still needed to reveal more. He revealed the sin but wanted the heart and underlying motive to be exposed and repented of. He faithfully and miraculously kept us together so we could get to the next layers of pain and repentance, which wasn't for another seven years. All we knew was that we had made a covenant before God in 1992 to stay married for better and for worse (we thought nothing could be worse than this), no back door, and God had told Mark very clearly to marry me—it was all we had to hold on to.

Some people will use this story against Mark and me, but we want to share it to help those of you who also are hurting and want to work through deep areas of sin in your marriage (or future marriage). I want God to be able to use all my story to help others, including the difficult, more "secret" sins. Every time I sat down to write for this book, I prayed what the Lord told Paul in 2 Corinthians 12:9: "My grace is sufficient for you, for My strength is made perfect in weakness."

Mark: I knew Grace loved me, but to hear her admit that she chose in our premarital counseling not to confess the entirety of her past sins because she knew I would not marry her made me feel like a furiously trapped animal. I had idolized Grace as a functional savior, and marriage and family as a functional heaven. When I discovered her sin against me and that she had punished me with resulting years of sexual and emotional denial, I felt like a total fool, and my world crashed around me. It seemed everything I had been striving for since I was a little boy was in vain. In idolizing marriage, I ended up demonizing Grace and doubting God.

Grace: Most people who know me now wouldn't believe I would commit such an act of sin, let alone hide it from my husband for years. Yes, I was instructed to "tell all" in premarital counseling, and the Holy Spirit nudged me to tell the truth, but I blindly believed the lie that it would hurt Mark too much to tell him, and it was just a one-time mistake anyway. I also chose to believe the lie that it wouldn't affect me, Mark, our marriage, ministry, or other lives in any way. This set up our life on a foundation of dishonesty, and it began to feed my fears that I didn't deserve Mark as a husband—he was too good for me. I did things to sabotage our relationship, like neglecting him sexually, staying emotionally distant, and serving others' needs obsessively—thinking I was protecting myself for when he left me. I gave into the Enemy's trap and was responsible for causing Mark to feel very alone. I knew something was wrong but wasn't willing to look at the effects of my sin as the cause of any pain.

Mark: I had been out of touch with my old pastor since graduation and had no one to talk to. Some friends tried to give us counsel, and they meant well and did their best, but ultimately they were of little help. So I put my head down, kept my pants on, and decided not to be the porn or masturbation or adultery guy. I worked about twice as many hours a week as I should have for the next decade, pouring all my energy into ministry and my children, while settling for a frustrating, lukewarm love life. Grace's identity, too, became serving others and the church.

I grew more chauvinistic. I had never cheated on a girlfriend, but I never had a girlfriend who did not cheat on me. And now I knew that included my own wife. So I started to distrust women in general, including Grace. This affected my tone in preaching for a season, something I will always regret.

We didn't know how to talk through these extremely hard issues without hurting each other even more, so we didn't talk about them at all. I just got more bitter, and Grace just felt more condemned and broken, like a failure. Occasionally we'd meet a Christian pastor or counselor who was supposed to be an expert in these areas, but we never spoke with them in much detail, because in time we found out they either had marriages as bad as ours or they had been committing adultery and were disqualified for ministry. We felt very alone and stuck.

Grace: I look back and wish I had listened to God's voice urging me toward repentance, but in the following years I continued to be wounded and to wound people I loved. Mark and I grew more distant in our marriage. Communication was at an all-time low, as was our intimacy, and we became unable to serve each other without demanding something in return. We dealt with conflict very differently: he chose harsh words, and I chose silence. We both chose bitterness. As you can imagine, nothing really got resolved. Fear, lies, busyness, and discontentment all kept us from intimacy.

Mark: In the second year of the church, we had a lot of single people getting married, and so I decided to preach through the Song of Songs on the joys of marital intimacy and sex. The church grew quickly, lots of people got married, many women became pregnant, and my counseling load exploded. I started spending dozens of hours every week dealing with every kind of sexual issue imaginable. It seemed as if every other young woman in our church had been sexually assaulted in some fashion, every guy was ensnared by porn, and every married and premarital couple had a long list of tricky sex questions. Day after day, for what became years, I spent hours meeting with people, untangling the sexual knots in their lives, reading every book and section of the Bible I could find that related to their needs.

Although I loved our people and my wife, this only added to my bitterness.

I had a church filled with single young women who were asking me how they could stop being sexually ravenous and wait for a Christian husband; then I'd go home to a wife whom I was not sexually enjoying. One particularly low moment occurred when a newly saved married couple came in to meet with me. I prayed, and then asked how I could serve them. She took charge of the meeting, explained how she really liked her body and sex, and proceeded to take out a list of questions she had about what was acceptable as a Christian for her to do with her husband. It was a very long and very detailed list. As I answered each question, she would ask related follow-up questions with more specific details. Her husband said very little, but sat next to her, looking awkward and smiling at most of the answers I gave. After they left the counseling appointment to get to work on the list of acceptable activities, I remember sitting with my head in my hands, just moaning and asking God, "Do you really expect me to do this as a new Christian, without a mentor or pastor, in the midst of my marriage, and hold on for the next fifty years?" Peter walking on water seemed an easier task.

By a miracle of God's grace, we stayed faithful to each other in our marriage, without infidelity of any kind. We did have mediocre sex that eventually resulted in five children and one miscarriage. We really did love each other and wanted to connect, but often did not. We still disagree on how often we had sex (I was bitter, and she was in denial, which skews the perspective), but we both agree it wasn't a healthy amount to support a loving marriage. We kept date night every week and checked the dutiful boxes of a decent, respectable Christian marriage that would not disqualify us from ministry. We were together, but both very lonely.

This became increasingly apparent as we raised our firstborn, Ashley. I have always absolutely adored and enjoyed her. She, along with my other children, owns a special place in my heart. Grace often commented that she had never seen a dad as good as me, but did so in an aching way, as she longed for the same kind of love from me. The beginning of a breakthrough came when God spoke a word to me. He said that He was Grace's Father and had chosen me for the important mission of rescuing, protecting, and loving His daughter. This felt like a noble divine assignment and began to change my motivation for pursuing Grace, because I saw her for the first time as the Father's daughter—the Father who loved her as I loved my own daughters.

Then, after more than a decade of marriage, a root issue was finally revealed. Grace's problem was that she was an assault victim who had never told me or anyone else of the physical, spiritual, emotional, and sexual abuse she had suffered. Hearing the details of her abuse broke me. Reliving her pain with her as we worked things through was healing. Yes, it hurt deeply. But at least the hurt was from a surgery that would cut out the cancer. In forgiving and walking with Grace, I realized that I was so overbearing and boorish, so angry and harsh, that I had not been the kind of husband whom she could trust and confide in with the most painful and shameful parts of her past. I was world-class at truth telling, but my words would tear her down rather than build her up. I spoke to her more as I would to a sinful guy, but where men stood up to my challenges, she fell down. My bitterness had continued to condemn Grace, and she kept shutting down more. In it all, God was gracious and gave me a deeper love for Grace than ever, and gave her a willingness to forgive and work with me.

As Grace began working on her root issues, I hit the wall physically, emotionally, spiritually, and mentally. I had been working way too many hours a week for more than a decade as the church exploded and became one of the largest and fastest growing in the nation, in one of the least-churched cities. I wrote books and spoke at conferences, traveling to make extra income so Grace could stay home with our children. My pay was still low, we had nothing in savings, and we accrued a bit of debt—in a city where the cost of living was high. I preached as many as seven times a Sunday for more than an hour each time, year in and year out, nearly every week of the year, until my adrenal glands and thyroid fatigued, and I finally came to the end of myself in my midthirties. I was breaking, and it seemed there was no help, relief, or sympathy.

My veneer of tough, self-reliant husband without any needs was gone. I really needed my wife in ways I had never told her and she was surprised to hear.

I needed a new life. I did not need a new job, but a new plan for that job. I also needed a new marriage, but wanted to have a new marriage with the same spouse. So we cleaned up the church, lost around one thousand people due to changes amid intense criticism, laid off a lot of people (many of whom were great), and decided everything would change or we would walk. I refused to die from stress or destroy my marriage and family for the sake of "religious" people and outgrown organizational systems. I found a good doctor and did what I was told to rebuild my health. Grace and I pulled back from many commitments, got some help, including someone to help her one day a week and someone else to clean the house every other week, and carved out some time to intentionally work on our relationship with Jesus and each other.

Since that season, we have been works in progress. We are now closer than ever and have a very healthy sex life. We work together as one. We repent and forgive quickly and well by God's grace. We are blessed to have been faithful to each other for the entirety of our marriage. Through it all, we've learned a lot. On a scale of 1 to 10, we'd say our marriage is somewhere around an 8+ or 9, when in years past it was a 3 or 4. Writing this book has been an absolutely unifying and trust-building project by God's grace. We have a lot of fun as friends, and we get a lot done in life and ministry. By God's grace and the Holy Spirit's power, we got a new marriage with the same spouses and avoided becoming yet another statistic.

It was 2007 when we decided to teach the Song of Songs again, about a decade after I had taught it the first time. We did not tell anyone the intimate details of our story. We did, however, tell folks the principles we have learned using a book of the Bible as a springboard to other books of the Bible, some cultural analysis, a few of our counseling insights, and some interesting sociological data. I preached the sermons, and Grace joined me onstage to answer two hundred questions texted in over the course of the series, which we titled "The Peasant Princess."[1] The series vaulted us to number one on iTunes for Religion and Spirituality, a place the podcast has been at or near every week since 2007. The series landed us on ABC's *Nightline* a few times, CNN, *Loveline with Dr. Drew*, and a bunch of other media coverage. It has also led to conferences around the United States.

I have also preached parts of this book's content in England, Ireland, Scotland, South Africa, Australia, India, and Turkey. I have stood in line, where Grace has joined me when she was able, around the nation and the world, talking for hours with hundreds of thousands of couples. This, along with the ministry in our church and church-planting network, has led to seemingly every possible kind of conversation related to sex and marriage, which helped us greatly in writing the book.

So, after years of learning, counseling, teaching, repenting, forgiving, and praying, we believe it's time for us to tell the story of what we've learned and what we are learning. The story is honest, helpful, practical, and biblical. We'll give date night tips, talk about how to set up a marriage, and discuss how to fix a broken marriage. We'll have pointed words for husbands and wives, answer the most tricky "can we do that?" sex questions, and give hope to people like us who entered into marriage a complete mess. And if you have unconfessed sin and/or a past of sexual sin, including pornography, fornication, sexual abuse, bitterness, and the like, we pray this book leads to the healing of your soul and your marriage.

2

FRIEND WITH BENEFITS

This is my beloved,
And this is my friend.

—Song of Songs 5:16

In the early morning hours one Easter, twelve young runaway nuns climbed into empty fish barrels and were smuggled out of their convent. Their unlikely hero was a renegade monk they had written to, imploring him to rescue them so they could marry and one day become mothers. The escape was a daring and successful adventure, and it led to a most unusual friendship and marriage. The hero monk? Martin Luther.

Luther is widely known as one of the leaders of the Protestant Reformation. Among the most important people to walk the earth, he lived from 1483 to 1546 as a contemporary of the printing press, Copernicus, Henry VIII, Leonardo da Vinci, Michelangelo, Christopher Columbus, and John Calvin. A copper miner's son, he was born in Germany some 120 miles outside Berlin.

After a powerful encounter with God in which he was nearly struck by lightning, Luther became a priest and a monk. This included taking vows of poverty, chastity, and obedience for the rest of his life. Examining his own sin with a brutal honesty and brilliant legal mind, he nearly drove himself mad seeking to make himself righteous in God's sight out of a terrifying fear of God. This included endless prayer, severe fasting that gave him significant intestinal problems, sleepless nights, freezing cold, and even beating his own body in an effort to atone for his sin.

But by the grace of God, Luther had an epiphany that changed not only his life but also the lives of countless others. While studying the Bible, he learned that righteousness is a gift God gives by grace from and faith in Jesus

Christ and not something earned or merited through human religious and moral performance.

Because of the prominence of Martin Luther the theologian, very little attention is given to Martin Luther the husband; however, constantly looming in the background of his works is the ever-present influence of his wife, Katherine von Bora Luther.[1]

Katherine was born on January 29, 1499. She was only six years old when her mother died, and she was sent to a Benedictine cloister to be educated. Around the age of nine or ten she moved to a convent, and by sixteen she was a nun. At this same time, miles away, Luther was beginning to disagree with the Catholic Church's teaching on the preferability of singleness and celibacy in honoring God above marriage. Though himself still a virgin, Luther began teaching and writing on marriage from the Bible, culminating in his booklet *On Monastic Vows*, which condemned much of the monastic lifestyle.

Among the readers of Luther's booklet were Katherine and the other nuns in her convent. They longed to escape, marry, and become mothers. So they wrote to Luther, asking the renegade monk to help them escape. To do so was an offense punishable by death. Nonetheless, after their rescue, three of the nuns returned to their families immediately, and the remaining nine were taken to Luther's Augustinian monastery in Wittenberg. Luther helped six of the nuns find a home, husband, or job. Eventually every one of the nuns was married with the exception of Katherine—whose devoutly Catholic family did not want her back.

Luther tried repeatedly to find a husband for Katherine, with no success. Being a very bold woman, she went so far as to tell Luther that if he could not find her a husband, she expected him to step up and become her husband. But Luther did not marry for many reasons, including the following: "Because I daily expect the death decreed to a heretic."[2] And he simply did not want to marry, saying, "Good God . . . they will never thrust a wife on me!"[3]

Much to everyone's surprise, eight years after leaving the priesthood, the ex-monk Martin married the ex-nun Katherine in the backwoods of rural Germany on June 13, 1525. One of the reasons Martin gave for his marriage was to spite the devil, which is perhaps the least romantic statement ever uttered. Their marriage was a public scandal and arguably the most significant marriage outside the Bible in the history of the world. They set in motion a model for Christian faith and maturity through marriage, sex, and children, rather than through singleness and celibacy.

What is perhaps most curious is that their marriage did not start with love or attraction, as Katherine was not physically attractive, but rather with a commitment to the principles of the Bible and service to God. One biographer said, "Martin and Katie did not get along very well because of their clashing temperaments and personalities." Certainly they were not romantically in love, and there is no evidence that any kind of courtship preceded their marriage. Martin even confessed to his friends afterward that of all the fugitive nuns, he found Eva von Schönfeld the most attractive, while the proud and haughty Katie alienated him. "I never loved Katie then for I suspected her of being proud (as she is), but God willed me to take pity on the poor abandoned girl."[4]

Making matters worse, their critics were relentless. A folktale in that day said the Antichrist would be born from sex between a priest and a nun, which led to wild speculation about what their children would be like. And Martin's nemesis, Erasmus of Rotterdam, spread a vicious rumor that they married only because Martin impregnated her out of wedlock. This was a lie he repudiated three months later, but the damage to the Luthers' reputation was done. Another powerful critic said, "You have truly sinned . . . nightly wanton and chamber with a nun . . . Obstinate and defiant wretch . . . captured by the net of eternal damnation; be merry until you descend into hell, as you surely will, where, infernal brand! you will burn forever, and be eaten alive by the never-dying worm."[5]

Even Martin's friends were not fond of Katherine. He reported that many cried with grief upon hearing of his hasty marriage.

On top of all this, the couple lived in great poverty with great responsibility. They had three boys and three girls during their first nine years of marriage. Tragically, one daughter died at the age of thirteen months and another at thirteen years in the arms of her devastated father. By all accounts, Katherine was a wonderful mother and Martin a loving and fun father who spent his evenings playing music for his children and teaching them the Bible, which was a welcome and joyous diversion from his busy and stressful life.

Martin's old forty-room monastery became their home, and Katie quickly went to work cleaning the bachelor pad, including throwing out the straw bed Luther had not changed in more than a year, decorating the home, planting a garden for fresh food, changing Martin's diet to nurse him to health and help overcome his legendary flatulence problem, and growing herbs, as she was a bit of a naturopath. Their home was bustling with activity. Martin was constantly studying and publishing to fuel the Protestant Reformation, preaching and teaching, working on translating the entire Bible into German, traveling, and keeping up a vast correspondence with ministers across many nations. Apparently Katherine often sat with Martin as he wrote letters, for they frequently included sections about what Katherine was doing at the time and the greetings she sent. Their home was constantly filled, and as many as twenty-five people lived with them at any one time, not to mention the eleven orphans they sheltered. Dinners there often fed more than one hundred people.

The couple's early years were reportedly awkward, likely because neither had spent much time in the company of the opposite sex during their monasticism. Martin reported, "Katie used to sit down next to me while I was studying and, not knowing what to say, would begin to ask questions like: 'Dear doctor, is the prime minister of Prussia the duke's brother?'"[6] Something that helped them learn to live together in love was their willingness to dish out and take a joke. They were known for being brutally honest with each other, poking fun at each other, and doing so as friends. For example, when one would start to nag, the other would commonly retort that perhaps a little prayer should occur before "preaching a sermon." His letters often teased her, but Katherine certainly could hold her own. Martin often struggled with severe depression, and it was very difficult to pull him out of his funk. But Katherine found creative ways to do so. On one occasion she dressed up like a grieving widow in black mourning attire and met Martin at their door upon his return home. "Are you going to a funeral?" he asked. "No," she replied, "but since you act as though God is dead, I wanted to join you in the mourning." Luther quickly recovered![7]

Through their years together, the Luthers built a genuine friendship. This is easily noticed in the letters we have from Martin to his wife. His favorite title for her was "Lord Katie." He also called her his "dear rib," "Sir Katie," "the empress," "my true love," "my sweetheart," and "a gift of God." In a romantic statement that perhaps only a theologian's wife could truly appreciate, Martin referred to his favorite book of the Bible, Galatians, as "my Katerine von Bora [sic]."[8]

When he suffered from catarrh, kidney stones, constipation, insomnia, dizziness, and a buzzing—"not a buzzing but a roll of thunder"—in his head, she nursed him back to health. When he would fall into his frequent bouts with severe depression, she would hold him, pray for him, comfort him, and read Scripture to him. She drove the wagon, looked after their fields and gardens, purchased and pastured cattle, brewed beer, rented horses, sold linen, helped edit his writings, prepared meals, kept house, raised kids, entertained guests, and was often awake by 4:00 a.m. and working until 9:00 p.m. She was such an incredibly hard worker that Martin had to frequently urge her to relax and even offered to pay her to sit down and read her Bible. She reportedly had a keen theological mind and often sat with Martin and visiting theologians to discuss and debate theology—something unusual for a woman in that day.

The tenderness with which Martin spoke of his wife increased throughout their marriage. He wrote, "I am a happy husband and may God continue to send me happiness, from that most gracious woman, my best of wives."[9] Luther's earlier teaching on marriage essentially portrayed marriage as a sort of necessary evil to stave off sexual temptation. But, as his loving marital friendship with Katherine grew, his perspective matured as suggested by statements such as, "The greatest gift of grace a man can have is a pious, God-fearing, home-loving wife, whom he can trust with all his goods, body, and life itself, as well as having her as the mother of his children."[10]

After preaching what would be his final sermon, Martin died at the age of sixty-two, while away from his beloved Katie. In his will he said, "My Katherine has always been a gentle, pious and faithful wife to me, has loved me dearly."[11]

———

Grace and I ran across the story of the surprising marriage of Katherine and Martin while we were researching this book. It underscored something we'd noticed: *marriage is about friendship*. All the talk about spending time and doing life together, making memories, being a good listener, growing old and taking care of each other, being honest, having the long view of things, repenting and forgiving can be summed up in one word—*friendship*.

In researching this book, we read all or part of 187 books on marriage, most written by and for Christians. Not one of those books had one chapter or major section of a chapter on marital friendship. As we dug deeper, we could find only one significant Christian book written on a theology of friendship, and that was written in the 1100s by a Christian monk commenting on Cicero's view of friendship.[12] In more recent years, only a few popular books have been written on friendship from a Christian perspective, and they do not reference friendship in marriage in any significant way.[13] Likewise, the most popular book written about the friendships of Christian women does not speak about a wife's friendship with her husband.[14] And every book for men I (Mark) have read that includes a section on friendship speaks only of friendships between men based upon Jonathan and David's friendship, while neglecting every marriage in the Bible as a possible example of friendship.

Husbands and wives who want their marriages to be enduring and endearing must be friends. One of the most respected sociologists studying marriage said, "The determining factor in whether wives feel satisfied with the sex, romance, and passion in their marriage is, by 70 percent, the quality of the couple's friendship. For men, the determining factor is, by 70 percent, the quality of the couple's friendship. So men and women come from the same planet after all."[15] He continued by saying,

> Happy marriages are based on a deep friendship. By this I mean a mutual respect for and enjoyment of each other's company. These couples tend to know each other intimately—they are well versed in each other's likes, dislikes, personality quirks, hopes, and dreams. They have an abiding regard for each other and express this fondness not just in the big ways but in little ways day in and day out. . . . Friendship fuels the flames of romance because it offers the best protection against feeling adversarial toward your spouse.[16]

Grace and I are friends. Since meeting, we've been friends. By God's grace, until our season of life under the sun is done, we will be friends. At times our friendship has been strained, but it is because of the friendship that we remain together. Our first dates together were not extravagant because we were broke teenagers, but they were fun because we just liked to hang out together. Our first date included a hamburger, a walk along the Seattle waterfront, and a long chat by a fire on the beach. We did not spend much money, but we each made a friend.

We drifted bit by bit as I (Grace) tried to hide the lie from Mark and after I realized he probably wasn't a Christian. I wanted the friendship but without the conflict. I didn't understand that true friendship involves healthy conflict and hard discussions as God reveals sin and repentance, and reconciliation takes place.

In those difficult days when our marriage struggled, and our growing church was sapping Mark's energy, he used to say he felt alone and always would because of the nature of ministry. It felt hopeless that we could ever return to that trusting, fun, free friendship. I tried to fight it, but I also partially believed he was right and found myself giving up hope too. It felt as if no matter how much I tried to become a good friend, he was determined to be alone, and yet was upset because of it. I was very confused. It wasn't until God had me tell Mark I wasn't his enemy that the light went on for him and he saw I truly wanted to learn how to be his friend and not make him feel so isolated. I clearly remember the fight we were having in the bathroom when I pleaded silently with God to give me words to explain and give Mark a heart to believe those words. God told me what to say, and I saw a physical change in Mark in that moment. He started to soften and want to trust me again. As I later walked through my abuse history, he became a friend again. In a good way I was forced to trust him, and he worked hard to respond lovingly.

As Mark has studied friendship, it has been an amazing gift to me, and hope has returned. We both needed to understand what a healthy friendship could be. I feel safe again, knowing we are *both* working on the friendship and building trust. It is easier for a woman to think of doing life with a friend than with a dictator or unemotional ruler. The husband is still the head, but a "loving her as Christ loves the church" head—a considerate friend.

Friendship is an integral part of a truly Christian marriage and a safeguard against emotional adultery. In our years together we have seen many couples, including pastors and their wives, commit emotional adultery. Emotional adultery is having as your close friend someone of the opposite sex who is not your spouse.

Sadly, too many books and sermons on marriage focus only on the Bible verses about marriage. They should also examine the mountain of Bible verses on friendship because those apply to the most vital human friendship of all with our very best friend, our spouse. The Bible itself weds marriage and friendship. A wife in Song of Songs says, "This is my beloved, and this is my friend" (5:16).

Perhaps the only major Christian theologian to speak much about friendship was Augustine (AD 354–430). He wrote often about friendship in his book *Confessions* as he lamented bad friendships earlier in his life, the death of a close friend, and what he learned about true friendship. In tender fashion he spoke of human friendship as "a nest of love and gentleness."[17] He also spoke of friendship in the most practical terms:

> To make conversation, to share a joke, to perform mutual acts of kindness, to read together well-written books, to share in trifling and in serious matters, to disagree though without animosity—just as a person debates with himself—and in the very rarity of disagreement to find the salt of normal harmony, to teach each other something or to learn from one another, to long with impatience for those absent, to welcome them with gladness on their arrival.[18]

We have a few true friends. There are people we do not choose to do life with but simply have them in our life by circumstance (for example, family, coworkers, classmates); those who are not godly, trustworthy, or loving; those who are not peers (both those ahead of and behind us in maturity and life lessons); and those with whom our lives happen to intersect but there is no intentionality to live life together (for example, neighbors we barely know).

But the word *friend* is too often used for relationships that are not friendships, including online "friends" on social networking Web sites. This can lead to unreasonable expectations or someone being hurt and disappointed. So the word *friend* needs to be used carefully. We are to be friendly toward all people, but only friends with a few.[19] We make a mistake when we call anyone we are friendly to a "friend." This is an especially important distinction for extroverts, those in ministry, and those in serving professions, where you know and help a large number of people.

Marital friendship requires both the husband and wife to be willing to invest what it takes to be a good friend. Friendship is costly in everything—time, energy, emotion, and sometimes money. Those who want their spouses to be friends without seeking to be good friends in return are selfish and demanding. And those who want to be good friends but do not help their spouses reciprocate are prone to be taken advantage of, abused, neglected, and suffer from their marriages.

In our marriage, we have made the mistake of assuming we were friends and not working on our friendship as we ought to. Instead, we invested countless hours on a long list of people we were trying too hard to make our friends. Over time, nearly all those people left. Only a few have remained and become true friends.

Through it all, we have learned that friendships take so much time, energy, and investment that you can only have a few friends—maybe two or three real friends. In the same way, Jesus had many foes, many fans, and only three real friends—Peter, James, and John—who had the most privileged access to Him. To be sure, Jesus in humility calls us His friends,[a] and as God now glorified in heaven where He is without any limitations, He alone can have innumerable friendships, whereas we are finite and limited to a few.

The sad truth is that we live in a world that encourages selfishness, independence, convenience, isolation, and using people rather than loving them. Curiously, people holding these same values simultaneously complain about the lack of community, kindness, hospitality, love, generosity, and friendship in our day. Perhaps more than ever, we must acknowledge that friendship is desperately needed, and the first step is not whining about our lack of friends, but rather becoming good friends. This is why Proverbs 18:24 says, "A man who has friends must himself be friendly."

Marriage often starts out as a journey between friends. It gets off course as friends become business partners trying to pay the bills, parents trying to raise the kids, caregivers trying to tend to aging parents, cab drivers trying to shuttle family members to various events, event planners trying to pull off everything from holidays to birthday parties, and lovers trying to keep the flames of passion hot. Perhaps the key is to always be working on the friendship, because in the end the rest of marriage seems to come together more easily and happily when you are working on it with your friend. As a fun way to look at the issue, here's what we believe it means to be married F-R-I-E-N-D-S:

a John 15:15.

F—Fruitful

Friendship with our spouses, like everything else, exists to glorify God and serve His kingdom. A portion of a love letter from the great Baptist preacher Charles Haddon Spurgeon to his wife illustrates this point well: "None know how grateful I am to God for you. In all I have ever done for Him you have a large share, for in making me so happy you have fitted me for service. Not an ounce of power has ever been lost to the good cause through you. I have served the Lord far more and never less for your sweet companionship."[20]

Marriage includes a spouse, and often children. But the goal, center, and purpose of marriage is not self, spouse, or children. The ultimate goal of marriage and family is the glory of God. Only when marriage and family exist for God's glory—and not to serve as replacement idols—are we able to truly love and be loved. Remember, neither your child nor your husband (or wife) should be who you worship, but instead who you worship with.

It was God Himself who not only created marriage, but also commanded that it "be fruitful." This explains why Satan did not even show up until Adam and Eve were married. Our enemy hates the fruitfulness that can come from a husband and wife serving God together.

In a letter to a newly married couple, from his prison cell in Nazi Germany, pastor, theologian, and martyr Dietrich Bonhoeffer wrote about God's glory as the ultimate purpose of marriage:

> Marriage is more than your love for each other. It has a higher dignity and power, for it is God's holy ordinance, through which he wills to perpetuate the human race till the end of time. In your love you see only your two selves in the world, but in marriage you are a link in the chain of the generations, which God causes to come and to pass away to his glory, and calls into his kingdom. In your love, you see only the heaven of your own happiness, but in marriage you are placed at a post of responsibility towards the world and mankind. Your love is your own private possession, but marriage is more than something personal—it is a status, an office. Just as it is the crown, and not merely the will to rule, that makes the king, so it is marriage, and not merely your love for each other, that joins you together in the sight of God and man.[21]

In marriage we have a duty to God, our spouses, the world, and future generations. But we are sinners. A husband and wife need to acknowledge that when the Bible speaks of fools, it is not just speaking about other people, but about them as well. Even the wisest among us has moments of folly. So God gives us spouses to serve as wise friends by praying with and for us, attending church with us, speaking truth, and providing Scripture along with good books and online classes, lectures, and sermons to nourish fruitfulness in our lives.

Life is so complex, dangerous, and stressful that the Bible often likens it to a war with the world around us, and the flesh within us betraying us to the Enemy. In light of this battle, what we need is a wise battle plan compiled by a multitude of counselors. Proverbs, the book of wisdom, speaks repeatedly of the importance of wise friends. Proverbs 20:18 says, "Plans are established by counsel; by wise counsel wage war." Proverbs 24:5–6 says, "A wise man is strong, yes, a man of knowledge increases strength; for by wise counsel you will wage your own war, and in a multitude of counselors there is safety." And Proverbs 13:20 says, "He who walks with wise men will be wise, but the companion of fools will be destroyed."

How has your spouse been a wise friend used of God to make you more fruitful? In what ways can you be a better and wiser friend to cultivate fruitfulness in your spouse? In what ways can you better use your spouse's wisdom to make your life and family more fruitful?

R—Reciprocal

While it only takes one spouse to be friendly, it takes both spouses to be friends. When both spouses are unfriendly, the marriage is marked by conflict and coldness. When one spouse is friendly and the other is unfriendly, the marriage is marked by selfishness and sadness. But when both spouses each make a deep, heartfelt covenant with God to continually seek to become a better friend, increasing love and laughter mark the marriage.

It is common to hear married people speak of "falling out of love" with their spouses and "falling in love" with someone else in adultery. In using the language of "falling," they are cleverly avoiding any responsibility, as if they were simply required to follow their hearts. But the Bible tells us not to follow our hearts, but rather "guard" them because they are prone to selfishness and sin.[a]

According to the Bible, love does not come from our hearts, but rather through our hearts. This is because "God is love," and in relationship with God through Jesus Christ, by the Holy Spirit, we receive God's love to share with others.[b] It is through the presence of God the Holy Spirit in our lives that we are able to love our spouses. Galatians 5:22 says, "The fruit of the Spirit is love." And Romans 5:5 says, "The love of God has been poured out in our hearts by the Holy Spirit who was given to us." Even when we don't feel loving with our spouses, we can give love to them and receive love from them if we live Spirit-filled lives.

In the Bible love is often a feeling. But rather than being a feeling that promotes action, it is often first an action based on obedience to God that results in a feeling for our spouses. This explains why the Bible commands husbands to love their wives[c] and wives to love their husbands[d] rather than commanding them to *feel* loving. This further explains why the Bible even commands us to love our enemies.[e]

In the Bible, love is also a verb; it is what we do. Like Jesus' love, it is a covenant commitment that compels us to act for the good of the one we love. This also explains why perhaps the most popular wedding Scripture of all time depicts love as active. First Corinthians 13:4–7 says, "Love suffers long and is kind; love does not envy; love does not parade itself, is not puffed up; does not behave rudely, does not seek its own, is not provoked, thinks no evil; does not rejoice in iniquity, but rejoices in the truth; bears all things, believes all things, hopes all things, endures all things."

Christian marriage is reciprocal acts of covenant love. This includes the little things. Perhaps some examples from people we asked will be helpful:

"He lovingly makes me coffee every single morning, and it means a lot to me!"

"He runs me a hot bubble bath when he knows I've had a tough day caring for our three daughters (all under five)!"

---

a Prov. 4:23 NIV; Jer. 17:9.
b 1 John 4:7–21.
c Eph. 5:25.
d Titus 2:4.
e Matt. 5:43–47.

"He prays for and with me and laughs at my jokes and we're silly together!"

"I cook, and he washes the dishes. It makes me think he appreciates my time that was spent cooking dinner, especially since we have two little ones."

"She lets me pick the TV shows and control the remote."

"[He] holds on to sentimental things—keeps them hidden where he thinks I will never find them. He has cards and notes I wrote him from when we first started dating."

"He calls home at lunchtime no matter what . . . just to reconnect and see if we are all doing okay at home."

"When my gas tank is low, he drives to the gas station and fills it. My husband has pumped my gas for almost twenty years. I appreciate that he notices and takes care of it for me!"

"A while back, I made a commitment to become more healthy physically. Among many changes was only having one soda a week. Every Saturday my wife goes out and buys me one Dr. Pepper so I will have it when I am finished preaching on Sunday."

"[She] surprises me with pizza and hot wings and a beer when I get home from work!"

"She leaves encouraging notes with my keys or on my car steering wheel in the mornings."

"We walk to the library hand in hand, choose books, read them, and then swap. Later that week, over wine on the porch, we discuss those books. My favorite thing ever."

"He opens the car door. I never had that before, and it means a lot to me."

"She's excited to see me every time I come home."

"[He] knows my favorite ice cream and just the right time for it."

"I have a lot of girlfriends whose husbands would never go to a grocery store with them or for them. My husband always goes grocery shopping with me to shop for our family of six instead of making me do it all by myself. He brings them in and helps put them away."

"We go hunting together, which he loves."

"My husband will not leave the house without kissing me good-bye. Sometimes I am in a rush and try to avoid him . . . but he will stand in front of my car, and climb in to make sure he does [kiss me]. His reasoning is, of course, first because he loves me, but if anything should ever happen to either of us, he wants to make sure that I know the last time we were together he kissed me and told me he loves me."

"I love it when she goes with me to a sports bar to watch a game even though she's not that into it, just because she knows I love it, and I love it when she's there."

"He rubs my back."

"He holds my hand."

"We were in an antique store, he was bored, and when a Frank Sinatra song came on, he grabbed my hand, twirled me around, and started to dance with me."

"We both take turns writing in a journal that we started when we were married in 2001. The entries range from silly to serious and from sweet to sexy."

What would you add to the list?

I—Intimate

In our teaching and counseling, we have seen people respond well to a simple explanation of three kinds of marriages—back-to-back, shoulder-to-shoulder, and face-to-face.[22]

A back-to-back marriage is one in which the couple has turned their backs on each other. As a result, they live separately and do not work together (shoulder-to-shoulder) or draw each other out in friendship (face-to-face). In such marriages the partners range from strangers to enemies, but are not friends.

A shoulder-to-shoulder marriage is one in which the couple works together on tasks and projects, such as keeping the home, raising the kids, growing the business, and serving the church.

A face-to-face marriage is one in which, in addition to the shoulder-to-shoulder work, the couple gets a lot of face-to-face time for conversation, friendship, and intimacy.

As a general rule, women have more friendships than men. And their friendships tend to be more face-to-face. This is because men commonly have shoulder-to-shoulder friendships around shared activity. If they take the time to reflect on whom they have considered friends in different seasons of their life, most men recall boys they played with on a sports team and guys they worked with on a job. But they often know very little about these guys they called friends, because their tasks consumed their time and conversation, as they talked about the task in front of them rather than the emotion between them.

Conversely, women's friendships tend to be face-to-face and built around intimate conversation. This explains why women do the sorts of things with other women that men do not do with other men, such as going out to lunch or coffee just to talk, sharing deep intimate feelings while looking each other in the face without a task bringing them together.

Wives, to be a good friend, learn to spend some time with your husband in shared activity. If he's watching a sporting event, sit down and share it with him. If he's working on a project, hang out nearby to help or at least ask questions and be a companion if nothing else. If he's going fishing, ask if you can come sit in the boat with him just to be in his world. For a wife to build a friendship with her husband requires shoulder-to-shoulder time alongside him.

Husbands, to be a good friend to your wife, learn to have deeper and more intimate conversations. Open up, telling your wife how you're doing and asking her how she is doing. Listen without being distracted by technology or a task (put your cell phone away), but instead focus on her, looking her in the eye for extended periods of time. Draw her out emotionally, and allow her to draw you out emotionally. Keep your advice to a minimum and learn to listen, empathize, comfort, encourage, and in so doing resist the constant male urge to find a problem and try to fix it. No wife likes feeling like a problem to be fixed rather than a person who wants to be intimate. For her, intimacy means "into-me-see," which means she wants to know her husband and be known by him. For a husband to build a friendship with his wife requires him growing in face-to-face skills.

Intimacy is ultimately about conversing. As an old proverb says, "The road to the heart is the ear." One book on friendship insightfully notes that there are really three levels of conversation—facts, opinions, and feelings.[23] Most of the conversations we have are about facts—the weather is hot or cold, we are tired, our sports team won, or gas has gotten expensive. As a relationship with someone becomes more intimate, conversations shift from facts to personal opinions. In this transition we are opening up a bit, allowing someone to get to know us more intimately. We talk about our opinions of such things as theology, politics, and other people. When a relationship becomes most intimate, we begin to share our feelings. We become vulnerable with someone, telling him or her not just what we do (facts) and what we believe (opinions), but who we are (feelings). As C. S. Lewis said, "Eros will have naked bodies; Friendship naked personalities."[24]

For me (Grace), friendship with Mark means his willingness to work through tough trials together and not give up or treat me like a project. It means patient correction; providing for and protecting the kids and me; praying with me; having patient intimacy and sex; holding me if I'm crying; having "understanding" or teaching conversations; spending time together (like having date nights, snuggling after the kids are in bed, and listening well); holding hands and taking walks; being generous with compliments or encouragement; and building memories together.

For me (Mark), like many men, I know a lot of guys and get along well with a wide variety of people. I have a lot of fans as well as foes, but until recent years few godly, safe, real male friends. There were not many people I would open up to, trust, and could not conceive of a life without. Some years ago, I sat Grace down and told her that I really needed her to be my intimate friend and "functional pastor." I think this surprised her on two levels. One, like most men, I project a sense of complete self-sufficiency, needing nothing, which is untrue because I hate feeling lonely and really need the intimate connection, conversation, and comfort of Grace. Two, while we do not believe a woman should be a pastor according to the Bible,[a] I asked Grace to be my functional pastor. As a pastor myself, I've never had a pastor since I left college. So I invited Grace to be the one who checked in on my heart, prayed for me, gave me wise counsel, and knew the most intimate parts of my past and present as well as my longings and fears about the future. And although Grace does not wish to hold any formal office in our church, she does hold the unofficial office in my life as my intimate friend who pastors my heart, something that has changed my life and our marriage.

---

a 1 Tim. 2–3; Titus 1.

E—Enjoyable

Often life is not much fun. Between the sins we commit and the sins committed against us—not to mention Satan, demons, and the curse—Jeremiah's lament, "Why did I come forth from the womb to see labor and sorrow" (Jeremiah 20:18), makes sense.

But a friendship with an enjoyable spouse can make a world of difference—someone who knows how to have a good time, relax, go on an adventure, or just toss it all to the side for a holy diversion. Any couple who hope to exit this life together still holding hands must be friends who have fun along the way and laugh a lot.

God commands married couples to:

> Go, eat your bread with joy,
> And drink your wine with a merry heart;
> For God has already accepted your works.
>   Let your garments always be white,
> And let your head lack no oil.

> Live joyfully with the wife whom you love all the days of your vain life which He has given you under the sun, all your days of vanity; for that is your portion in life, and in the labor which you perform under the sun. (Ecclesiastes 9:7–9)

The big idea is that life is short. In the original language, the word *vain* is the Hebrew word *hebel*. The word occurs some thirty-eight times in the twelve chapters of Ecclesiastes and is variously translated as *meaningless* (NIV), *vanity* (KJV, NASB, NKJV, RSV, NRSV), or *emptiness* (NEB). How one translates that word affects his or her entire view of not only Ecclesiastes, but also the very purpose of life, as that is the central question of the book. While it is difficult to know the exact meaning of *hebel*, it seems that *vapor*, or *breath* is the best translation of the word. Life does not have to be meaningless, vain, or empty—though it can be, apart from faith and repentance.

However, life is short. It is fleeting, like a breath on a cold morning that you see for only an instant before it disappears. Life moves quickly. Married life can seem as if it's only five days long. The first day you meet, the second day you marry, the third day you raise your children, the fourth day you meet your grandchildren, and the fifth day you die first or bury your spouse to go home alone for the first time in many years.

God in His grace gives us spouses as enjoyable friends. And He expects us to get dressed up now and then and have some fun with our friends, eating and laughing to God's glory and our good. There will always be work to do, and once in a while we need to stop working and start worshipping by enjoying the friends God gave us. We are convinced that the couples who pray and play together stay together.

Last, an enjoyable friend helps routines become rituals. If your spouse is an enjoyable friend, suddenly a cup of coffee together, a walk after dinner, and a trip to the grocery store become sacred rituals filled with meaningful opportunities to have some fun with the friend you are married to.

Date night is a ritual for me (Grace). It is weekly, but it is different each week because the conversation, food, and activities change. Sometimes we go to dinner and a movie, sometimes we find a great spot on the beach and chat, sometimes we do a fun activity or getaway, sometimes we come back home and snuggle up, but we always try to keep that time about us. Family night, every Saturday, is a similar ritual (sabbath time with the family doing various low-key things).

For me (Mark), I've learned to see many of the things Grace does for our family and for me as a series of sacred rituals. She is far more Martha than Mary. This hardworking woman devotedly serves and manages a busy home with five kids, ministry demands, and a high-maintenance, drama queen of a husband. But when we were not as emotionally connected in prior years, I did not value her service because it felt as if she was doing things *for* me rather than *with* me. As our friendship has grown, I have come to see her service differently—more as sacred rituals motivated by love than as tasks performed by a business partner.

One example in particular happens every Sunday morning. I leave the house around 7:00 a.m. and do not return until 10:00 p.m. because I preach all day. In recent years we have developed a ritual. Grace gets up early to make me breakfast (French press coffee sweetened with raw honey and huevos rancheros with chorizo and green chilis are my favorites), and together we connect before I head out to preach. Between services, Grace and the children join me for lunch in my office, and I get a bit of time to connect with my family—I miss them when I am away from them. These Sunday rituals mean the world to me and have made a big difference in my life and ministry as well as in our family.

N—Needed

In the beginning there was God.

Before there were date nights or divorce lawyers, there was God.

One gloriously happy, completely united, altogether loving God. In fact, before there was anyone or anything, there was one God in three persons living in unbroken union and eternal communion.

Then, God said, "Let Us make man in Our image, according to Our likeness . . . So God created man in His own image; in the image of God He created him; male and female He created them."[a] God made the man first, and for the first time in recorded history, something was declared to be "not good," even though sin and the curse had not yet entered the world. God declared, "It is not good that man should be alone; I will make him a helper comparable to him."[b] The man had God above him, and creation beneath him, but no woman alongside him to walk as an equal partner, lover, and friend to reflect something of the mystery of the Trinity of Friends. God's solution was a friendship in the covenant of marriage. Subsequently, the first human friendship was between a husband and wife, meaning your nearest and dearest friend is to be the one you are in covenant marriage with. So, unlike the rest of creation that God spoke into existence, God crafted the woman with His proverbial hands as the gift of a friend.

Curiously, God made the woman from a rib taken out of the man's side. Perhaps this was because she belongs at his side as an intimate equal and not in front of him as feminism would teach or behind him as chauvinism would teach. For Grace and me, this may also explain why she likes to snuggle burrowed into my side and why it feels like home to her.

a Gen. 1:26–27.
b Gen. 2:18.

We need human friendships in addition to friendship with God. And God's answer is first a spouse and then other godly friends of our same gender. For a man, this means he must jettison the stereotype of a "true man" standing alone against the world. God said it best: "It is not good that man should be alone; I will make him a helper comparable to him."[a] Anyone who tells his or her spouse, "I don't need you" is in fact calling God a liar. A man needs his wife as his companion and friend. And a wife needs to be helpful by God's design. The more his need for her and her need to help him are celebrated as gracious gifts from God, the faster oneness and friendship blossom in the marriage. Any religious person who says he does not really need human friends because God is his friend is calling God a liar, because He's the One who says we also need human friends.

D—Devoted

A devoted friend is dependable through varying seasons of life. The Bible speaks a lot about times and seasons. Wisdom is about knowing what season someone is in and responding accordingly. This takes humility, discernment, and attentiveness. A bad friend is one who always has to be happy and have a good time, as if life were a never-ending party; or who always has to be sad, somber, and serious, as if life were a continual funeral. A devoted friend agrees with Ecclesiastes 3:4, which says there is "a time to weep, and a time to laugh."

To be a devoted friend requires wisdom from the Holy Spirit, accompanied with an emotional sensitivity to others. Rather than first thinking about yourself, Philippians 2:3–4 says, as a good friend you need to "in lowliness of mind . . . esteem others better than [your]self. Let each of you look out not only for his own interests, but also for the interests of others." As we do, we are able to obey Romans 12:15 and "rejoice with those who rejoice, and weep with those who weep."

The opposite of a devoted friend is a fake friend. Proverbs speaks a great deal about fake friends. Fake friends are what the Puritan Matthew Henry called "swallow friends" who "leave when winter comes." Fake friends are with

---

a Gen. 2:18.

us so long as they get something from us—be it the sense of worth they receive from us needing them when we are suffering, to the benefits they accrue from our seasons of blessing. A real friendship is about both people giving and taking in every season without keeping a record of what is given and taken. A fake friendship is about one person doing all the giving and the other doing all the taking. Fake friends quickly desert us when life with us becomes complicated, costly, inconvenient, or no longer meets their needs. Proverbs 18:24 says, "A man who has friends must himself be friendly, but there is a friend who sticks closer than a brother."

It is in the darkest seasons of life that God reveals to us our most devoted friends. These kinds of friends seem to rise up to the challenge of trouble just as Proverbs 17:17 says: "A friend loves at all times, and a brother is born for adversity." Someone has said that a friend is the person who walks in when everyone else walks out. In marriage, being a devoted friend in all life's seasons is key to building oneness, intimacy, and trust.

We had to learn to do this by listening well and being attentive, so that our responses were authentic. For me (Grace) this included learning what a friend truly is. I wrongly considered nearly anyone and everyone a friend. I served people tirelessly, even though most of my "friends" did not reciprocate in any way. Such people are not friends, but rather people God asks us to serve for different seasons, encouraging them toward maturity and serving others.

Grace and I observed devotion in marriage early on in our relationship. Her uncle John was a frail elderly man whose wife, Gladys, had to be placed in a home because of her declining health and decimated memory due to Alzheimer's. John rented an apartment close to her care facility so he could faithfully visit her multiple times every single day for years, until the day he died. Although Gladys did not remember John or any of the days they had shared over the course of many decades, he faithfully sat with her for hours every day because—despite their marriage being difficult—she was his best friend and he loved her dearly. John could have moved on with his life, divorced her, married a woman he enjoyed, and never visited her again, and she would have been completely unaware because she remembered so little. But he loved her faithfully as a devoted friend, every day staring into the eyes of his wife who could not remember who he was or even his name.

Grace loved her uncle John very much, and they were close. When we began dating in high school, I, too, enjoyed getting to know John. Occasionally, Grace and I would join him as he went to visit Gladys. The night before we married, I stayed at John's apartment, and he asked me to promise that I would love Grace and remain devoted to her no matter what. I gave him my word, and after watching his example knew exactly what he meant, as he was asking me to covenant to being Grace's best friend.

S—Sanctifying

Author Gary Thomas asked the vital question, "What if God designed marriage to make us holy more than to make us happy?"[25] We truly do not know how selfish and sinful we are until we live with someone in marriage. Most of our dating time is spent pretending to be people we are not, and after a few years of marriage, our spouses start to discover who we truly are rather than the characters we have been acting like. The same is true for them.

Regarding our selfishness and sin, our spouses do not change us as much as they reveal us. Once we're exposed, we have to decide if we will be changed for the good, what the Bible calls being sanctified. A husband and wife need to accept that they each are, and are each married to, a weak, failed, flawed sinner who needs loving help and patient endurance. As sinners, we all fall into sin, and without a friend we are often simply stuck, unable to get up and move on with our lives. This is why Ecclesiastes 4:9–10 says,

> Two are better than one,
> Because they have a good reward for their labor.
> For if they fall, one will lift up his companion.
> But woe to him who is alone when he falls,
> For he has no one to help him up.

True friends are revealed when someone has failed and fallen into sin. Those who rush to help them up—knowing full well whom they are helping and what they have done—are true friends. We may say we are someone's friend, but unless we are quick to pursue them in the sin they have fallen into, we are not really much of a friend. We know that we are considered a godly friend when the person in sin trusts us enough to come clean with us, be honest, and ask for our help. This is particularly true of our spouses, who need us to pursue them most diligently when they have fallen most grievously.

As sanctifying friends, a married couple needs to lovingly, humbly, graciously, and kindly speak the truth in love so they may grow to be more like Jesus Christ. This kind of truth telling that calls us out of our sin rather than pushing us deeper into shame is what Proverbs 27:6 means: "Faithful are the wounds of a friend, but the kisses of an enemy are deceitful." A spouse who only showers you with praise, never disagrees with you, and avoids conflict at all costs, is an enabling rather than a sanctifying friend.

A godly friend loves God and loves us enough to hate our sin and speak truthfully about it with us. This is why Proverbs 27:9 says, "Ointment and perfume delight the heart, and the sweetness of a man's friend gives delight by hearty counsel." The word *hearty* simply means "to be honest." This means that one of the God-given duties of our spouses as friends is to be honest with us for God's glory and our good. Sometimes this requires that they sting us with a rebuke—what some people affectionately call "stabbing us in the front." And if we are wise, we will love our spouses all the more for loving us enough to risk our friendship for the sake of our good. Proverbs 9:8 says, "Rebuke a wise man, and he will love you."

—

In closing, the earnest pursuit of a good marriage can quickly become overwhelming because there are so many things to work on. We, too, have felt this anxiety: *Where do we start? How can we possibly work on spirituality, communication, scheduling, sex, spirituality, finances, family-of-origin issues, and so forth, all at once?* But we've also found that by always working on our friendship, the rest of marriage seems to sort itself out in time. So we would commend to you the goal of devoting the rest of your life to being a better friend to your spouse.

3

MEN AND MARRIAGE

When I became a man, I put away childish things.
—1 CORINTHIANS 13:11

This chapter is primarily for men.

My tone will be as a man to men.

Were I writing to women, my tone would be considerably different. So, while women are welcome to read this chapter, they are also forewarned that it may get a little rough. To be fair, not every man is the caricature I critique throughout this chapter. And I invite you men not to take offense, but rather pray for and speak to the men you know who are guilty of not manning up to their responsibilities.

For most of human history, a male would go through two life phases: boy, then man. The transition from boy to man was comprised of five events that happened almost simultaneously or in very close succession. As a man you were to

1. leave your parents' home;
2. finish your education or vocational training;
3. start a career-track job, not a dead-end-Joe job;
4. meet a woman, love her, honor her, court her, and marry her;
5. parent children with her (Gen. 2:24).

But the fools' parade hijacked the march to manhood. Rather than moving from boyhood to manhood by this succession of sociological transitions, we've created a third life stage in the middle called adolescence, or what I call "boys who can shave." Today adolescence starts somewhere in the teen years and, in many cases, continues indefinitely. The problem with adolescence is we guys don't know when we're ever going to grow up and be men, and no pressure is exerted on us to do so.

Is it when we are old enough to legally drive, vote, join the military, or drink alcohol?

Is it when we graduate from college?

Is it when we get married? Is it when we have kids? Is it when we buy a house?

No one knows. We are left with indefinite adolescence and a Peter Pan syndrome epidemic where some men want to remain boys forever. If we do make the transition to manhood, many husbands and fathers revert back to adolescence with something called a *midlife crisis*. Even some old men revert back to adolescence, trading in their wives for the youngest girlfriends they can.

There is nothing wrong with being a boy, so long as you are a boy. But there is a lot wrong with being a boy when you are supposed to be a man. To paraphrase Paul: "When I was a boy, I talked like a boy, I thought like a boy, I reasoned like a boy. When I became a man, I put childish and boyish ways behind me."[a] A lot of guys fight the transition from boy to man because they despise responsibility.

Enabling this type of guy are a legion of moms and girlfriends who pay his bills, pick up his mess, lend him their cars, and keep him supplied with alcohol and a steady diet of snacks.

Men are supposed to be producers, not just consumers. You are defined by the legacy, the life, and the fruit that come out of you, not by what you take in. But most guys are just consumers.

Paul said a man is "the image and glory of God."[b] He is to reflect the truth, goodness, love, and mercy of Jesus, his God and Savior. He is the glory of God.

If you recognize yourself, even a little bit, in what I've described, take heart. I have hope for you, because you are the glory of God. God wants His glory to shine through men. God wants His kingdom to be made visible through them. God wants them to be His sons. God wants us to follow, by the power of the Holy Spirit, in the example of Jesus.

---

a 1 Cor. 13:11.
b 1 Cor. 11:7.

I don't really care if you buy man toys, or if you play video games or rock out on your guitar. The problem is when those are prevalent, predominant, and preeminent in your life. Some of you would argue and say, "It's not a sin." No, but some things that are not sinful are still just dumb. If you got fired because you were up trying to get to the next level and become a guild leader, that's dumb. If you work only one part-time job so you can have more time to play guitar or Frisbee golf, that's dumb. If you spend all your money on a new car or truck, or toys, or gear, or gambling, or clothes, or fantasy football, that's dumb. There are a lot of things that Christian guys do that aren't evil; they're just dumb and childish and foolish.

Men are to be creators and cultivators. God is a creator and a cultivator, and you were made to image Him. Create a family and cultivate your wife and children. Create a ministry and cultivate other people. Create a business and cultivate it. Be a giver, not a taker, a producer and not just a consumer. Stop looking for the path of least resistance and start running down the path of greatest glory to God and good to others because that's what Jesus, the real Man, did.

Tough and Tender

Being a man like Jesus is about being both tough and tender.

As men, we are to be tough in defending the weak, oppressed, abused, and poor, fighting for justice and mercy. We are to be tough (and honorable) when competing in business because we are competing in order to feed our families. We are to be tough in defending truth and combating false teaching and error. We are to be tough with stiff-necked, hard-hearted men who bully others around. We are to be tough in carving out safety and protection for women and children in a world that abuses them.

As men, we are to be tender in comforting the hurting, encouraging the downcast, and teaching the simple. We are to be tender with our wives, loving them as Christ does the church. We are to be tender with our children, kissing them on the head, often telling them we love them, and providing continuous assurance that we truly consider them gifts from God. We are to be tender with those who are already broken by their sin and needing godly counsel and help.

Jesus was tough enough to go to the cross without shedding a tear. And Jesus was tender enough to weep over the death of His friend.

But men who are mainly tough without also being tender are commonly tough chauvinists who only understand masculinity in part. Do you know any of these guys or recognize any of their habits in yourself?

Tough Chauvinists

"No Sissy Stuff" Sam believes being a man is simply being the opposite of a woman. He lacks emotion other than anger used for bullying and intimidation because other emotions are a sign of weakness. He is not very verbal because he has little interest in opening up or getting drawn into a deep conversation with his wife because he's selfish. And he is not physically affectionate other than when he wants sex from his wife, because he sees affection as effeminate and sex as a masculine activity more akin to hunting, scoring, or conquering. He needs to learn that being a man is not the opposite of being a woman, that both are made in the image of God and express the same emotions in masculine and feminine ways.

Success-and-Status Stewart believes being a man is about what you have and do rather than who you are and how you serve. Like a foolish ex-jock, this fellow is forever talking about and consumed by any score keeping that he can use to show his superiority over others—for example, the beauty of his wife, his strength, appearance, health, car, income, degree, skills, university he graduated from, children's performance, and possessions. You never have to ask this guy what his latest victory is, because he'll make sure to tell you what a winner he is.

"Give 'Em Hell" Hank thinks men are solely warriors, brawlers, and tough guys. He is prone to a short temper, and his wife is often afraid of upsetting him and the wrath she might endure. The simplest way to understand this guy is that he's a controlling bully. Bullying has worked for him, so he feels no need to change. He's been able, for the most part, to get through life finding weaker people who avoid conflict and then bullying them around. His children feel no close connection to him, and his wife is left with the horrible choices of leaving the fool; sticking around to toughen up like a man and fight back; or just bowing her head, shutting her mouth, and doing what she's told, not unlike a pet.

"I'm the Boss" Bob loves to be in authority and tell others what to do, but he hates being under authority and doing what he's told. Wherever he finds himself, he appoints himself king and lord. He loves to be in charge, boss people around, and bark out orders. He's happy so long as he's the boss and gets his way but becomes quite contentious, or even a whiney baby, when he does not get his way. Men like Bob go from church to church declaring they cannot find a good one, and by "good church" they mean one led by a pastor dumb enough to take orders. Their wives are often weary women, and it shows in their faces. Their children grow up to despise them or parrot them, either of which is a tragedy.

———

The problem with blockhead tough chauvinists of all sorts includes how they read the Bible. When they read about men being the "head" of their families, they miss all the other parts about repentance, friendship, love, humility, and being like Jesus.

The opposite of tough chauvinists are tender cowards. These are the kinds of guys who are too soft, too amiable, and too effeminate.

Tender Cowards

Little-Boy Larry never grew up—like Peter Pan. He tends to be disorganized and has a hard time getting his life together for an extended time. Getting and keeping a job are always tough because he's not very ambitious and finds that ongoing responsibilities tend to get in the way of his hobbies and friends. He's immature; his interests and mannerisms are those of a boy and not a man. Unable to pay his bills or look after himself, he tends to borrow money from other people who keep an eye on him in ways an adult looks after a child. Women are attracted to him in the way a mother is attracted to a helpless baby.

Sturdy-Oak Owen goes to work and comes home, cuts the grass, mends the fence, pays the bills, turns on the TV, and checks out. He is physically present but emotionally absent. He's always working on his car. He's always on the Internet. He's always in his study. He's always in the garage. He's always in the yard. He's always doing something other than connecting with his family. His hobbies tend to be solo activities, like fishing, hunting, or motorcycle riding. Or they may include a few of his buddies but not his family. He does not hug. He does not speak. And he's ultimately a coward afraid of being emotionally involved in the life of his own family.

Hyper-Spiritual Henry is the guy with the Christian T-shirts and Christian bumper stickers, always listening to praise music and reading the latest trendy Christian book. He embarrasses his wife and children. The kids don't bring friends over to the house because they fear their father will have a Ned Flanders episode where everything has to be connected to some out-of-context Bible verse, theological position, or downright odd spiritual lesson.

Good-Time Gary is super fun, the life of the party, and a really nice guy, so no one really ever puts a finger in his chest as they ought to. He is funny; he is charming; he is winsome; he is entertaining. There's always a crowd of people around him. Everybody likes him. He gets along with everybody, and here's the key: everybody likes him, but nobody respects him. Every time something happens in his life, he turns it into a joke. He doesn't realize that his life is the joke. He can't hold a job, can't pay his bills, can't get out of bed in the morning, can't follow through on a commitment, can't stay organized, can't see anything through to completion. He'll draw a crowd, but they won't follow him because he's not going anywhere; he's not a leader. For the wife who's married to this guy, eventually he becomes not so cute, not so funny, and not so clever. He becomes profoundly annoying. She tires of the jokes and the good times and the "everything's funny, and aren't I clever and cute?" She wants a king of a man she can depend on and not a court jester for a husband.

———

None of these guys are the kind of men Jesus wants us to be. The key to understanding masculinity is Jesus Christ. Jesus was tough with religious blockheads, false teachers, the proud, and bullies. Jesus was tender with women, children, and those who were suffering or humble. Additionally, Jesus took responsibility for Himself. He worked a job for the first thirty years of His life, swinging a hammer as a carpenter. He also took responsibility for us on the cross, where He substituted Himself and died in our place for our sins. My sins are my fault, not Jesus' fault, but Jesus has made them His responsibility. This is the essence of the gospel, the "good news." If you understand this, it will change how you view masculinity.

You may not be physically big, strong, or tough. [But if you are rightly tough and tender, and you take responsibility for yourself and others, then you are truly a man's man, a godly man, and by grace you are being conformed into a man like the perfect God-man, Jesus Christ.]

This is what the Bible means when it says that a husband is the head of his wife as Christ is the head of the church. It means that he lovingly, humbly, and sacrificially leads by being a blessing and taking responsibility not only for himself but also for others—beginning with his wife.

Men are like trucks—they drive smoother and straighter with a load. Adolescence delays this load carrying indefinitely. Wise men know this and load themselves up early in life to get their education, careers, families, and ministries started as soon as possible because it gives them a good head start on the fools. So load yourself up. Take responsibility for yourself. Take responsibility for your wife (and children if or when you have them). Take responsibility for your church. Take responsibility for your company. Take responsibility for your city. Real men don't look for other men, organizations, and governments to carry their load. Real men carry their own load.

A Wife's Perspective

When you consider how many men are really just boys who can shave, think about how terrifying it must be for a woman to marry. As a man, you may never have seen marriage from your wife's perspective. First Peter 3:1–6 speaks about the proclivity of wives to be afraid about marriage and filled with fears about the dependability and affection of their husbands. Those fears are legitimate.

When a woman marries a man, she's trusting that for the rest of her life he won't hit her, cheat on her, rape her, or kill her; that he'll work hard, pay the bills, love their children, finish the race well, and walk with Jesus till the end; that if she gets sick, he'll look after her; that if she is dying, he will be faithful to her. Gentlemen, it is a terrifying thing for a woman to trust a sinful man. Will he take responsibility or dump it all on her? Will he be too tough and crush her? Will he be too tender and allow her to be crushed?

As a man, I don't think I fully understood this until I had daughters, and now I have some understanding of that fear. The thought of walking my daughters down the aisle and handing them to a man and trusting that he will love them and protect them and serve them and care for them and look after them causes me fear and grave concern.

It is the responsibility of the husband to hear and obey God continually so that these fears are diminished. This is why in 1 Peter 3:7, we read, "Husbands, likewise, dwell with them with understanding, giving honor to the wife, as to the weaker vessel, and as being heirs together of the grace of life, that your prayers may not be hindered."

Wives have legitimate fears. Husbands need to help alleviate those fears by loving "in an understanding way, showing honor." Every man who reads this, even the best man among us, has areas of repentance and growth that are required. Consider the following ways to honor your wife.

Honor Your Wife Physically

Peter said that the woman is the "weaker vessel." What that means is, generally speaking, if a husband and a wife get in a cage fight, he'll win.

Do you ever hit her? Do you ever shove her? Do you ever push her? Do you ever grab her, restrain her? Do you ever raise a hand and threaten her? Do you ever threaten her with physical violence? Do you give her that look, that pierced, glazed, violent, angry, don't-push-it-now's-a-good-time-to-shut-up look? Do you tell her, "I'm getting very angry; you should just shut up right now or it's gonna go bad for you"? Do you get right in her face? Do you intimidate her with your presence? Do you play the role of the bully to push your wife around?

You honor your wife physically by being safe for her, protective of her, and tender with her. In this way she will see your physical strength as a blessing instead of a danger. This is important to learn. In sports, men are taught to find a weakness in their opponent and exploit it. But since a husband is one with his wife—who is not his opponent—her weakness is his weakness, which means he needs to honor and protect it rather than exploit it. Because she is a crystal goblet and he is a thermos means she is not only delicate but also precious.

Honor Your Wife Emotionally

Some men say, "I'm not emotional; I don't connect." This is a lie. Men and women have the same emotions; they just express them in masculine and feminine ways. Your wife needs intimacy. She wants you to know her. She wants to know you. She wants you to open up. She wants you to be passionate and loving and honest. The Bible says that Adam was with his wife, and he "knew her."

There are too many guys who turn marriage into a job description. He does his responsibility, she does hers, and there's no emotional connection whatsoever. This is a sin of omission. "I didn't hit her; I didn't yell at her." But you didn't love her. You didn't connect with her. You didn't encourage her. You didn't pursue her. So ultimately, you failed her. Not only do women initiate most divorces; they often do so because they have lost hope that their emotionally flaccid husbands will ever change, and so they walk away forever.

One Christian author used the idea of "love languages."[1] His thesis is that people give and receive love differently. For some people, love is words—verbal or written—of encouragement, adoration, appreciation, and the like. For others, love is received or given in gifts large and small that convey generosity and affection. Love may be service and practical deeds of help; time alone together, uninterrupted; or touch, both sexual and non-sexual, that conveys closeness, safety, and companionship.

We may have more than one love language, or see our love language change in different seasons of life. For example, a wife who used to enjoy touch may find that with a newborn nursing baby, her body needs a break, and what she would really appreciate from her husband is some service in the form of help with the baby. The problem is that most of us give and receive love according to our own love language without considering the love language our spouses prefer and loving them in their language. For husbands, this means we must pay attention to our wives and also ask them how we can honor them emotionally, even if it doesn't come naturally to us.

We cannot demand to be loved only in the ways we want to receive love, but also need to be willing to see the different ways our spouses are expressing love. For example, if you like touch and gifts, but your spouse loves to serve you through time and acts of service, be willing to accept those and encourage her to be creative in other forms as well. This takes attentiveness and was something we did not do well in the early years of our marriage. For example, I (Mark) love touch, but Grace prefers service, so I would sit on the couch alone at night and stew while she was busy doing chores rather than simply being with me. Meanwhile, I would buy her nice gifts when what she really wanted was service—she was sometimes overwhelmed with the demands of young children. God has helped us to understand and take better care of each other, so things have changed.

Too many men are more like conquerors than explorers. They get married—which is akin to landing on the beach of an unexplored land—yet fail to explore the landscape and all its wonder. Our wives do not want to be conquered; they want to be explored emotionally.

Honor Your Wife Verbally

How do you speak to your wife? Do you have nasty nicknames for her? Do you raise your voice? Do you threaten her? Do you give backhanded compliments? Some men say, "I would never hit a woman." How about with your tongue? (Both in speaking to your wife and about her.) When your wife is not there and you're with your buddies, how do you speak about her? What do you say about her? Your children will pick this up as well. If you start saying critical, cutting, demeaning, cruel, or disrespectful things about your wife, your children will be left in the awful position of choosing between their mother and father. Invariably some of your children will despise their own mother and speak evil of her in an effort to remain loyal to their father. They're casualties of war.

As a man, you could defuse this and take away that fear by honoring your wife verbally and speaking honestly, respectfully, and lovingly to her and about her. God hears everything; you are not getting away with anything.

Honor Your Wife Financially

Admittedly, many men hit tough economic times due to unemployment or injury. They want to work but have a hard time finding a decent job. Such men need encouragement to keep seeking gainful employment and the humility to take whatever job(s) they can to feed their families. My own dad was a construction worker who often had seasons without work due to the economy, and I deeply respect the fact that he would seek side jobs and do most anything to make ends meet. When he finally broke his back, he reinvented himself by going to college, getting a degree, and pursuing a new career. Through it all, my mom stayed home to raise five kids and, although times were tough, we got through it without ever going into debt.

The Bible plainly says, "If anyone does not provide for his own, and especially for those of his household, he has denied the faith and is worse than an unbeliever."[a] In Genesis 3, as a result of sin, the woman's curse was in relation to being married and having children. This means that a woman will be stretched and sanctified as a wife and mother. Much of the frustration and pain, as well as joy and satisfaction, will come from her husband and children. The man's curse was providing for his family. This means that a man will always find it very difficult not to idolize or demonize his work and to do it unto the Lord as an act of worship, which God has chosen to mature and grow him as a man. And what the weakest, most worthless men among us do is say, "Oh, my load is heavy. I know yours is heavy, but I need you to carry half of mine too." Men, you have to work harder and smarter than the other men if you want to feed your family. That's your responsibility as a man. If you want any men to respect you, if you want your wife to respect you, if you want your children to respect you, you pay the bills.

Admittedly, a wife working before kids are born, or who finds a way to make money from home without neglecting her first God-given responsibilities of Christian, wife, and mother is acceptable. But men, you should make money. You should feed your family. One study found that "American wives, even wives who hold more feminist views about working women and the division of household tasks, are typically happier when their husbands earn 68% or more of the household income."[2]

We live in a time where there are guys telling their wives that they don't want to have children because that would mean they would need to step up to provide for their families and stop acting like children themselves. There's nothing sadder than a woman who loves Jesus and wants to be a mom, but the husband keeps saying, "I'm the head of the home. No." What he's saying is, "I'm in charge, and I command you to sin," to deny all your maternal instincts.

The latest statistics reveal that 40 percent of all children are born out of wedlock. It is now at the point where women aren't even pretending they will ever get married. They go to college, get good jobs, get pregnant, and have children alone. They've lost any hope of ever finding a guy who can actually carry the load, and that's tragic.

A 2007 Pew Research Center study found that only 20 percent of mothers with children under eighteen want to work full-time.[3] It also has become

---

a 1 Tim. 5:8.

increasingly common for the media to feature stories on stay-at-home dads as if this role reversal were common. But less than 1 percent of America's 22.5 million married families with children under fifteen had a stay-at-home dad in 2008, according to the U.S. Census.[4]

Not only should a man make money, he also should steward it well. He should have a wise budget that accounts for spending, saving, investing, retirement, tithing, and being generous to his family as much as he is able. And if your wife is going to work outside the home when the children are small, you must account for all the costs financially and practically. Will all the increased costs for Mom working (another car, eating out, cell phone, day care, increased tax bracket, etc.) really be worth it? Will the quality of child care anyone else provides rise to the level that comes from a godly mother in the daily life of her child(ren)? Would it be wiser to downsize your lifestyle than downsize the care of your child?

Honor Your Wife Technologically

Are you constantly checking your phone? Do you spend hours surfing the Internet? Are you always checking game scores? Do you bring your phone to the dinner table? Do you have a television at the foot of your bed? Do you take your laptop, phone, and other technology with you on vacations and date nights? Do you spend your free time sitting in front of a screen? Do you spend your date nights not speaking to your wife but watching a movie? Turn it off; unplug it; move it; leave it. Be present with your wife, speak with your wife, connect with your wife, and cultivate your wife rather than ignoring her.

I've had to work on this so that my wife and children know they are my priority. There is always a seemingly urgent need seeking to take my time, but breaking bad habits and ensuring that our family is my highest priority is essential.

Covenant Marriage

Understanding *contract* versus *covenant* is essential to marriage. In a contractual marriage two people with two lives negotiate the terms of their marriage. This tends to make marriage more like a business deal where two individuals living parallel lives monitor each other's contributions to see if the terms of the marriage negotiation are being upheld. For many men and women, the questions are: Is my spouse keeping up his/her looks, making his/her share of the income, doing an equal amount of the chores, and having enough sex with me, or not? And if at any point I do not believe my spouse is keeping up his or her end of our business arrangement, I simply nullify the deal and file for divorce according to the terms of a prenuptial agreement in which the divorce was organized before the marriage began.

A covenant is not like a contract. This is important for men to understand because most men, especially professionals, think contractually, which is fine for business but death to a marriage. The concept of covenant appears literally hundreds of times throughout the Bible. At the most basic level, a covenant is a loving agreement between two parties that bonds them together.[a] Some covenants are made between God and people, such as the new covenant of salvation.[b] Other covenants are made between people, such as the covenant of marriage.[c]

The concept of covenant is referred to in various terms throughout the Bible, but the main one is *hesed*. It is often translated as *covenant love, loving-kindness, mercy, steadfast love, loyal love, devotion, commitment, loyalty,* or *reliability*. Perhaps *The Jesus Storybook Bible* for children says it best, describing covenant love as "a Never Stopping, Never Giving Up, Unbreaking, Always and Forever Love."[5]

Safeguarding every covenant is a head, a leader responsible for the keeping of the covenant terms. The Bible repeatedly says that Jesus Christ is the capital-*H* covenant "Head."[d] Regarding the family, the Bible also repeatedly says that the husband is the little-*h* "head" of covenant marriage and family.[e] This assignment of the husband to the role of covenant head is not something rooted in culture that can be changed, but rather something rooted in creation that is unchanging. The Bible evidences this in five ways.

---

a Gen. 26:28; Dan. 11:6.

b Jer. 31:31–34; Matt. 26:28; Luke 22:20; Rom. 11:27; 1 Cor. 11:25; 2 Cor. 3:6; Heb. 7:22; 8:8–13; 9:15; 12:24.

c Prov. 2:16–17; Mal. 2:14.

d Col. 1:18; 2:10, 19; Eph. 1:10, 22; 4:15; 5:23.

e Gen. 2:18, cf. 1 Tim. 2:11–15; Gen. 5:2; 1 Cor. 11:2–16; 14:33–34; Eph. 5:21–33; Col. 3:18; Titus 2:3–5; 1 Peter 3:1.

1. God called the race "man" (Gen. 1:26) and "mankind" (Gen. 5:2).
2. By naming Eve, Adam was exercising authority over her as God commanded (Gen. 2:23).
3. Although the woman sinned first, God came calling for the man (Gen. 3:8–9) and held him responsible because he failed to lovingly lead and protect his family from Satan and sin. Sadly, our first father, like many of his cowardly sons, sat idly by and did nothing while his wife was being deceived (2 Cor. 11:3; 1 Tim. 2:14).
4. It is Adam's sin that is imputed to the human race, because he is our head, and only Jesus, who is called "the last Adam," can remove that sin (Rom. 5:12–21; 1 Cor. 15:45).
5. Echoing the creation account of our first parents, the Bible repeatedly declares that husbands are to lovingly, humbly, and sacrificially lead their homes as Christlike heads, and that wives are to submit to their husbands (Gen. 2:18, cf. Gen. 5:2; 1 Cor. 11:2–16; 14:33–34; Eph. 5:21–33; Col. 3:18; 1 Tim. 2:11–15; Titus 2:3–5; 1 Peter 3:1).

This does *not* mean that a husband is in ultimate authority. God is. And other authorities are over the man, such as the state and church governments. It also does not mean a wife can't have independent thoughts or seek to influence her husband, or has to obey her husband's command to sin, or that she is less intelligent or competent than her husband. This *does* mean that a husband and wife are equal with complementary roles (like a left and right hand that work together, though one is dominant); wives are to submit to their husbands as Jesus does to God the Father; husbands are to lovingly lead their wives as Jesus does the church. A single woman should only marry a man she respects and trusts enough to follow. Marriage is supposed to reflect something of the Trinity and the gospel, where Jesus pursues us in love and takes responsibility for us as an example to husbands and fathers.

Despite sin entering the world, the duty of the husband to be the loving covenant head of his marriage and family remains. When the Bible says that the husband is the head of his wife, it is not stating that a man *should* be the head, but rather that he simply *is* as Jesus is the Head of the church. The only question, therefore, is whether or not a husband is a good or bad head.

For Adam and his sons since, God promised that everything under their dominion would be cursed and fight against them; providing for their families would be a cursed experience that would show us how difficult it is for God to be our Head when we disobey Him.[a]

A husband who is a good head will not abuse, abdicate, abandon, or avoid responsibility. Instead, he will accept it humbly and seek by God's grace and the Holy Spirit's power to obey God's command in Ephesians 5:25–28, "Husbands, love your wives, just as Christ also loved the church and gave Himself for her, that He might sanctify and cleanse her with the washing of water by the word, that He might present her to Himself a glorious church, not having spot or wrinkle or any such thing, but that she should be holy and without blemish. So husbands ought to love their own wives as their own bodies; he who loves his wife loves himself."

A godly man is continually learning that to be the head of his home means to take responsibility for the well-being of his wife and children much as Jesus Christ has taken responsibility for him. As the covenant head, you cannot remain distant, unwilling to get involved in the messiest parts of your family life, or tell your wife to get her act together apart from your loving inclusion. This is not to say that your wife bears no responsibility for her own sin, but that you bear it with her out of love. We see this perhaps most clearly in Genesis 3, when the first married couple sinned. Though the wife sinned first and was held accountable by God, the husband was called out by God and held responsible for both his sin and his wife's sin.

Being the responsible head does not mean that a man does everything in the family, but rather that everything gets done. This includes him lovingly carrying his load for the family, helping his wife do the same, and making sure the children do as well. This means that whoever is best at something and is willing to do it assumes that responsibility. For example, if your wife is a great accountant and you are not, she can run the family finances. Or if you're a chef and she cannot make a peanut butter and jelly sandwich, you may do a lot of the meal planning and preparation, help teach her, or encourage her spiritual gift of picking up takeout. And if you do not have the time or skills to work on the cars, you can do as I do and pay someone else to do it.

As a general rule, when a man does accept the responsibilities God requires

---

a Gen. 3:17–19.

of him as the lovingly humble servant leader of his home, his wife and children flourish. When he does not, the results are not pretty. Sadly, a myth has become quite popular that there is no difference between the quality and holiness of Christian and non-Christian marriages and that the incidence of things such as adultery and divorce are essentially the same between the two groups. This myth is based on some research that only asked people if they were Christians and failed to ask any follow-up questions.[6] Jesus Himself predicted that many who would profess faith would in fact not possess faith.[a] Therefore, in addition to asking people what they believe, we must ask them how they behave to ascertain if they are truly Christians. And when all the facts are included, it becomes very clear that those who both profess *and* practice Christianity have markedly different and better marriages than those people who do not.

W. Bradford Wilcox has conducted the most helpful research done on the difference active Christian faith makes in a marriage. He is widely recognized as one of the most distinguished sociologists in America.[7] Wilcox has undertaken the massive project of determining what effects religious belief and participation have for men regarding their wives and children. He classified religious men in categories of Catholic, more liberal mainline Protestant, conservative evangelicals, and unaffiliated men without religious connections or convictions. He also factored in "religious participation" (church attendance).

Mainline Protestants were said to hold to "Golden Rule Christianity," which means they are primarily committed to loving God and people through such things as acts of justice and mercy. They had a lower commitment to other things that conservative Protestants or evangelicals hold to, such as the belief that the Bible is the inerrant, perfect Word of God, which serves as the moral guide to all of life. They also hold that Jesus is the only means to salvation. Wilcox's findings only confirm what the Bible says: that Christian men (Catholic and Protestant) who lovingly and biblically lead their homes as head have considerably better marriages and families.

While there is no silver bullet to ensure all goes well in marriage, the following things make a big difference: get involved in a good church, agree on what the Bible says, and worship together at home.

---

a Matt. 7:21–23.

Get Involved in a Good Church

There are many benefits of a husband being involved in a Bible-believing, Jesus-loving, conservative Christian church.

Churchgoing husbands express more positive emotion to their wives, are more attentive to their marriages, serve their wives more, take more time for date night and time together, and invest more in their wives.[8] This is due, in part, to the constant stressing in a good church that selfishness is a sin, and we are called by God to live for the glory of God and good of others, which helps safeguard a marriage from selfishness.

The combination of preaching, teaching, modeling of godly men, negative examples from sinful men, accountability, praise for godly behavior, and discipline for ungodly behavior all help keep husbands pursuing their wives in love.[9] The church also helps create a "canopy of meaning" where daily life activities are connected to God and purpose. It also closes the back door on adultery and divorce, forcing men to work on their marriages and to take a long-term view, even to future generations.[10]

> Churchgoing conservative Protestant family men are soft patriarchs. Contrary to the assertions of feminists, many family scholars, and public critics, these men cannot be fairly described as "abusive" and 'authoritarian' family men wedded to "stereotypical forms of masculinity." They outpace mainline Protestant and unaffiliated family men in their emotional and practical dedication to their children and wives and in their commitment to family, and they are the least likely to physically abuse their wives.[11]

In fact, "evangelical married men have the lowest rates of reported domestic violence of any major religious or secular group in the United States."[12] However, "nominal conservative Protestant husbands are the group . . . most likely to commit domestic violence."[13] "Nominal" refers to those who profess Christianity but do not practice it with such things as regularly reading the Bible, praying, and attending church.

Godly men make the best fathers. The research confirms that "conservative Protestant married men with children are consistently the most active and expressive fathers and the most emotionally engaged husbands."[14] And men who are regular churchgoers are more likely to spend time in youth-related activities such as coaching sports, hugging and praising their children, disciplining them rather than forcing Mom to do it all by default, keeping tabs on their children, playing games with them, and helping out with homework. They also yell at their children less frequently than other fathers.[15]

Couples who regularly attend church together report greater marital happiness, marital support, and romance in their marriages.[16] The positive impact for husbands is even greater than for wives. "For men, 70 percent of husbands who attend church regularly report they are 'very happy' in their marriages, compared to 59 percent of husbands who rarely or never attend church."[17] In light of the above statistics it is not surprising that the wives of godly men report the highest levels of marital happiness.[18]

Couples who regularly attend church together are far less likely to separate or divorce, which is the most common eventual result of separation. Couples who "frequently attend religious services are only about half as likely to separate."[19] Also, the "rate of marital dissolution [divorce] is 2.4 times higher among couples where neither spouse attends than among couples where each spouse attends religious services every week."[20] One study found that couples who attend church together regularly were approximately 35 percent less likely to divorce, compared to their married peers who rarely or never attended religious services.[21]

What do all these statistics mean to you? If your marriage is in trouble and you are not in a good church, connecting with one is an urgent matter. And if your marriage is not in crisis, then please seek to stay connected in community at a good church to help safeguard your marriage. In choosing a church, it must be a church that the husband wants to attend. Too often the wife is the one choosing the church because it meets her emotional desires and the children's programming needs. Subsequently, the husband is not interested in church because he sees it primarily for women and children. This, in part, explains why the majority of church attenders are women. To curb this trend, you, the husband, need to take the initiative to find a church that you also find challenging, one that is filled with men you respect, enjoy, and would pursue godly relationships with.

This all begins with the preaching pastor, because a man chooses a church not so much because of style or programming but rather because he admires the senior leader and is willing to submit to him, follow him, and emulate him.

So husbands must find a church led by a man who believes the Bible, loves Jesus, and leads his home and church well as a man's man.

Once you are in a local church, do not merely attend events anonymously; get connected to community. Good churches encourage and provide opportunities for couples and their children to spend meaningful time together, from serving to small groups and retreats. Good churches have other families that can become great friends of your family as you encourage and support one another to honor God in all of life. These relationships are incredibly important because they provide for a husband and wife same-gender relationships and accountability. For example, Grace and I have a handful of very wise, godly couples both in and out of our church whom we depend on for earnest counsel and loving rebuke. These relationships have been life changing and marriage saving. Good churches also have wise people who can help you learn how to care for a newborn, sort out your finances, purchase a home, deal with an illness or death, get a job, and handle other challenging life seasons and circumstances. Last, a good church provides ministry opportunities for a husband and wife to serve God together, which is incredibly meaningful, purposeful, and uniting.

Agree on What the Bible Says

You and your wife will be well served to agree on your theology of marriage. Couples who do not do the hard work of studying what the Bible says about life and marriage may believe in God, but they fail to enjoy the kind of oneness that He intends for them. Rather than fighting *with* each other about what is right and wrong, together you fight *for* each other, seeking to honor your shared biblical convictions. You will have a great advantage if you not only attend the same church but also have the same theological convictions on the big issues, including marriage. This is proved statistically in the following ways.

One, couples who are part of the same Christian denomination are 42 percent more likely to be very happy than couples who are not. Moreover, higher rates of attendance and theological conservatism are also associated with greater marital happiness—especially when spouses have similar beliefs and attendance patterns.[22] Conversely, couples who do not share the same religious denomination or who have no religious affiliation are significantly more likely to divorce.[23] And couples with different religious backgrounds are more than 120 percent more likely to divorce.[24]

Two, theological agreement is more important than an equal sharing of chores in the home. In past generations, chauvinism was common because some husbands did not respect their wives as equal or value their contributions. In reaction, feminism then came into vogue, seeking to get women out of the home and into the workplace, and to make the husbands do half the chores at home. This method has been called an *egalitarian marriage*. Despite a lot of egalitarian effort, the evidence concludes that whether or not a wife works outside the home, she still does most of the chores in the home. What is curious, however, is that it does not seem to be the determining factor in whether a wife thinks she has a high-quality marriage. The researchers studying this

> find no support for the theory that egalitarianism (conceptualized as approving or disapproving of women working when [they] have children, whether or not the wife participated in labor force, whether husband or wife earned more, and how equally household labor [was] divided) promotes wife's marital quality. It is more important for wife's marital happiness that husband and wife have shared ideas about marriage, that they both commit to the institution of marriage, that they are integrated into an institution (like the church) that also has these same ideas about marriage, and that the marriage and the husbands are emotionally invested in marriage.[25]

For engaged couples, these findings underscore the importance of rigorous biblically based premarital counseling in a local church that includes a community of support. Couples who do not theologically agree on what will and will not happen in their marriage wind up fighting about it, sometimes for the rest of their lives. But couples who do agree on their roles in marriage as taught in the Scriptures embrace their roles and find them meaningful.

For the wife, this means that so long as the husband expresses great thankfulness for her work in the home and is willing to help out as needed, she does not usually feel slighted.[26] And the husband who considers it his duty to be the primary if not the sole breadwinner does not begrudge this fact but rather embraces it as a God-given duty. Furthermore, he is genuinely aided by a wife who thanks him for working hard to take care of their family and appreciates his work outside the home as much as he appreciates her work in the home.[27] Mutual appreciation and encouragement is key, especially in a culture that doesn't regard biblical roles positively. Similarly, a marriage in which both spouses work outside the home requires that they agree on how their life is organized and each is encouraging and thankful for the various contributions the other makes to their family. The key is always agreement and appreciation.

Worship Together at Home

The Bible expects husbands and fathers to lovingly function as pastors to their wives and children. The Bible commands husbands to be in the Scriptures with their wives regularly.[a] The Bible invites studious wives to take their biblical and theological questions to their husbands with the assumption that they know their Bible. If a husband doesn't have an answer, he should lovingly do his homework to help his wife grow spiritually.[b] The Bible also commands fathers as "pastor dads" to spiritually raise up their children.[c]

The evidence concludes that "the frequency with which couples engage in regular in-home worship activities (for example, prayer and scriptural study) was also a positive link with relationship quality."[28] Men, as the head of your homes, this is ultimately your responsibility. To be sure, as your helper, your wife should participate. But as the leader, it is your God-given duty and privilege to lovingly and humbly make the well-being of each member of your family your responsibility, starting with yourself, then your wife, and then your children and grandchildren.

A Few Tips for the Guys

Here are a few practical tips for husbands in addition to some of the things mentioned above:

1. As the family leader, model humility, honesty, repentance, service, study, and worship. Your life preaches at least as loudly as your words, so teach and model humble godliness by the grace of God.

---

a Eph. 5:25–26.
b 1 Cor. 14:35.
c Eph. 6:4.

2. Make sure everyone in your family has a good, age-appropriate Bible that they regularly read. Read the Bible yourself and with them so they are encouraged to read on their own.

3. Make sure you have some basic Bible study tools available for your family in either print or digital form and that everyone learns to use them. If you do not know where to begin, ask your pastor or a godly student of Scripture in your church about things like a good Bible commentary, concordance, dictionary, and atlas.

4. Buy good Christian books for everyone in your family to read. Include Christian biographies among those books.

5. Choose good books that you and your wife can be reading together, including books of the Bible, and discuss what you are learning.

6. If there are Bible-based classes offered in your church, attend with your family.

7. Redeem your commute by listening to good sermons and classes, many of which you can download for free.[29]

8. Have dinner together with your family most nights, and use that time to pray together, keep a journal log of prayer requests for other people, and read a portion of the Bible and talk about it together.

9. Pray for each member of your family every day and let them know you are praying for them.

10. Place a hand on the head of each of your children every day and pray over them. Then kiss them on the head and make sure they often get a loving hug.

11. While either snuggling or holding hands, pray with and for your wife every day and remember to include the reasons you are thankful to God for her that day.

If these things have not been common in your home, it is very likely that your family has been aching for them and will be thankful for your loving leadership as the head of your home.

Your wife gets to be the umpire on the content of this chapter. If it helps you remember that fact, buy her a white-and-black-striped shirt to wear to bed at night—she'll look cute, and it will serve as a reminder. You may read this chapter and think you are loving and leading well. But it is your wife who gets to make the call on your performance.

Ephesians 5:22–33 is perhaps the clearest section of the Bible on the role of husbands to lead their families as the head and wives to respectfully submit to them. When a wife is critical of her husband's performance as a loving leader, he may be prone to dismiss her by telling her she is simply wrong and needs to submit. But the verse that sets up the responsibilities of husbands and wives, Ephesians 5:21, commands them to be "submitting to one another." This means she gets to decide if you are loving and leading well as the head, and you get to decide if she is respecting and submitting well as the helper. And if one of you should come to believe the other is simply wrong or unreasonable, a mediator in the form of a pastor or Bible counselor needs to play the role of referee and make the call. Until then, without defending yourself for any shortcomings, start asking your wife how you are doing at loving and leading and what you can do to improve your game in those areas.

As men we bear a greater burden before God for the well-being of our families. Our wives and children (should God gift us with them) should flourish under our loving leadership. My hope is that you would not find this condemning, but challenging. By the grace of God you can be who God has called you to be, do what God has called you to do, and love as God has loved you. As men, we will never in this life experience perfection, but by the grace of God we can experience progress every day until we enter perfection in the life to come. So don't sulk, don't sin, and don't settle, but instead strive.

4

THE RESPECTFUL WIFE

Let the wife see that she respects her husband.

—EPHESIANS 5:33

Long ago, there was a believing woman who was married to an unbelieving man. Because of his power, she was made to marry him, though she did not know him. He divorced his first wife for disrespecting him in public. This new wife was given a very powerful position by virtue of marrying him, and she trusted that God was going to give her wisdom and strength to humbly love him and learn from him. She desired to be obedient to God first, and she was going to be asked to risk her very life for God's plan. In her culture, women (wives) weren't allowed to make requests of powerful leaders without being called by the man first. Can you imagine having to wait for your husband to call upon you to talk to him or ask anything from him? Amazingly, when she had an extremely urgent request, she respectfully waited outside his room to be heard. She didn't barge in and demand that he do what she wanted. She didn't back down from the request because it was too much effort or risk. She didn't disregard his need for respect, even if it seemed extreme. She humbly prayed, acted in godly faith and wifely respect, and saved the lives of her people!

Esther is an amazing example of a godly woman in the hardest of circumstances. She took a risk by doing the right thing, in the right way, at the right time, for the right reasons. Her example illustrates the repeated command across all Scripture that wives respectfully submit to their husbands, and it removes any excuse we have for disrespecting our husbands.[a]

---

a Gen. 2:18, cf. 1 Tim. 2:11–15; Gen. 5:2, 1 Cor. 11:2–16; 14:33–34; Eph. 5:21–33; Col. 3:18; Titus 2:3–5; 1 Peter 3:1.

Were you hoping I (Grace) wouldn't address this issue, or were you going to skim through this chapter because you think you already respect your husband well? Many of us have read chapters and books on this topic, but for some reason most of them seem to be written by men![1] I want to honestly look at what the Bible has to say versus what the culture has to say and encourage you to live in the freedom that comes when we are obedient to God and His Word. Mark has written to the men on their responsibilities, and I believe it is wise for me to do the same for the women, because they go hand in hand.

Do you want to have a joyful and unified marriage that glorifies God? In order to obtain oneness and worship our Lord in our marriages, we need to correctly understand the need for respect. Men and women were created with equal worth but different roles. God created and called the man to lead and love his wife, and when he doesn't do that in a holy way, he is sinning. God created the woman to help[a] and respect her husband, and when she doesn't do that in a holy way, she is sinning. Oneness is not accomplished through sinning against our spouses and our God! Esther obeyed God *and* respected an ungodly husband. God protected her, and her king husband loved her through honoring her request. This is exactly what Ephesians 5:33 intends for your marriage as well: "Let each one of you in particular so love his own wife as himself, and let the wife see that she respects her husband."

Respect **Defined**

We need to know what a word means before we can start to practice it. To *respect* is "to notice, regard, honor, prefer, defer to, encourage, love, and admire." Can you think of someone you respect? As women, we often respect other women. But what things do you respect about your husband, and does he know what they are? Do you consider yourself respectful toward your husband? Would he agree with your assessment?

Respect includes your head, heart, *and* hands. As I began this chapter, I was struggling (pridefully) to think of examples of how I disrespect Mark. I'm guessing if you know anything about Mark's character as a man, he tends to naturally command respect, so you might assume that I'm a naturally respectful

---

a Gen. 2:18.

wife. I thought that was true for a long time, and the first time Mark told me I was a disrespectful wife, I laughed and said, "Me? What are you talking about? I'm always nice to you." I could see he was frustrated and serious, and from that point on I started to question how I was disrespecting him.

When I recall my initial response, I can clearly see now that it was completely prideful and disrespectful because it claimed no fault and disregarded his rebuke. It is important to pray about our issues with respect and listen to our husbands' concerns. My disrespect included my head, heart, and hands. My head sinned by not desiring to listen and potentially repent; my heart sinned with prideful disregard for how Mark felt; my hands sinned by not reaching out to him both physically and emotionally.

Heads of Respect

Respect starts in our heads and includes our minds and thoughts. Disrespect also starts in our heads and can begin with a very subtle temptation that over time affects our hearts and hands. James 1:14–15 describes it perfectly: "But each one is tempted when he is drawn away by his own desires and enticed. Then, when desire has conceived, it gives birth to sin; and sin, when it is full-grown, brings forth death." Disrespect starts when we think things like: *That was a dumb decision he made; I can do better than that. I wish he were more like _____. I'll just fix all the things he does wrong. I hope the kids don't grow up to be like him. When he is out of town, life is easier. I won't ask him because he won't understand.* If you are thinking this way toward your husband and let it continue, it will seep into your heart and eventually come out in your words and actions toward your husband. We need to stop disrespectful lies and sinful thoughts before they "give birth."

In 2 Corinthians 10 we are reminded to continually bring "every thought into captivity to the obedience of Christ" (v.5). Every thought? That seems impossible. We can only do this through prayer and, as Romans 12:2 says, letting God renew (replace with holy thoughts) our minds with Scripture and His wisdom. As Philippians 4:8–9 says,

> Finally, brethren, whatever things are true, whatever things are noble, whatever things are just, whatever things are pure, whatever things are lovely, whatever things are of good report, if there is any virtue and if there is

anything praiseworthy—meditate on these things. The things which you learned and received and heard and saw in me, these do, and the God of peace will be with you.

What an honor it is that He allows us to speak to and listen to Him anytime we want! We need to take full advantage of that opportunity throughout our days, while we are working, exercising, driving, cooking, cleaning, waiting for the kids at school. God is always available to help us. Subsequently, our days must be filled with truth from God and prayer to God if we hope to grow as respectful wives.

Many of us read about respect and are inclined to agree that it is a vital character trait for a wife to cultivate by the grace of God. But some of us are more inclined to bristle and disagree. Unfortunately, it's an issue that has been used by some—at times from the pulpit itself—to demean women or cause them to feel less valued. We may have experienced things in our lives that caused us to build emotional walls to protect ourselves and create systems of thinking that give us a false sense of safety. Often we are not aware that we are doing this."[2] This was true in my life, as I didn't have brothers and had very little understanding of guys. Some of you may not have had a father or, if you did, not a godly example of a man. Roughly four out of ten kids growing up today go to bed without a father in their lives. A fatherless girl can grow up to be more vulnerable to ungodly men because her father was not there to protect her, and because she did not have an example of what a godly, safe man is like. For me, this has meant working hard to take down walls and develop godly ways to work out issues of disrespect in my marriage.

If we have wrong thinking or bitterness toward the word *respect* and what the Bible says, we need to start with repentance and ask God to give us respectful thoughts toward even His authority. If we continue to feed our old way of thinking with lies and fears, the sin of disrespect will control us. I hear many women say there is nothing they respect about their husbands, and they have many complaints instead. If you married him, you must have seen something you appreciated and admired about him. We can develop new habits of biblical thinking by being thankful for our husbands' gifts and strengths, rather than being bitter about their weaknesses and shortcomings.

Mark and I are opposite in literally everything (except our theological convictions), right down to him liking the big potato chips and me preferring the little pieces. Sometimes we just have to laugh that God put us together with everything different about us. We can either choose to be constantly frustrated by being opposite, or be willing to grow and learn from each other and appreciate our differences. These things can actually, by God's grace, complement our marriage and help us serve each other and others more fully. Sadly, we know far too many people (including us for many years of marriage) that let the differences lead to disrespect and division, but it doesn't have to be that way.

Where do you start the respect process? Confess your sin of disrespecting authority to God and your husband, and be willing to listen to the Holy Spirit's conviction for change. By taking time to observe your husband closely, you can start to journal or make a list of things you appreciate about him, such as working hard, staying faithful to you, spending time with you and the kids, being a friend, and doing specific tasks. Mark appreciates both verbal and written encouragement; so telling him and writing notes about how I appreciate him are ways I can show him I respect him.

Think about how you feel when your husband encourages you or thanks you for something you did. This doesn't mean you are overlooking his sin, but if you are caught in the cycle (as I was) of disrespectful thinking about him, you need to stop walking down the path of disrespect and in repentance go the other direction, toward respect. As we obey God's command to respect our husbands, faith and wisdom will rise up in our hearts and replace fear. There will be a difference in your words and actions if your mind is growing in respect first toward God and His Word and then toward your husband.

Hearts of Respect

If our hearts are working toward respect, our mouths will follow because "out of the abundance of the heart the mouth speaks."[a] If our hearts abound with disrespect, our mouths will spew disrespectful words. Our words as women are often motivated or withheld because of our emotions. Do you tend to respond to your husband with criticism or with silence? When you talk about him in public or with others, do you tear him down or build him up? Are you careful not to gossip about him, or do you freely share your issues

---

a Matt. 12:34.

with others? This includes prayer requests, women's Bible studies, and female accountability relationships that degenerate into gossip, busybodying, and disrespecting our husbands in the name of ministry.

The respectful Proverbs 31 woman "opens her mouth with wisdom, and on her tongue is the law of kindness."[a] Are your words to and about your husband marked by "wisdom" and "kindness"? Or, do you instead use words as a form of control because you don't know how to, or just don't want to, have healthy conversations with your husband about your frustrations? When we speak disrespectfully, it is often because we are seeking to be in control, to manipulate or bully our husbands. A biblical counselor rightly said, "If my words don't flow out of a heart that rests in [God's] control [sovereignty], then they come out of a heart that seeks control, so I can get what I want."[3]

We don't want to be talked to harshly, so we need to desire the same for our husbands. Also, it is important to remember, we don't change our husbands; the Holy Spirit does! Use your words to pray for him and help him instead of belittling him. Or use your words to pray for yourself that you will practice self-control. When you want to speak, remember Ephesians 4:29: "Let no corrupt word proceed out of your mouth, but what is good for necessary edification, that it may impart grace to the hearers." Are you a wife who criticizes, contradicts, or sneers at your husband? Do you do this in front of other people? Do you "joke" about his lack of abilities or his way of doing things? Do you cut him down in front of the kids? My fear is that we may be doing this without even paying attention to it, because it is so common in our culture. Popular situational comedies on television degrade the husbands and make them look like idiots in comparison to their wives. Ask yourself how you would feel if your husband was disrespectful to you, or remember how devastated you have felt when he responded to your disrespect with disrespect.

Our battle with words goes all the way back to the garden of Eden when Eve used her words to ask her husband to sin with her. Her intention was not to bless him but to excuse her sin and have him join her in it. We continue to fight the same war with our mouths today, but God gives us the Holy Spirit for wisdom and strength to continue being redeemed. Sometimes we don't even hear ourselves, because our words can be subtle disrespect, so we might

a Prov. 31:26.

need others whom we trust to help us assess our hearts and mouths. Ask your husband or a godly woman, or both, if your words are respectful, and be willing to listen without blame shifting or excusing your sin. We cannot grow in respect if we disregard those who point out our disrespect.

Hands of Respect

God created women to be helpers, which is a reflection of His character. God said, "It is not good that man should be alone," so He created a helper for Adam.[a] It is important to note that the word *helper* does not denigrate the wife; in fact, God is also referred to as our helper.[b] We need each other, not so we lose our identities, but rather so we can reflect our identity in Christ to our spouses as the Holy Spirit makes us more holy. As a helper, a wife is called to become a companion in her husband's God-given calling. This is what 1 Corinthians 11:7–9 means, saying, "[Man] is the image and glory of God; but woman is the glory of man. For man is not from woman, but woman from man. Nor was man created for the woman, but woman for the man."

Upon marriage, a woman's life changes as she joins her husband in his life's course. That looks different for me than it does for your marriage because all our husbands are unique. For starters, prayerfully consider the following ways to have respectful hands:

Hands That Pray. Prayer softens both our hearts and their hearts, by trusting God to make us teachable and to work in *both* of us. If you only pray for him to change, then you won't see your own sin too. Prayer reminds us of our total dependence on God. When I pray for Mark, he feels respected and loved. I look at his calendar for the day and pray for teaching sessions, meetings, appointments, safety, wisdom, and other things God brings to mind. We also enjoy prayers of thankfulness together when we see God's grace in our lives. When Mark is sad, upset, stressed, or discouraged, I offer to pray out loud with him.

Hands That Touch. Physical affection is key to intimacy. If he enjoys touch, you probably can't go overboard on this one, but if he is more reserved, you can still express comfort through holding hands, neck rubs, and meaningful

---

a Gen. 2:18.
b E.g., Pss. 10:14; 118:6–7; Heb. 13:6.

kisses. Sex for the purpose of oneness usually doesn't just "happen" at the end of a long day without working toward it throughout the day. Don't get into a habit of only touching him when he is leaving the house once a day; rather, learn to enjoy playfulness that leads to deeper intimacy and sex. Try meeting him for lunch appointments when possible. Greet him at the door with a hug or kiss instead of demands when he arrives home from work. Text him during the day to let him know you are thinking about him.

Hands That Feed. Take the time to plan a menu for the week (or month) so you aren't throwing unhealthy things together for dinner or tempted to always eat out. There are many recipe and cooking Web sites (for example, allrecipes. com and foodnetwork.com) that offer healthy meal ideas. He will have more mental, physical, and emotional energy if he is not eating simple carbs and sugar all day. I'm not saying he can't cook if he likes to, but be attentive to nutrition, and educate yourself so you are stewarding the health of your family well. And sitting down to regularly enjoy good meals together is a welcoming way to nurture your friendship with your husband.

Hands That Hunt And Fish. Be unselfish. I'm actually the one who likes to fish, and Mark doesn't hunt, but the point is to do activities that he likes to do sometimes and have fun with it. Mark loves baseball, so I have attended many games and learned how baseball works. I often watched him play in high school. Our three boys also love baseball, so I spend countless hours at the field for all their games. In return, Mark knows I don't like to shop alone, so he takes me to my favorite stores every so often and helps pick out what looks nice. He also loves to study the culture by watching some of the popular TV shows, so I watch shows with him that wouldn't be my first choice. There is always something I learn from the shows as well.

Hands That Open The Bible. Grow your relationship with Jesus. If you aren't getting fed through Bible reading, prayer, and personal repentance, it will be impossible to know how to serve and respect your husband. Since respect is a command, God will give us the wisdom and strength to carry it out and not leave us alone to figure it out. We *have* to stay connected to Jesus in order to keep our husbands a priority over tasks, kids, other people, and the pull of culture. I tried respecting Mark without keeping Jesus first, and it was a disaster no matter how hard I tried. I used to think I didn't have time for daily Bible and book reading, but we just need to use the time that God already gives us for it. As a mother of five, I learned to pray for God to show me moments throughout the day to use for reading, and He has been faithful to do that. Anytime the order of godly (1) woman, (2) wife, (3) mother, and (4) friend gets switched, we commit idolatry and end up in misery.

———

The Bible provides principles for how to respectfully help our husbands, but it does not give us many methods. Women are prone to ask other women what methods they use as respectful helpers, or to read books such as this one, seeking to be told what to do. Indeed, some good methods can be gathered in this way. But the best thing is to simply ask your husband. Start by telling him that you want to be a wife who "does him good and not evil all the days of her life."[a] Then respectfully ask him where you are doing this well and where you could do this better, and make note of his answers. Ask him how he needs you to be a helper. Respectful conversations can lead to respectful actions in your marriage.

Communication can either encourage or discourage change in your marriage. As I mentioned in an earlier chapter, Mark and I didn't start out knowing how to communicate well. He came from a vocal family, and I came from a silent family. You can only guess how we collided when we got married! Mark would abruptly voice his comments, and I would become silent. He used to say it was like trying to volley the ball over the net, but it would never get returned. I felt squashed and he felt neglected. We went around in this cycle for years before we realized it was only getting worse, and we were becoming more divided. He had to learn to draw me out by loving me, even if he was angry with me about something; and I had to learn to engage in respectful conversation by not being silent. I had to learn (and am still learning) how to disagree, pray, counsel, submit, and encourage respectfully. It has been an interesting process of going from silent to fighting back to prayerfully considering my words. God is still showing me how to be "swift to hear, slow to speak,"[b] so I wanted to share some of the lessons I have learned from mistakes I have made over the years.

———

a Prov. 31:12.
b James 1:19.

Disagreeing Respectfully

Many people ask Mark and me if we ever fight. Yes. We believe that if you never fight, you probably aren't having heartfelt conversations that often lead to disagreement. We've never known a couple to agree on everything and live in perfect harmony unless they were in denial or didn't want to allow change or healthy conflict in their own lives. The key is to fight as friends and not as foes. Friends do fight, but they fight lovingly and respectfully. If your husband is verbally or physically abusing you, he is not loving or respecting you. If this is an ongoing issue, it should be addressed and stopped immediately by a pastor or trustworthy leader who will listen to you both. We never condone abuse (nor does the Bible), and if you don't get help, you could be in danger. There is further discussion of abuse in chapter 7 if you would like to have more information. If you are not in an abusive relationship, viewing your husband as a friend should help you engage respectfully rather than defensively.

There are two extreme types of women during times of disagreement with their husbands: the silent, compliant wife or the loud, contentious wife.

When faced with conflict, the silent, compliant wife supports everything her husband says and does, thinking she is practicing holy submission, but instead she is making her husband into an idol that she worships. In so doing, she is not being a helper, but rather an enabler. Women like this see their lives get progressively sadder and harder as their husbands make foolish decisions. One woman I know has a husband who continually made foolish business decisions that have bankrupted their family, left them destitute, and indebted them to many fellow Christians. All of this happened while she said very little to him. Another woman has a husband who demands that she submit to his authority, while he repeatedly refuses to submit to any church authority. As a result, their family has moved from church to church, since anytime a ministry leader broaches sin in the husband's life, he becomes divisive and leaves the church. Subsequently, she is no longer in any meaningful fellowship and is quite lonely and hurting. She has never really stood up to her husband and should do so in a respectful way because she is supposed to be a helper. Proverbs 19:14 says, "A prudent wife is from the LORD."

A silent, compliant wife is guilty of the sin of the "fear of man." Proverbs

29:25 says, "The fear of man brings a snare, but whoever trusts in the LORD shall be safe." Noted biblical counselor Ed Welch said,

> Fear in the biblical sense . . . includes being afraid of someone, but it extends to holding someone in awe, being controlled or mastered by people, worshipping other people, putting your trust in people, or needing people. . . . The fear of man can be summarized this way: We replace God with people. Instead of a biblically guided fear of the Lord, we fear others. . . . When we are in our teens, it is called "peer pressure." When we are older, it is called "people-pleasing." Recently, it has been called "codependency.[4]

When we fear someone wrongly, our identity, joy, value, and security are tied to that person above the Lord. As a result, we avoid his or her rejection or disappointment at all costs. But in so doing we are not loving that individual by respectfully standing up to his or her sin; rather, we are doing harm by compliantly enabling that person's sin.

For women, it is common to worship our husbands by fearing them wrongly. In fact, "fear not" is the most common command in the Bible.[5] Many women allow their marriages to be governed by their fears. For some women, this fear in their minds and hearts leads to symptoms of anxiety in their bodies—everything from chronic illness to panic attacks and depression. For such women, Jesus' words are to be heard as a loving invitation more than a stern command. In Luke 12:22 Jesus says, "Do not worry about your life." And, in Luke 12:25, Jesus says, "Which of you by worrying can add one cubit to his stature?" My life scripture is Philippians 4:5–7: "The Lord is at hand. Be anxious for nothing, but in everything by prayer and supplication, with thanksgiving, let your requests be made known to God; and the peace of God, which surpasses all understanding, will guard your hearts and minds through Christ Jesus."

If this describes you, or you have experienced fear when disagreeing with your husband, please remember the verse from 1 Peter regarding Sarah, "Do what is right and do not give way to fear" (3:6 NIV). Pray for the Holy Spirit to convict you of your sin so you don't breed pride in your husband and hold him in a place of perfection that only God should be. It is not a sin to have a different opinion from your husband or to see sin or folly in your husband. You need to learn freedom in respectfully expressing these things to him. A good way to start is to pray first; then ask questions rather than make accusations or strong statements. Pray for God to give you a humble boldness.

On the other hand, if you are the loud, contentious wife, you tend to fight back with cutting remarks when you are faced with conflict.

Proverbs has a lot to say about such women:

A foolish woman is clamorous;
She is simple, and knows nothing. (9:13)

Better to dwell in the wilderness,
Than with a contentious and angry woman. (21:19)

As a ring of gold in a swine's snout,
So is a lovely woman who lacks discretion. (11:22)

[A wife] who causes shame is like rottenness in his bones. (12:4)

Better to dwell in a corner of a housetop,
Than in a house shared with a contentious woman. (21:9)

A continual dripping on a very rainy day
And a contentious woman are alike. (27:15)

Fighting disrespectfully and unrepentantly puts your husband in a lose-lose situation. This is doubly true if you do so in front of other people, especially your children. If he walks away, you win. If he stays and fights angrily, you win. This is a form of manipulation to get your way. You want control, and you are going to get it by breaking him down, whether it's little by little or all at once! Men refer to this kind of wife as a "ball breaker." I don't usually use terms like this, but I believe you need to understand the seriousness of how this feels to your husband. In the end, ask yourself if you have more or less respect for him when you've "won" the fight. If you cause him to want to "live in the wilderness or on the corner of the roof" rather than with you, you haven't won anything; rather, you have caused division in your marriage. Pray for the Holy Spirit to convict you of your sin so you don't destroy your husband and put him in a place of submission to you. Women with this tendency complain that their husbands won't lead, but often the wives won't let them. Honestly, underneath a controlling attitude there is usually a major fear that a wife needs to work through, such as from past abuse or a neglectful father or the fear of being seen as a "doormat." It is common to place our past experiences on our spouses, but we need to repent and let them earn fresh trust in our marriage.

I have also heard both types of women, compliant and contentious, use the excuse of it being "just my personality" or "just the way I am" that is perceived as disrespectful. I want to clarify that I know women with quiet personalities and outgoing personalities who are equally respectful to their husbands. You can be outgoing and bold in personality, but there are ways to do that with respect. You can be quiet and shy, but there are ways to do that with respect. Please don't allow your personality to be a way to excuse yourself from changing; rather, allow the way God created you to be redeemed into a quiet or bold submission. Truthfully, each woman can learn from the other how to practice both types of submission, as I've had to learn that different issues require different character qualities, and we need to be willing to mature respectfully in both of them.

———

What fears do you have about your husband? What fears do you have about letting God change you? What fears do you have about your marriage? What fears do you have about your future?

It's normal for us to have concerns, but when they rise to an unhealthy level, some women rush in to rule over their husbands in an effort to serve as functional saviors and avoid whatever it is they are afraid of. But women who succeed in ruling over their husbands through disrespect, eventually despise those same men who allow themselves to be yelled at and bossed around like pets. Or the wife finds herself in an ongoing battle with her own husband until he simply starts spending more and more time away from her, as Proverbs predicts.

As wives, our goal cannot be to have our husbands control us or for us to control them. Instead, we are to be controlled by the Holy Spirit to follow our husbands' leadership as respectful helpers. This allows us to disagree with our husbands in ways that are truthful, helpful, and respectful. We can and should influence them toward God and God's purposes for our lives together. There is a balance between being submissive and participating in the marriage as an equal bearer of God's image. Finding that balance requires humility and wisdom.

Again, we need to be quick to listen and slow to speak, but what do you do if you are dialoguing and trying to work toward agreement, but still don't agree? First of all, you need to both agree that you are on the same team and want to work toward oneness rather than division. For several years, Mark truly felt as if I were his enemy because of my lack of support and constant criticism during trials in our marriage. God showed me in one of our "stuck" fights that I needed to tell him I was not his enemy but wanted to learn how to be his friend. This changed something in him as he saw me open to learning how to be a safe confidante and start being an ally. Following are three practical options for resolution that have been helpful to us as we learn to communicate in loving and respectful ways.

Option 1

The husband prays over an issue, discusses it with his wife, and either patiently waits for his wife to come to agree with him through her prayer and processing, or God changes his mind and he comes to see the wisdom in her disagreement. This is how most differences are settled in a healthy marriage.

OR

Option 2

The husband appeals to a higher authority, such as a pastor or Bible-based counselor who is not a relative or biased friend. The husband and wife each present their case to the mediator, who then makes a decision that they both obey. If this is a common occurrence, there is a serious underlying problem in the marriage, likely due to significant theological disagreement or personal distrust.

OR

Option 3

The husband makes the decision and the wife follows it. If the husband's decision is found to be wrong, he needs to be willing to admit that humbly, and the wife needs to be careful not to denigrate him by continually reminding him ("I told you so"). If the husband's decision is found to be right, the wife needs to be willing to admit that she was wrong. This shows humility and builds trust in future decisions.

———

Every disagreement is an opportunity for oneness or division. Every day we are either drawing together or drifting apart. As wives, we can be a tremendous blessing if we continually seek, by the grace of God, to be respectful helpers fighting against being either silently compliant or loudly contentious, and fighting for the glory of God and the good of our husbands.

Counseling Respectfully

What comes to mind when you think of counseling? A therapy session with someone asking you personal questions, a wise person in your life—how about a war image? When the Bible speaks of Jesus as our "Wonderful Counselor,"[a] it uses the imagery of a kingdom at war, led by a valiant king who makes battle plans with wise counsel. The Bible often says that life is a war. With our flesh in us conspiring with the world around us, and the Enemy against us, we need our Wonderful Counselor and a wise battle plan compiled by a multitude of counselors. Proverbs 20:18 says, "Plans are established by counsel; by wise guidance wage war." Proverbs 24:5–6 says, "A wise man is strong, yes, a man of knowledge increases strength; for by wise counsel you will wage your own war, and in a multitude of counselors there is safety."

How does this relate to marriage? As helpers, we are to be wise counselors to our husbands. Not *the* Wise Counselor or the only earthly counselor, as men need other men for wise help as well. Your role requires constantly praying for wisdom and knowing how and when to share it with your husband. Sometimes

———

a Isa. 9:6.

your husband will ask you for counsel. Sometimes you should kindly and respectfully ask how you could give your counsel, and see if he is open. If not, pushing it will not help, but praying for God to open his heart is wise. If he is not interested in your counsel, he will likely learn a few things the hard way. When this happens, he will be waiting for you to shame him and remind him of how right you were. But if you are respectful, he will be more likely to seek your counsel in the future. In doing these things, a wife takes time to earn her husband's trust and learn to seek God's wisdom for herself in the process.

It has taken several years for Mark and me to see the fruitfulness in considering each other's counsel. If I am anxious about something, God has taught me how to pray and wait to speak or trust Him to use others to bring wise counsel. I can honestly say that, after being married for almost twenty years, I have seen God use the most random ways to speak into Mark's life when I didn't know how. It has grown my own faith and taught me much about God's sovereignty. There will be some trial and error if this hasn't been a healthy pattern in your marriage, but it can bring great oneness as you wage the war together instead of against one another. In what ways can you be a more helpful, respectful, and wiser friend? In what ways can you make better use of your spouse's wisdom to make your life and family more fruitful?

Encouraging Respectfully

Do you have the spiritual gift of encouragement? Is encouragement something that comes naturally to you, or do you have to work at it? Does your husband consider you to be an encouraging helper and friend? We all know people who have a way of making us feel cared for and hopeful, even when pointing out sin and folly in our lives. A wife is the most powerful person in her husband's life, with a great opportunity to encourage her husband toward godliness through her words, actions, and body language. Several years ago, Mark told me that my encouragement means more than anyone else's, which surprised me. He explained that since I know everything about him, good and bad, when I encourage him, he knows it is authentic. Some people encourage for selfish reasons; others think they are encouraging, but they aren't. I used to think that being Mark's greatest critic was encouraging because I was "helping" him see his problems. I couldn't have been more wrong. If your husband is aware of his problems, he will be tempted to cover them up unless he feels safe to bring them to you, his wife, and invite you to help him overcome them.

Do you think nagging or slipping into "mom mode" and lecturing him like a child is at all encouraging? What about backhanded compliments? Aren't they partially encouraging? Everything, for a man, is viewed as respect or disrespect. For a woman, everything is seen as loving or unloving. I can honestly tell you that all my pushing, nagging, telling him to read this or do that, and failing to pray for Mark made things worse. He felt totally disrespected, not encouraged, by me, and felt as if I was trying to fix him by making him into what I wanted instead of who God wanted. I wasn't encouraging him toward what God had, but demanding what I wanted him to be and do.

I found that once I started praying for him, and praying for God to reveal my own heart, God gave me tenderness and patience toward Mark. I also started to see my own sins (instead of just focusing on his all the time) and was convicted to work on those. The Bible says it is God's kindness that leads us to repentance, so we need to follow that example of kindness with our husbands. If they have unrepentant sin that needs to be addressed, we need to invite them toward change through our encouraging words and actions, rather than demanding change and disrespecting them.

The clearest section in all Scripture commanding a husband to love his wife and a wife to submit to her husband, Ephesians 5:21, talks about "submitting to one another in the fear of God." We believe this means the husband gets to decide when he feels disrespected, and the wife needs to honor that. And the wife gets to decide when she feels unloved, and the husband needs to honor that. For example, we have conflict when Mark says, "I was loving you when I said or did _____" and I disagree. If I don't feel loved, then I get to make that call, and he needs to work on how he can be more loving with me. On the other hand, I sometimes disagree when Mark says I am talking to him disrespectfully, but because he is the one who feels disrespected, then I need to trust him and change my tone, body language, or method of how I am talking to him.

Submitting Respectfully

Unfortunately, *submission* is often a misunderstood word for men and women. The culture's lie is that a woman's worth decreases when she submits to her husband. The truth of the Bible is that a woman's value does not increase or decrease if she submits, because her value comes from being created in God's image, just as Adam and Eve were.[a] Our value comes not from what we do; rather, what we do comes from our value as God's image bearers. For example, my five children don't have any less value than I do just because they submit to me as a parent; they were created in the image of God and merely depend on me for care and instruction. As Christians, this is why we believe the unborn and born, young and old, healthy and sick, educated and uneducated, rich and poor, and women and men are all equally valuable. A husband and wife are equals on the same mission with different roles and responsibilities. We are both reliant on God's grace, and both called to obedience and responsibility.

The Bible frequently commands that a wife submit to her husband.[b] Before explaining what this means, we must first explain what this does not mean.

First, a husband is not in ultimate authority over his wife. For this reason, if he asks her to sin, she must not, because she needs to be in submission to her highest authority, the will of God as revealed in the Word of God. For this reason, if her husband commits a crime, she can call the police; and if he commits a sin and remains unrepentant, she can call the pastor. The husband's authority is derivative. This means authority does not come from him, because he is not a god, but authority comes to him from God.

Second, a husband is not, by his God-given authority, automatically more valuable, gifted, competent, or intelligent than his wife. Thus, a husband is not always right, and his wife is free to have her own independent thoughts. Because God created man and woman equal in the sense of bearing His image equally, we also carry equal spiritual worth as we partner together, and the man's primary responsibility is to lead the marriage in a God-glorifying direction. If you have different theological convictions, you need to study and pray for common beliefs, without compromising, so that you can make decisions that are from the same foundation.

Third, the Bible *never* commands women to submit to men in general. This would lead to horrendous abuse. Instead, the Bible commands husbands

---

a Gen. 1:27.
b Gen. 2:18, cf. 1 Tim. 2:11–15; Gen. 5:2, 1 Cor. 11:2–16; 14:33–34; Eph. 5:21–33; Col. 3:18; Titus 2:3-5; 1 Peter 3:1.

to love their wives with the kind of patience, affection, devotion, and humility that Jesus demonstrates toward the church as her friend. As a godly author, Bible scholar, pastor, and husband of more than thirty-eight years (with one of the best marriages we have ever seen), Raymond C. Ortlund Jr. said, "The model of headship is our Lord, the Head of the church, who gave Himself for us. The antithesis to male headship is male domination. By male domination I mean the assertion of the man's will over the woman's will, heedless of her spiritual equality, her rights, and her value."[6] We in no way accept domination. And the Bible commands wives to submit to their husbands by respectfully following their leadership. In so doing, a woman is protected from the abuse of other men because of her loving relationship with her husband. Ortlund went on to say, "The 'natural outcome' of godly male headship is female fulfillment, not a denial of female rights."[7] A wife flourishes with a loving husband, and a husband becomes courageous with a respectful wife.

A husband reflecting the gospel by loving his wife as Jesus does the church isn't something that happens overnight with a man, unless he has had godly manhood training by his parents, and even then it is tested and further learned through circumstances in the marriage. The same is true regarding respectful submission for a wife. Since we are all sinners, for leadership and submission to grow in a marriage, it takes time, prayer, Scripture study, communication, humility, and a desire to serve your spouse. Ideally you are both working on your biblical command so you can grow in your oneness.

For women, the key to growing in respectful submission is to look to Jesus Christ. In the very nature of the trinitarian God of the Bible there is functional submission through what is called "ontological equality." What this means is that although the Father, Son, and Spirit are different persons, they are also equal and one while practicing submission. Similarly, a husband and wife are equal and one while practicing submission. For example, more than forty times in John's gospel alone, we learn that God the Father sent God the Son to earth. And while on the earth, Jesus practiced submission by teaching us to pray, "Your will be done"[a] and Himself praying, "not My will, but Yours, be done."[b] Jesus also said that while on earth He only did what the Father told Him to do

---

a Matt. 6:10.
b Luke 22:42.

and said what the Father told Him to say.[8] Jesus said this was because "I can of Myself do nothing. As I hear, I judge; and My judgment is righteous, because I do not seek My own will but the will of the Father who sent Me."[9] Importantly, Jesus' submission was both emotional and vocal. He said what He felt, as when He prayed in the Garden of Gethsemane before His crucifixion. This means that a woman can simultaneously be respectfully submissive and vocally honest with both her husband and God about how she's feeling.

If your husband isn't working on his part of loving, you are still called to work on your part of submitting, knowing that God hears your prayers and honors your obedience. This doesn't mean if there is abuse or harm you are to endure it. But, as a helper on mission, you are supposed to respectfully discuss how he can be loving and ask how you can be respectful. Biblically these go hand in hand, and you are to help each other understand how to live out what love and respect mean. These should be regular conversations and actions if you want your marriage and friendship to mature. You might want to start with one area for each of you to work on so you don't get overwhelmed and discouraged. It requires time alone together and focused listening to mutually benefit the relationship. If you don't plan for these times and just wait for things to blow up, you will continue to hurt each other and the marriage. This is a time for humility, not pride, to look for ways to grow closer to Christ and your husband.

One woman, an example of a compliant wife who is painfully learning about godly submission instead of enabling, told me, "In my own sin, I chose to falsely flatter that which wasn't honorable in my husband, selfishly hoping I'd get a better experience. My sins of giving way to fear [of conflict and of her husband's disapproval] led me to submit dutifully while becoming more enslaved in my husband's self-focused desires rather than the Lord's desires." Our sin makes things messy.

Conversely, a contentious wife who resists submission said, "My sin of constant disrespect and lack of submission has caused a part of my husband to die. I've made him afraid to lead me. He avoids talking to me so I won't argue with him and doesn't trust my love for him. He sees me as his enemy instead of a wife and friend because I am quarrelsome. I thought if I took control I would respect him more, but it didn't work."

These were very painful realizations for these women, but there is hope for God to forgive and reconcile these couples. We've seen miraculous things happen in our own marriage and for many others whom God has given us the opportunity to counsel. It's never too late to turn from sin, but the longer you wait, the more painful it can be—so I encourage you to start now. Our marriages only seem "unfixable" if we are unwilling to repent. We'll be covering repentance in more depth in chapter five.

In closing this chapter, I can't emphasize enough the importance of respect. I could give you pages of examples of marriages that are miserable because the wives are unwilling to see their disrespect. Unfortunately, we live in a day and age where women in the workplace with your husband sometimes show more respect to him than you do at home. We need to protect our husbands from that false form of flattery, and if they are neglected at home, it leaves them vulnerable. It doesn't excuse any form of them straying from the marriage, but we need to be aware that there is even a name for these kind of work relationships—"work spouse"—because it is so common. "A work spouse is a co-worker of the opposite sex with whom you have a close platonic relationship. In many ways, these relationships can mirror a real marriage."[10] If you are a woman working outside the home, and your marriage is struggling, you also need to be alert to this temptation. Because this is a newly studied issue, the number of people who claim to have this type of "work spouse" relationship ranges from 30 to 60 percent![11] I think the 30 percent is shocking enough, but 60 percent is a devastating number, if true, for our marriages. Someone else may be willing to step into the role of spouse for your husband, but only for the eight hours she sees him at work.

I urge you, as I do myself, to constantly examine how you can be a better helper to your husband and image bearer of God to those around you through your marriage. After years of the hard work of letting God break our sinful habits, Mark and I can honestly say we are more thankful than ever for each other. When I am respectful and he is loving, there is nothing better than the oneness and friendship it creates. It is worth every ounce of suffering it may take to get there! Nonetheless, our goal cannot be to fix our husbands or even to save our marriages, but rather to glorify God by submitting to our husbands, trusting that His commands are those of a loving Father who not only wants our lives to work but to be ones of worship.

5

TAKING OUT THE TRASH

Confess your trespasses to one another,
and pray for one another.

—James 5:16

E very home accumulates trash, so we must take it out often. Failure to do so stinks up the entire home. Sin is like trash, and every home has it too. Repentance and forgiveness are how a couple takes their trash out.

If you are married, you will have conflict. You cannot avoid it because marriage is an unconditional commitment to an imperfect person.

$$1 \text{ sinner} + 1 \text{ sinner} \neq 0 \text{ conflict}$$

You will sin against your spouse, and your spouse will sin against you. Couples who claim to never fight are either lying or living completely passionless, independent, parallel lives, so emotionally distant that hurting each other is virtually impossible. You will fight. The question is, will you fight well to the glory of God and the good of your marriage?

Dr. John Gottman has become world renowned for his work observing the ways couples respond to each other. Over the course of sixteen years on various occasions, he observed forty-nine married couples in an apartment-laboratory and recorded everything from their facial expressions to their heart rates in order to investigate what triggers might suggest a propensity for divorce. He said, "In 91 percent of the cases where I predicted that a couple's marriage would eventually fail or succeed, time has proven me right."[1]

Echoing the apocalyptic language of the Bible, he said that when conflict arises, there are "four horsemen" who are certain to multiply relational pain and result in marital death.[2] This is especially true when a discussion begins with a "harsh startup" where tempers are flaring and the tone is more contemptuous, because the beginning of a conflict sets it in a direction toward war or peace.

Horseman number one is criticism. A complaint is simply pointing out something in your spouse that you find annoying, displeasing, or frustrating. Unlike a complaint, a criticism goes deeper to attack someone's character or personality. Simply, a complaint attacks the problem, whereas a criticism attacks the person.

Horseman number two is contempt. Contempt is showing disgust for your spouse with such things as name-calling, mocking, condescending humor, belittling, demeaning, and body language (rolling your eyes, huffing, glaring, and sneering). Contempt grows over time if conflicts are not resolved, and we come to despise our spouses because our unresolved and unforgiven troubles stack our negative thoughts into a mountain of disgust. Contempt can also include belligerence, which is an aggressive action marked by provoking our spouses to harm us, or threatening to harm them in some way. Contempt invariably leads to more conflict and pushes a couple further from reconciliation.

Horseman number three is defensiveness. Defensiveness occurs when the guilty person refuses to apologize or back down from the conflict. Instead, the guilty person excuses his or her behavior and even blames the other spouse in an effort to be the morally superior one who presides over the conflict as judge. Defensiveness results in a standoff between enemies rather than a truce between allies.

Horseman number four is stonewalling. Stonewalling is when we stop working for oneness and settle for two lonely, parallel lives. This can include separate financial lives, social lives, spiritual lives, and even separate bedrooms. Acts of stonewalling include tuning out to ignore your spouse, turning your back and walking away from a conversation, and simply disengaging emotionally and verbally by checking out, surfing the Internet, turning up the television, or just plain ignoring your spouse. Husbands do fully 85 percent of stonewalling.

When the four horsemen—criticism, contempt, defensiveness, and stonewalling—take up ongoing residence in a marriage, statistically it will end in divorce. Are any of these four horsemen riding around your home, slashing your marriage to pieces? What can be done about it beyond just learning to coexist, trying not to upset your spouse, or accepting that your marriage is a war and your spouse is your enemy?

Sin is the problem. The gospel of Jesus Christ is the answer.

Sin includes both omission, where we do not do what we ought to, and commission, where we do what we ought not to do. Sin includes our thoughts, words, deeds, and motives. It includes godlessness, which is ignoring God and living as if there were no God, or as if we were God. Sin is invariably idolatry, which is replacing God as preeminent with something or someone else—most often ourselves, so that we live for our own glory rather than God's and our own good rather than our spouses'.

There is a marked difference between sins and temptations. The Bible says that Jesus was tempted, but never sinned.[a] Therefore, when our spouses or we are tempted and do not give in, we have won the victory, and nothing needs to be repented of.

Repentance

She really wanted to buy some things that she technically did not need. The problem was, they did not have the money to pay for them. So she secretly applied for a credit card, made her purchases, and planned to pay off the balance before her husband ever found out. But rather than paying it off, she started buying more things and during the course of many months, dollar by dollar, racked up a very large debt. Frantic to cover her sin, she started selling things on eBay and through consignment stores, hoping to earn enough extra money to pay off her debt without her husband ever finding out. But after she missed a payment, her interest rate increased, fees were added, and she could see she was getting into real trouble. So she sat her husband down and, with tears running down her cheeks, told him the whole embarrassing story.

Jesus never sinned, and so He never repented. But unlike Jesus, we sin all the time. Therefore, we need to repent often. *Repentance* is a favorite word of God's prophets throughout the Bible, including Jesus' cousin John the Baptizer and even Jesus Christ Himself. Because Jesus died for our sin, we can put our sin to death by the power of the Holy Spirit. That is repentance. We can kill our sin, or sin will kill our marriages. Those are the only options.

---

a Heb. 4:15.

To best understand what repentance is, let's look at what repentance is *not*.

- *Repentance is not getting caught but coming clean.*
  What does your spouse not know about you?

- *Repentance is not denying our sin.*
  What sin is in your life and marriage that you have simply not accepted as sin that has to be dealt with honestly?

- *Repentance is not diminishing our sin.*
  What have you partially confessed without telling the whole truth about? What have you downplayed as a minor sin that if not put to death will only grow to damage your marriage greatly?

- *Repentance is not managing our sin.*
  What sin are you trying to keep under control or not let your spouse or other people you respect see?

- *Repentance is not blame-shifting our sin.*
  What ways have you blamed others for your sin rather than accepting responsibility for it? Who or what do you, like Adam and Eve in the garden, blame—God, your spouse, your parents, the culture, your personality, stress?

- *Repentance is not excusing our sin.*
  What excuses do you most commonly use to justify and excuse your sin?

- *Repentance is not about someone else's sin.*
  When conversing with your spouse, which sins of theirs are you most apt to bring up, rather than speaking about your own sins?

- *Repentance is not about manipulating God or people for blessing.*
  In the past, how have you faked true repentance in an effort not to put your sin to death out of true sorrow, but rather in an effort to manipulate God or people to bless you for being a good person?

- *Repentance is not worldly sorrow.*
  Even non-Christians can and do feel bad about their sin but do not see it as an offense against God and do not hate it out of love for Him

and others. Have you simply shed a few tears, looked sad, and said you were sorry, but not really repented?

- *Repentance is not solely grieving the consequences of your sin but is hating the evil of the sin itself.*
  How have you lamented the consequences of your sin and what it has cost you but not truly come to hate it, fight it, war against it, and put it to death?

- *Repentance is not mere confession.*
  How many times have you said you were sorry with no real, deep, heartfelt commitment to change, and what confusion has this caused your spouse?

———

True repentance is a combination of three things.

- *Repentance includes confession.*
  In confession, you agree with God that you have sinned. Confession includes both your mind and mouth.

- *Repentance includes contrition.*
  In contrition, you feel what God feels about your sin. Confession includes both your emotions and expressions. Your heart is affected, not just your words.

- *Repentance includes change.*
  In change, you stop sinning and start worshipping. Change includes your will and works.

———

Every married couple has to continually practice repentance of sin if they hope to have any loving, lasting life together. As one writer wisely said, "Couples don't fall out of love so much as they fall out of repentance."[3]

Forgiveness

Fortunately, the wife who had racked up secret debt confessed the whole truth to her husband and—as an act of repentance—cut up the credit card, never to repeat that sin again. And he forgave her. He communicated his appreciation that she had finally told him the truth and admitted that her keeping a secret from him hurt him more than spending the money. Together, they devised a plan to pay off the debt and did so. He never speaks of the matter, as he does not want to shame her for something he has forgiven. And the only reason we know the story is that she tells it freely. Because once she repented and he forgave her, a burden was lifted, thereby enabling her to be honest without feeling condemned or ashamed.

When we sin against our spouses, we cause them to suffer. When we sin, we are supposed to apologize, ask forgiveness, and try to make things right.

When we are sinned against, we need to forgive quickly. Jesus' words on this are haunting: "Forgive us our sins, for we also forgive everyone who is indebted to us."[a] We cannot simply ask God to forgive our sins; we must also extend that same forgiveness to others.

Forgiveness is a gospel issue. In our hurt and woundedness, we can lose sight of the truth that no one has been sinned against more than God. No one has been more wounded, grieved, hurt, betrayed, and mistreated than God. Furthermore, we each have contributed to the pain that God experiences, as all sin is ultimately against God.[b] This means that God could be the most embittered person.

Instead, He came as Jesus and took our place to suffer for our sins, pronouncing forgiveness from the cross.

Therefore, our forgiveness of our spouses has very little, if anything, to do with them. Instead, it has everything to do with God. As an act of worship, we must respond to our sinful spouses as God has responded to our sin—with forgiveness—because it is a gospel issue. We cannot accept forgiveness from God without extending it to our spouses.

The Bible commands spouses to be in the ongoing habit of "forgiving one

a Luke 11:4.
b Ps. 51:4.

another, even as God in Christ forgave you."ᵃ How did God forgive believers in Christ? We caused Him to suffer unjustly, and He received it without bitterness, forgave us, pursued us, and wants good for us. This means that if I accept God's forgiveness of my sins but refuse to forgive my spouse of his or her sins, I am in effect saying by my actions that my spouse's sin against me is worse than my sin against God.

It is important to note, however, what forgiveness is *not*:

- *Forgiveness is not denying, approving, or diminishing sin that is committed against us.*
  We cannot say we are fine, that it was no big deal, or that, since it was in the past, we've just moved on. We must be honest about the reality of the sin if we want the forgiveness to be equally earnest. In forgiving, we are, in fact, saying our spouses are wrong, we do not approve of their sin, and that it really is a big deal and not a trivial matter to us.

- *Forgiveness is not naivety.*
  Naive people are prone to live as if the world were not filled with depraved sinners capable of evil; they often become naive by not really looking at the sinfulness of sin, including their own. Such people are not forgiving sin as much as they are ignoring it.

- *Forgiveness is not enabling sin.*
  To forgive people is not to remain stuck in their cycle of sin, thus being complicit and enabling their continued transgression.

- *Forgiveness is not waiting for someone to acknowledge sin, apologize, and repent.*
  The sad truth is that some people will never fully repent, and others never at all. Others we will never see again, or they will die before we hear an apology. We forgive because it is what God requires and what we need, not because our offenders have apologized.

- *Forgiveness is not forgetting about sin committed against us.*
  It is actually impossible to completely forget such things. This is why

---

a Eph. 4:32.

when God says, "Their sin I will remember no more," it does not mean that He has no memory, but rather that He continually chooses not to bring it up or keep it in the forefront of His thinking.[a] Indeed, because God is omniscient (all-knowing) it is, in fact, impossible for Him to actually forget something.

- *Forgiveness is not dying emotionally and no longer feeling the pain of the transgression.*
  Rather, forgiveness allows us to feel the appropriate depth of grievous pain but choose by grace not to be continually paralyzed or defined by it.

- *Forgiveness is not a one-time event.*
  Those who have been sinned against commonly have seasons when they feel afresh the pain of past hurts and have to forgive their transgressors yet again.

- *Forgiveness is not reconciliation.*
  It takes one sinner to repent, and one victim to forgive, but it takes both to reconcile. Therefore, unless there is both repentance by the sinner and forgiveness by the victim, reconciliation cannot occur, which means the relationship remains continually broken until reconciliation does occur. Forgiveness is the beginning of potential reconciliation but is not in and of itself reconciliation. Forgiveness takes a moment. The trust that reconciliation requires is gained slowly and lost quickly.

- *Forgiveness is not neglecting justice.*
  In fact, if a crime has been committed, we can simultaneously forgive someone and call the police to arrest him or her. God will deal with every sin of every human being justly. For those who repent of sin and come to faith in Jesus Christ, justice came at the cross of Jesus, when our Savior suffered and died in our place for our sins. For those who do not repent of sin and come to faith in Jesus Christ, their justice will come in the punishment that is assigned to them

---

a Jer. 31:34.

in the conscious eternal torments of hell. By not seeking vengeance, we are not neglecting justice, but rather trusting God for perfect justice and getting ourselves out of the middle between the sinner and God. Romans 12:19 instructs precisely this: "Beloved, do not avenge yourselves, but rather give place to wrath; for it is written, 'Vengeance is Mine, I will repay,' says the Lord." We know that we are not bitter when we actually want those who have sinned against us to be maturing Christians and, in addition to praying for them, we forgive them in hopes of showing them the gospel of grace.

———

Forgiveness is loving despite sin. Just as God forgives not just undeserving but ill-deserving sinners, we must too. We do not forgive our spouses because they are good or deserving, but rather because God is good and deserving. Forgiveness includes wanting good for the spouse who sinned against you, being able to pray for his or her well-being, and not keeping a record of wrongs against your spouse like a pile of rocks to throw when convenient. Forgiveness is an ongoing lifestyle that is incredibly costly to us and lived out of love for God and others.

Bitterness

As a little boy I can still recall the first time I tried to remove a small tree I did not like from my parents' yard. I took my father's handsaw from the garage and sawed away until it fell. Assuming the tree was forever removed, I was surprised to later discover that it was growing back. It was then that I learned about roots. Because the life of a tree is in its roots, unless you pull up the unseen roots, the tree will continue to grow until, in time, it returns to its former size and may even exceed it.

Like a tree, the Bible tells us, bitterness has roots.[a] Consequently, we can saw away at our frustrations, disappointments, angers, hurts, and sadness, but unless we dig up our root of bitterness, it only returns, sometimes bigger than ever.

———

a Heb. 12:15.

The only alternative to forgiveness is bitterness. And the only alternative to bitterness is forgiveness.

The true test of whether or not we are bitter is our tongues. What do we say about our spouses? Do we pray for them? This explains why Paul said, "Let no corrupt word proceed out of your mouth, but what is good for necessary edification, that it may impart grace to the hearers. And do not grieve the Holy Spirit of God, by whom you were sealed for the day of redemption."[a] Even when the spouses we are bitter against are not present, God the Holy Spirit is, and He grieves when we speak ill of them.

Bitter spouses are prone to give demeaning and contemptuous nicknames to people they are bitter against. Bitter spouses cannot constrain their tongues, but rather the "root of bitterness springing up cause[s] trouble, and by this many become defiled"[b] This means that children are impacted by their parents' bitterness, generations are affected, circles of friends are poisoned, and entire churches can be consumed with the demonic drama that proceeds from one tongue speaking on behalf of a bitter heart. Making matters even worse in our day are the innumerable opportunities that technology affords us to spew our bitterness to the world.

We can sometimes be blind or indifferent to those we have embittered. How might your spouse be bitter against you? What can you do to help your spouse overcome that bitterness?

As a general rule, those who are bitter have good reason to be angry—they have been sinned against. The sin may have been something catastrophic, such as adultery, abuse, assault, major theft, a horrible lie, great injustice, or damaging gossip. Or the sin, in and of itself, may not seem to be a big deal, but the pain it causes is severe because the person who caused it was someone you loved, trusted, and gave privileged access to your soul. Because that person betrayed you, you are devastated.

Bitterness is often unrelated to the magnitude of a sin, but instead correlates to how much you love the offender. If a stranger sins against you in a significant way, you are likely to be angry, but not bitter. If a spouse sins against you—even in a little way—however, you are likely to get bitter because

a Eph. 4:29–30.
b Heb. 12:15.

you have higher expectations for your spouse's relationship with you. And we can even become bitter against God, like Naomi (meaning "pleasant"), who changed her name to Mara (meaning "bitter") because "'the Almighty has dealt very bitterly with me.'"[a]

In dealing with potential bitterness, Paul exhorted us to "[put] away lying" and "speak truth."[b] To do that, we must be honest about deep heart pain. It means asking ourselves some soul-searching questions so we can get beyond simply saying we are fine, or pretending that the past solely remains in the past and that we've moved on when we have not.

We are all bitter at various times in our marriages. Sometimes the issue is seemingly small, other times large. In our years of ministry together, we have seen hundreds and maybe thousands of examples of spouses who are bitter— bitter because they feel unappreciated, neglected, not cared for or pursued; and bitter because they have been sinned against, leaving them feeling betrayed, alone, or foolishly taken advantage of.

In seasons of bitterness, we have a proclivity to blame others, most likely our spouses, for our bitterness, as if they placed it in us through their transgression. The truth is people, even the worst of them, do not embitter us. Rather, they provide an opportunity, or temptation, to choose bitterness, for which we remain morally responsible.

A common misunderstanding among many who give advice to bitter people is that people should not be angry about the wrongs they have suffered. That counsel, however, is both unbiblical and unhelpful. God Himself does get angry throughout the Bible in response to sin, even though we are told that His wick is long and He is "slow to anger."[c] Furthermore, Jesus got angry on different occasions recorded in Scripture.[4]

The truth is, righteous anger is the right response to sin and far more consistent with God's character than faking happiness, approval, or acceptance. The Bible, on many occasions, gives us examples where human anger is justified.[d] This is why Paul did not tell us, "Do not get angry," but rather, "Be

---

a Ruth 1:20.
b Eph. 4:25.
c Ps. 103:8.
d Ex. 32:19; see also Ex. 11:8; 16:20; Num. 16:15; Lev. 10:16; 1 Sam. 11:6; 20:34; 2 Sam. 12:5; Neh. 5:6; Mark 3:5; Luke 14:21.

angry, and do not sin."[a] He accepted anger as a legitimate emotional response to being sinned against. But he also warned us to be careful not to combine righteous anger with unrighteous bitterness.

Everyone gets angry. Some people stuff it and make themselves sick through stress while appearing closed, odd, emotionally stunted, dull, or fake. Others become passively hostile, often making snide comments under the auspices of kidding, when they really intended to be cruel. And still others stack up their bitterness by not dealing with it until they explode in an instant—perhaps completely overreacting to a small frustration by unleashing the arsenal of anger they have been storing.

Instructing those who are angry and tempted to bitterness, Paul exhorted us to have a sense of urgency in dealing with our anger, not to wait even a day to respond to it or risk becoming consumed by it. Failure to do so, he said, actually grieves God the Holy Spirit, who desires to help us work through our anger and bitterness so that Satan does not have a foothold in our souls and marriages. In an era without electricity when the day started to wind down at sunset, the phrase "do not let the sun go down on your wrath, nor give place to the devil" meant that resolution needed to be pursued that day.[b] This does not mean it is unacceptable for someone who is confused or raging to take an hour or two to pray, clear his or her head, calm down, seek wise counsel, and jot down a few thoughts so that person can engage his or her spouse constructively. It does mean that, since sin separates people from one another until it is dealt with, the longer we wait, the more ground we give our Enemy in his war against our marriages.

Perhaps one of the most painful examples of mutual marital bitterness comes from one of history's famous Christian leaders. John and Charles Wesley were brothers and the founders of Methodism, from which came the charismatic, Pentecostal, and holiness movements that include multiple Christian denominations. Charles and his wife reportedly had a loving marriage that included Charles staying home much of the time to be with his family and write most of his six thousand famous hymns. His brother John, however, had a very bitter marriage that was exacerbated by his constant travel and itinerant preaching.

---

a Eph. 4:26.
b Eph. 4:26–27.

John Wesley had poured his life into his ministry of Methodism. But in February 1751 things changed when, at the age of forty-eight, the never-married John Wesley was crossing London Bridge when he slipped on ice and broke his ankle. He was then taken into the home of forty-one-year-old Molly Vazeille, a wealthy widow with four children. Without even a passing mention in his journal, the two were married eight days later. Some biographers have since referred to their ensuing marriage as the "thirty years war." During the course of his ministry, John traveled some twenty-five thousand miles on horseback and preached some forty thousand sermons. He also believed that his marriage should in no way reduce his travel or ministry, saying, "I cannot understand how a Methodist preacher can answer it to God . . . to preach one sermon, or travel one day less, in a married than in a single state."[5]

Molly tried to travel with him for the first four years of his ministry but stopped after she experienced seemingly constant illness, seasickness, and fear from the dangerous mobs who would sometimes seek to assault John. She wanted him to greatly reduce his itinerant ministry. She was bitter that he refused to travel less, and he was bitter that she desired him to travel less. Sadly, rather than repenting and forgiving, they became bitter enemies.

She returned home, and he continued to travel extensively. On one occasion she fell ill, and John received word she was near death. He arrived at her bedside at 1:00 a.m., and when her fever lifted within the hour, he immediately left to return to preaching.

In an effort to sabotage his ministry, Molly broke into her husband's office to open his personal mail. She sent damaging letters to his critics and the press, and even sent letters from her own hand undermining her husband and seeking to destroy his ministry. This included accusing him of adultery with his housekeeper, a charge he continually denied. Their bitter conflict seems to have escalated to violence. A visiting minister reported that he witnessed Molly ripping John's hair out (though John denied it ever happened). And in one of his own letters to his wife, John seemingly admits to assaulting her, saying, "I took you first by ye Arm, & afterward by ye Shoulder, & shook you twice or thrice" admitting it "might have made you black & blue. I bless God, that I did not do this fifty times & that I did nothing worse. I might have given you an unlucky Blow."[6]

Her bitterness, made worse by John's extensive ongoing letter writing to multiple women, caused Molly to become insanely jealous, which led to erratic and volatile behavior. Their final years were spent apart, as she never once set foot in his personal residence. What is believed to be his final correspondence to her reveals their profound bitterness. Dated October 2, 1778, his letter says he is not bitter, but it seems untrue: "As it is doubtful, considering your age and mine, whether we may meet anymore in this world, I think it right to tell you my mind once for all without either anger or bitterness . . . If you were to live a thousand years, you could not undo the mischief that you have done. And till you have done all you can towards it, I bid you farewell."[7]

Molly died on October 8, 1781. She was dead and buried a few days before her husband was even notified. Today she is buried under a road in London, far away from her husband. The painful story of the Wesleys reminds us that there are no loving marriages apart from repentance and forgiveness. Marriage either gets bitter or gets better.

The gospel is the only helpful answer to the bitterness and anger that victims feel. Paul said, "Be kind to one another, tenderhearted, forgiving one another, even as God in Christ forgave you."[a] Admittedly, when people are bitter and angry, words like this can sound like the kind of hyper-spiritual platitudes that come from annoying religious types and only push victims to defend their angry bitterness by recalling to mind and sometimes even aloud all the valid reasons for their hurt. By doing so, they are defending their angry bitterness by appealing to a sense of justice—that to simply forgive a spouse who has not apologized, changed, or made amends is tantamount to condoning evil.

In those moments we are able to recall intricate details of exact circumstances surrounding the sin(s) that contributed to our hurt and anger. We can remember where we were when sinned against, exactly what was said, and other similar details, such as what the perpetrators were wearing, the tone of their voices, and their expressions. Our memory is keen in these moments because we have recounted the event(s) over and over in our minds, digging up the past to emotionally relive it over and over in the present, which is what Paul told the

---

a Eph. 4:32.

Corinthians is an unloving record keeping of wrongs.[a] If not repented of, our bitterness begins to so cloud our entire view of the past that history gets revised with war words like "always" and "never." Bitter people have a filter through which everything (past, present, and future) is viewed negatively.

A Good Fight

The key to having a good fight that ends in reconciliation rather than a bad fight that ends in bitterness is to learn to fight as friends and not enemies. The following rules of engagement are offered to help you fight to the glory of God and the good of your marriage.

First, you have to decide if your spouse has committed a sin. If so, you have to decide whether or not you are going to say something. Should you just overlook it, pray for your spouse, or just wait for a more opportune time to speak with him or her? We can become so frustrated with the sin of our spouses that we deal with the right issue in the wrong way or at the wrong time, which can only make matters worse.

Second, decide how you want to deal with the conflict. People respond to conflict with a "fight, flight, or fright" instinct. Fight mode creates a harsh startup to a conflict, which quickly escalates when someone accepts and heightens the conflict in an effort to bully, punish, and/or "defeat" his or her spouse. Those of us who choose flight respond by wanting to retreat, withdraw, and avoid the conflict. Some people experience fright, where they simply freeze, have a hard time thinking on their feet, and get stuck. Knowing how you and your spouse respond to conflict will help you know how to lovingly engage each other when frustrated.

Third, do not fight when either of you has any substances in you, such as alcohol, that alter your emotional state.

Fourth, before you fight, stop to pray, asking God to be in the midst of your fight, controlling your tongue, and helping you fight for the marriage by attacking the problem and not the person.

Fifth, do not use fighting with your spouse as your release valve or lightning rod. A release valve is something that relieves pressure from the stresses

---

a 1 Cor. 13:5.

of life. Ideally, this would be a physical exercise or a relaxing activity with your hands. A lightning rod is a person you choose to just listen to you, thereby grounding out the storm of fury in your life so that no one gets hurt. A lightning rod does not seek to comfort or counsel as much as he or she simply listens and lets you get all the frustration out. If life has you frustrated, you will be tempted to use a good fight with your spouse as your release valve or lightning rod. Do not do this. Find something else to do to relieve your stress productively, and a godly friend of the same gender to listen and ground out your storms, especially storms with your spouse.

Sixth, sometimes a couple simply cannot come to an agreement on an important issue, and it affects their oneness and unity, possibly including their sexuality. In such circumstances humble servants need to ask whether or not the issue is really worth holding their ground on, or if in love with a clear conscience they can defer to their spouses. And, if they think the issue is important enough to retain their contrary position, they need to seek outside authority. The couple needs to agree on a godly authority (for example, a pastor or biblical counselor) to whom they will each present their case, allowing that mediator to make a decision for them that they will then submit to. As we stated earlier, this should be a very rare occurrence involving a neutral, godly person who is not a close friend or relative. In short, when all else fails, get a referee and let him make the call.

———

What do you need to repent of to your spouse? What do you need to forgive your spouse for? Are you bitter against your spouse in any way? How can you have more God-glorifying fights?

To conclude this chapter, we should technically share an epic story of a couple who have experienced reconciliation after sin. We could tell you stories, including some from our own marriage, that apart from the saving work of Jesus Christ make no sense at all. But instead, we have chosen to pray for you. We are hoping that rather than admiring another couple's redemptive story, you will make your own by God's grace and the Holy Spirit's power. Even better than reading an amazing gospel story is having one. So we felt it fitting to close this chapter with a hymn by Charles Wesley that also works as a prayer for you and your spouse:

Weary of wandering from my God,
And now made willing to return
I hear and bow me to the rod
For thee, not without hope, I mourn:
I have an Advocate above
A Friend before the throne of love.

O Jesus, full of truth and grace
More full of grace than I of sin
Yet once again I seek Thy face:
Open Thine arms and take me in
And freely my backslidings heal
And love the faithless sinner still.

Thou know'st the way to bring me back
My fallen spirit to restore
O for Thy truth and mercy's sake,
Forgive, and bid me sin no more:
The ruins of my soul repair
And make my heart a house of prayer.

The stone to flesh again convert,
The veil of sin again remove;
Sprinkle Thy blood upon my heart,
And melt it by Thy dying love;
This rebel heart by love subdue,
And make it soft, and make it new.

Give to mine eyes refreshing tears,
And kindle my relentings now;
Fill my whole soul with filial fears,
To Thy sweet yoke my spirit bow;
Bend by Thy grace, O bend or break,
The iron sinew in my neck!

Ah! give me, Lord, the tender heart
That trembles at the approach of sin;
A godly fear of sin impart,
Implant, and root it deep within,
That I may dread Thy gracious power,
And never dare to offend Thee more.

Part 2

SEX

6

SEX: GOD, GROSS, OR GIFT?

They were both naked, the man and his wife,
and were not ashamed.

—GENESIS 2:25

We only had fifteen minutes between teaching sessions at a marriage conference to say hello to people and expected that perhaps a few would come up and introduce themselves. Instead, they lined up more than a hundred deep to drop the bomb of their sex lives on us in a minute or less. Women who were molested as children, weeping so hard they could not breathe; husbands who had been caught, yet again, viewing porn; a married couple who had not had any sexual contact in more than a decade; a woman who had sex with her husband twice a day and was still unsatisfied, wanting more; a few couples who had been married more than a year and were still virgins; one woman who had not told her husband she had dozens of partners before they met; a wife who asked if her husband was guilty of raping her; and a Christian couple who wanted to know if they should keep watching porn together. And those are just a few of them.

Getting back up to teach was difficult, to say the least. Our hearts were broken. We felt completely overwhelmed. There was an epidemic, and people were suffering more than we could have possibly imagined. Worse still, they were desperate for answers, and they had nowhere to turn. How did sex, which is a gift from God to married couples, turn into such a curse for so many of us?

We have to begin in the beginning. In the beginning God created our first parents and brought them together to meet. For Eve, it was a big day. She had just been created, met God, and was going to her first "date" and wedding naked. Upon seeing his wife for the first time, Adam was overwhelmed and uttered what are the first recorded human words in all history. In response to

Eve's glory, Adam sang what is in Hebrew a rhythmic and poetic love song, not unlike an epic musical, in which he named her "woman."

As her father walking her down the aisle, God brought Eve to Adam. And as their pastor, He officiated the first wedding ceremony, declaring them husband and wife.

God blessed them because He is altogether good, and He invited our first parents to make some babies, steward creation, rule over lower life, and make a culture that reflected His glory for our good. When God was done creating the world and our first parents, He declared it all to be "very good."

God then established a threefold process as the pattern and precedent for marriage that both Jesus and Paul quoted in their teachings. First, a guy needs to grow up by moving out of his parents' house, paying his own bills, worshipping his God, and taking care of himself. Second, a man is then able to pursue a noble woman in a noble way. The truth is that guys want to have sex, and the Bible teaches that sex is for men and not for boys and calls them to only have sex as husbands with their wives. Third, as husband and wife, a man and woman are to become "one flesh." In consummating their marriage, a husband and wife become "one" in a way that is akin to God the Father, Son, and Spirit being "one." Curiously, this threefold process is exactly the opposite of our culture of hook up, shack up, and break up.

The Bible then records sex that is "very good," saying, "They were both naked, the man and his wife, and were not ashamed."[a]

Sex was good. God was glorified.

From the opening pages of the Bible, we learn seven sex essentials.

One, God created us male and female in His image and likeness with dignity, equality, value, and worth. Men and women are different and complement one another.

Two, love is more like a song than a math equation. It requires a sense of poetry and passion to be any good at it, which is why people who are stuck in their heads struggle and are frustrated by it, and lovers prefer songs to syllogisms.

Third, marriage is for one man and one woman by God's design. This is the consistent teaching of the Bible from the table of contents to the appendix and the teaching of Jesus Christ Himself.

---

a Gen. 2:25.

Fourth, God created sex. God made our bodies "very good" with "male and female" parts and pleasures. When our first parents consummated their covenant, God was not shocked or horrified, because He created our bodies for sex. The reason that sex is fun, pleasurable, and wonderful is because it is a reflection of the loving goodness of God, who created it as a gift for us to steward and enjoy.

Fifth, sex outside of marriage is a sin. Sinful sex includes homosexuality, erotica, bestiality, bisexuality, fornication, friends with benefits, adultery, swinging, prostitution, incest, rape, polygamy, polyandry, sinful lust, pornography, and pedophilia. For married people, the following sexual acts with anyone other than your spouse qualify as sin: masturbating someone else, oral sex, anal sex, heavy petting, dry humping, cybersex, and phone sex. In the New Testament, the Greek word *porneia* (from which we get the word *pornography*) is translated into English as "sexual immorality" and encompasses all sorts of sexual sins. It is frequently used as a junk drawer in which every sort of perversion is thrown because people are prone to invent new ways of doing evil.

Sixth, sex is to be done in such a way that there is no shame. Many people experience shame in regard to sex. Sometimes shame is a gift from God in response to our sexual sin, sometimes it is the devastating feeling we bear because we have been sexually sinned against, and other times we have not sinned or been sinned against sexually but feel shame because we have wrong thinking and feelings about sex in general, or a sex act in particular.

Seventh, your standard of beauty is your spouse. Of all the principles we have shared with people around the world regarding sex, this is perhaps the one we get the strongest positive response to. And it alone could save many marriages. God made one man and one woman. He did not ask them if they wanted someone tall or short, light or heavy, pale or dark skinned, with long or short hair. In short, He did not permit them to develop a standard of beauty. Instead, He gave them each a spouse as a standard of beauty.

One of our culture's powerful lies—fueled by pornography, sinful lust, and marketing—is that having a standard of beauty is in any way holy or helpful. God does not give us a standard of beauty—God gives us spouses. Unlike other standards of beauty, a spouse changes over time. This means if your spouse is tall, you are into tall. If your spouse is skinny, you are into skinny. If your spouse is twenty, you are into twenty. When your spouse is sixty, you are no longer into twenty, but rather into sixty. And if your spouse used to be skinny, you were into skinny, but now you are into formerly skinny. We are to pour all our passion and pursuit of sexual pleasure into our spouses alone, without comparing them to anyone else in a lustful way.

But the Bible does not end after Genesis 2 with our joyful, naked, and unashamed first parents. In the next chapter God's Enemy, and ours, shows up to tempt them. He twists God's words. Our mother Eve's sin of commission was, in a proud effort to become like God, partaking of that which God had forbidden. Our father Adam's sin of omission was failing to intervene as he sat by quietly, idly, and timidly watching the Enemy deceive his wife as so many of his cowardly, passive, silent sons have done ever since.

Rather than living as one, they separated as two sinners. Rather than welcoming God, they hid from Him in the garden. Rather than being naked without shame, they covered their nakedness, making clothes for themselves. Rather than repenting of their sin, they blamed everyone else. And every wedding since has happened outside Eden, even those hosted in gardens as if to pretend that things were not so.

This fall of humanity into sin has infected, polluted, and corrupted literally every aspect of life on the earth. This includes sex, concerning which—perhaps more clearly than any other aspect of life—we have become utterly confused. The result is that people tend to think that sex is god or gross to varying degrees, rather than a gift.

Sex as God

He had a beautiful wife but was never sexually satisfied. His mind was filled with sinful fantasies from pornography he had viewed, as well as sexual experiences he had enjoyed, before marriage. Some would have been sinful to do even with his wife, others were not sinful, but she was opposed to them because they violated her conscience. Over the course of some years in their marriage, rather than killing these sinful desires, he occasionally nurtured them by daydreaming about what it would be like to make his fantasies realities. One day he did—with another woman.

He decided to never tell his wife because, in his flawed mind, it was better for her not to know the truth and be devastated. He actually considered his lying somewhat loving. But she could tell something was different, so she pressed him for answers. Eventually he confessed. As we met during their counseling session, while his wife wept continually, he tried to downplay what had happened by saying it was only one day of their life, he did not love the other woman, and similar inane efforts to make his sin seem less sinful.

Nothing seemed to get through to him until I (Mark) simply told him he was not only an adulterer, but had become an adulterer because he was first an idolater. The first commandments are that we are to worship God alone. If we obey, we then do not worship other people and things as functional gods. When we disobey, we then continue to worship but do so as idolaters treating people and things as gods. His sin was not just sleeping with a different woman, but sleeping with another woman as a worship act to another god. Sex was his god, a bed was his altar, their bodies were their living sacrifices, and he was a pagan priest committing idolatry.

The worship of anyone or anything other than the God of the Bible is by definition idolatry. Idolatry happens when a good thing (like sex) becomes a god thing (like adultery), which is a bad thing.

Idolatry begins in the heart before it reaches our hands, the prophet Ezekiel told us.[a] Someone or something becomes the center of our lives, the pursuit of our desires, the ground of our identities, and the source of our hopes. We must have it or them, and if we do not, we will be miserable. Once we obtain it or them, if lost, we become inconsolably despairing because our god has departed. So we make sacrifices to obtain and retain our idols. Our thoughts, words, deeds, health, dollars, and days are consumed with religious zeal for the cause of our idol.

Paul flatly stated in Romans 12:1 that worship is offering our bodies as a living sacrifice. In 1 Corinthians 10:7–8, Paul made this connection between sexual sin and idolatry, explaining what sounds like a rousing night at the ancient club: "Do not become idolaters as were some of them. As it is written, 'The people sat down to eat and drink, and rose up to play.' Nor let us commit sexual immorality, as some of them did."

Sex is deeply spiritual.

Throughout history God's people have maintained a very special view of

---

a Ezek. 14:3.

sexuality. In the days of the Old Testament, most of their neighboring religions in the Middle East taught that God was to be experienced through nature, particularly through sexuality. Because of this thinking, many of these religions had sexuality and temple prostitution as integral components of their spirituality and religious ceremonies. In contrast, God's people were strongly opposed to such thinking because they held that God could not be reduced to something He had created.

More contemporary examples include Hinduism, which maintained temple prostitutes until quite recently. Hinduism's Kama Sutra sex manual serves as one example of many such weddings of illicit sexuality and religion that can also be found in Islam, Buddhism, and Confucianism.

Greek and Roman societies also had sexuality as a major element in their worship activity. Their temples had male and female ritual prostitutes available for sexual worship. The temple of Aphrodite in Corinth was one such temple that was renowned for having more than one thousand temple prostitutes.

Conversely, God's people have always held that sex was created by God, and for the glory of God, but did not serve as a means of reaching God. They held that sex was to be appreciated but never worshipped or elevated to the level of idolatry frequently found in other religions.

The worship of sex as a god is as passionate as ever. The Bible predicted this tragedy. In Romans 1:24–25, Paul wrote that people either worship God our Creator and enjoy His creation—including our bodies—or people worship creation as a god, and in sexual sin offer their bodies in worship. Paul went on to explain that those who worship creation invariably worship the human body and its pleasures through sinful sex, including homosexuality and lesbianism, because it is the apex of God's creation.

The Porn Plague and Prostitution

The sexual revolution of the 1960s and '70s radically altered the sexual landscape of our nation, so that today sex before marriage and viewing pornography are the culturally accepted norm. Subsequently, we are in the midst of a sexual social experiment the consequence of which no one truly knows.

Only by seeing sex as a god we worship are we able to make sense of the porno plague. The statistics paint an ugly picture. Annual pornography revenues are more than $90 billion worldwide.[1] In the United States, pornography revenues were $13 billion in 2006, more than all combined revenues of professional football, baseball, and basketball franchises[2] or the combined revenues of ABC, CBS, and NBC ($6.2 billion).[3] Porn sites account for 12 percent of all Internet sites.[4] Every day 2.5 million pornographic e-mails are sent.[5]

A staggering 90 percent of children between the ages of eight and sixteen have viewed pornography on the Internet, in most cases unintentionally.[6] The average age of first Internet exposure to pornography is eleven.[7] The largest consumer category of Internet pornography is boys ages twelve to seventeen.[8] Youth with significant exposure to sexuality in the media were shown to be considerably more likely to have had intercourse at ages fourteen to sixteen.[9] The mean age of first intercourse in the United States is now 16.4.[10]

Porn addiction has also found its way into the lives of Christians; 57 percent of pastors say that addiction to pornography is the most sexually damaging issue to their congregations.[11] The most popular day of the week for viewing porn is Sunday, the day of Jesus' Resurrection and the Christian Sabbath.[12] Tragically, one survey revealed that one-third of evangelical pastors admitted to viewing Internet pornography.

Perhaps the most damaged among us are prostitutes whose bodies have been sacrificed to the god of sex. The vast majority of young women involved in prostitution were sexually abused as children; estimates range from two-thirds to 95 percent.[13]

The life of a prostitute is incredibly dark: 62 percent report having been raped in prostitution. In one study, 75 percent of women in escort prostitution had attempted suicide; prostituted women comprised 15 percent of all completed suicides reported by hospitals.[14]

Please take this as a loving warning. If you, or your spouse, tend to view sex as god, you are in grave danger. You are on a path that leads to death. The further you venture down that path, the darker and more damaging it becomes. Your idol is lying to you. There is no freedom, comfort, joy, pleasure, or life at the end of the path you are traveling on. But it is not too late. You need to be honest, you need to tell the truth, you need to get help, and you need to turn around and run for your life. So be honest with your spouse and get the help you need from a pastor or biblical counselor.

If not, you will end up doing tragic things, as Solomon did. The man richer than Bill Gates, smarter than Albert Einstein, more powerful than an

American president, and more influential than the pope amassed a harem rivaled only by men who are porn addicts who collect women in their minds. Despite having sexually sinful parents who conceived his older brother through adultery, he did not learn his lesson. Despite being the wisest man to ever walk the earth other than Jesus Christ, he did not learn his lesson. Despite marrying a beautiful and sexually free woman who loved him, as recorded in the Song of Songs, he did not learn his lesson. Instead, he intermarried with seven hundred godless pagan women and kept three hundred additional sexual concubines from many other nations who helped turn his sinful heart away from God so that he worshipped false gods, even building pagan altars where sexual sin was conducted in worship to demon gods.[a] This includes his support of Ashtoreth, the Canaanite demon goddess of sex worshipped around male phallices symbolized by poles around which orgies occurred.

He also funded the worship of Molech, the demon god who demanded children be sacrificed by fire; and of Chemosh, the Moabite god who demanded child sacrifice not unlike abortion. Solomon's example reveals that the longer we wait to repent, the more damage we do. Solomon himself wrote an entire book of the Bible, Ecclesiastes, in part to repent and warn us not to follow his folly.

Sex as Gross

Often in an overreaction to the worship of sex as god, people adopt the position of sex as gross. As such, sex is viewed as a sort of necessary evil for procreation but otherwise a rather vulgar, repulsive, and off-putting act.

The thinking of the Greek philosopher Plato may have had as much influence on Christian thought regarding sexuality as any system of thought. Platonic thought was very dualistic and did not see people as unified wholes, but instead as a divided combination of material body and nonmaterial soul. This led to viewing the material body as an evil prison that housed the more pure soul. Since sexuality was passionate and physical, Christians steeped in Platonic thought began to teach that passion and sexuality were inherently sinful. This also led to a very low view of women, since men viewed them as the cause of their lusts.

---

a 1 Kings 11:1–43.

The "sex as gross" view often reduces sex solely to an unfortunate means by which procreation occurs. Thus, for sex not to be sinful, it needs to be done with the possibility of conception occurring. On this point, a theologian said, "In the postapostolic period marriage was generally viewed as being for procreation. Clement of Alexandria [AD 150–215] expresses this attitude when he says, 'Intercourse performed licitly is an occasion of sin, unless done purely to beget children.'"[15] Some of the early church fathers held worldly views of sex informed by erroneous Greek thinking and sadly set in motion a precedent of seeing sex as gross. Theologian Wayne House said,

> In Stoicism, emotions were downplayed and self-control was exalted. This even became true in marriage, where passion was considered suspect. Marriage must have another purpose, namely, the continuance of the human race. In the words of the Stoic philosopher Ocellus Lucanus, "We have intercourse not for pleasure but for the purpose of procreation. . . . The sexual organs are given man not for pleasure, but for the maintenance of the species."[16]

Tertullian (AD 155–220) and Ambrose (AD 340–397) were said to prefer extinction of the human race to continued sexual intercourse. Origen (AD 185–254) was so convinced of the evils of sexual pleasure that he not only allegorized the Song of Songs but also took a knife and castrated himself. Gregory of Nyssa (AD 335–394) taught that Adam and Eve were created without sexual desire, and if the fall had not occurred, the race would have reproduced itself by some harmless mode of vegetation. Chrysostom (AD 347–407) said that Adam and Eve could not have had sexual relations before the fall. Jerome (AD 347–420) threw himself into thorny brambles to overwhelm himself with pain when he began to desire a woman sexually. He also beat his chest with a stone to punish himself for feeling sexually tempted. And he believed that a husband was guilty of adultery if he engaged in unrestrained sexual passion with his wife.[17]

Augustine (AD 354–430) was sexually active before his conversion and later decided that sex within marriage was not sinful, though the lust and passion associated with it was sinful. Because of this, he often commended married couples for not engaging in sex and referred to it as a form of animalistic lust.[18]

Saint Francis made women out of snow and then caressed them in order to quiet the lust that burned in him. Thomas Aquinas (AD 1225–1274) taught that sex was only permissible for purposes of procreation. Aquinas saw sexual intercourse as duty alone. Anything beyond this was immoral. He wrote, "For if the motive for the marriage act be a virtue, whether of justice that they may render the debt, or of religion, that they may beget children for the worship of God, it is meritorious. But if the motive be lust . . . it is a venial sin."[19]

Catholic moral instruction, following the tradition of Thomas Aquinas, cautioned that marital relations of husbands and wives could only be justified as a matter of "duty," certainly not as a matter of "desire."[20] The Catholic Church's view through the Middle Ages was that sexual love, both in and out of marriage, was evil. By the fifth century priests were forbidden to marry, which has, at least in part, resulted in a global scandal as sexually unhealthy and unholy men entered pastoral ministry.

Early in the sixth century, Pope Gregory the Great wrote that although marriage was not sinful, "conjugal union cannot take place without carnal pleasure, and such pleasure cannot under any circumstance be without blame."[21] The Church eventually began to limit the days on which sex was permissible and continued adding days until half the year or more was prohibited, with some priests going so far as to recommend abstinence from five to seven days a week. Medieval Catholicism even provided priests with detailed manuals to aid them in taking sexual confession. Some priests would inquire of intimate sexual details and attempt to regulate the frequency, positions, and sensations of marital intercourse.

Not solely an ancient issue, sex as gross continues in Catholicism to some degree even today. A 2011 pastoral letter on chastity from the Canadian Conference of Catholic Bishops for married couples said, "The value of sexual intercourse does not lie in recreation, or physical gratification. . . . That is why the sexual act has to be unitive and procreative and why some kinds of sexual activity are not chaste. Though pleasure may be present, some acts are a misuse of sex when they fall short of what God intends."[22]

A modern Protestant version of this error includes one female author speaking against marital sex purely for pleasure and even orgasm, calling it "sexual gluttony." She said, "Nowhere does the Bible say that the purpose of marital sex is climax, much much [sic] less climax at the expense of fruitfulness and oneness."[23]

The belief that sex is gross has even affected how the most erotic, passionate, and sexual book of the Bible has been interpreted and misinterpreted. Until around AD 100, the Jewish rabbis interpreted the Song of Songs in a literal way as a series of love songs between a husband and a wife, using figurative language. The Song of Songs was read at the Passover liturgy, and the songs were often sung in the pubs to celebrate marital love and intimacy within a covenant relationship.

But early in the history of the Christian church, as allegorical methods of Bible interpretation became fashionable, the Song of Songs was explained as being about our relationship with God instead of being a passionate poem about a husband-and-wife relationship. In studying love and intimacy, you will find that some principles may indeed correspond to our relationship with God, though this is not the primary intention of the Song. Those who consider, to varying degrees, sex as gross drive this misuse of Scripture. And rather than renewing their minds to agree with the Bible, they instead change the meaning of the Bible to fit their own error, as they simply cannot fathom that God would speak in detail positively about sexual pleasure.

In our experience, one common source of the sex-as-gross view is religious and sexually prudish older women who, in the name of mentoring, teach younger women that sex is for husbands and babies but not for personal pleasure. Subsequently, they instruct other women to endure sex as part of marital duty but not for marital delight. Perhaps the most extreme examples I (Mark) have encountered were multiple young couples from strict religious upbringings at a conference in Minnesota. In conversations throughout the course of the day, I repeatedly had Christian couples who had been married a year or more asking when I thought they should consummate their relationship and have sex for the first time. They had no sexual contact of any kind before marriage, or even after marriage, because they considered it gross and were actually somewhat scared of sex. Most wrongly thought that sex was for procreation alone and not pleasure.

If sex is only for procreation, it would mean that apart from the fertile days a woman experiences each month, sexual intercourse in marriage would be sinful. Furthermore, this would mean that intercourse with an unfertile husband or wife or sex with a postmenopausal wife would also be sinful. All of this is incredibly nonsensical, unbiblical, and impractical for many reasons. A woman's clitoris is a nerve center created by God for only one purpose—pleasure, not reproduction. God also made women multi-orgasmic for the joy of sexual pleasure in marriage. Proverbs 5:19 reveals that a wife's breasts are not solely for baby food but also for husband fun: "Let her breasts satisfy you at all times."

What is also curious is the frequent hypocrisy of those who most vocally purport the sex-as-gross position. Such people speak with great passion about the evils of sex. Perhaps the most obvious are the hypocritical preachers who preach against sexual sins that they themselves are guilty of concurrently committing. To be fair and compassionate, sometimes the sex-is-gross position is also the result of sexual sin and abuse. Those who have sinned and been sinned against sexually and have not worked through their issues biblically and thoroughly often see sex as gross. One young woman, for example, told us that after being molested repeatedly as a child, she had lived her life believing that everything below her neck was "gross." In chapter 7 we will discuss sexual abuse and how it affects married couples. There is healing, help, and hope for them to in time increasingly embrace and enjoy sex as a gift from God.

Sex as Gift

Contrary to their much-maligned image, the Puritans marked a shift in thinking about sex. Church historian Belden Lane stated, "Puritan marriage manuals by English writers like William Whately and William Gouge forthrightly defended 'mutual dalliances for pleasure's sake' within the marriage covenant, urging 'that husband and wife mutually delight each in the other,' maintaining a 'fervent love' in their regular yielding of that 'due benevolence' one to another which is warranted and sanctified by God's word."[24]

The change of thought by the Puritans from previous Christian teaching was due to their return to the Bible. The Bible teaches that while sex can be received as a god and rejected as gross, it can also be redeemed as a gift. Because sex is a gift that God gave, it is His intent that we steward and enjoy that gift, like every gift He gives, in such a way that is glorious to Him and good for our marriages.

Sex is a powerful gift that God gives to married couples. Furthermore, it provides six good and glorious benefits.

Sex is for pleasure.

Throughout the most erotic book in the Bible, the Song of Songs, children are never mentioned, as the entire focus of the book is simply marital passion and pleasure. Pleasures in the Song of Songs include kissing (1:2), oral/fellatio—her initiative (2:3), manual stimulation—her invitation (2:6), erotic massage—his initiative (4:5), oral/cunnilingus—his initiative (4:12–5:1), striptease (6:13–7:9), and new places and positions, including outdoors—her initiative (7:11–13).

Sex is for creating children.[a]

Birth control use is not always a sin if abortive methods are not used, and the heart's motives are not sinful, as we examine in chapter 10. But children are repeatedly considered a blessing throughout Scripture. God created a husband and wife to conceive children at the moment of deepest connection.

Sex is for oneness.[b]

New Life Community Church says,

> Sexual pleasure is one of the most intense human experiences. Physically speaking, when a man or woman reaches sexual excitement, nerve endings release a chemical into the brain called "opioid." "Opioid" means opium-like and is a good description of the power of this chemical. Apart from a heroin-induced experience, nothing is more physically pleasurable than sex. This is a wonderful thing in a committed marriage relationship, because it helps to bond two people together and bring joy to living together and building a relationship.[25]

A faithfully married couple with a free and frequent sex life are literally bonded together as one, physically and chemically by God's design. This oneness is expressed in such things as having one last name, living in one house, sleeping in one bed, attending one church, sharing one bank account, and worshipping one God.

---

a Gen. 1:28.
b Gen. 2:24.

Sex is for knowledge.[a]

In the act of sex, and the related intimacy that surrounds it, a couple learns to know each other in a way that they are not known by anyone else. This sacred and experiential knowledge means that a faithfully married couple has an intimacy and connection that is not only exclusive but also unprecedented in all their other relationships.

Sex is for protection.[b]

While there is no excuse for sexual sin, there are factors that can increase the temptation for sexual sin. Perhaps chief among them is a marriage in which at least one of the people is sexually dissatisfied because the sex is not free or frequent enough. If one person feels sexually denied and discouraged, it increases the temptation to wander outside the marriage for sexual satisfaction. But free and frequent sex within marriage helps safeguard and protect the marriage from such sins as bitterness, adultery, pornography, and secret masturbation.

Sex is for comfort.[c]

There are seasons in life when nothing can be said or done to comfort a suffering spouse. In those moments it is the ministry of touch that allows us to connect with our spouses in a way that lovingly serves them and binds us together in the suffering. We knew a couple who suffered the death of their young child. They were understandably devastated. The husband was unsure what to say or do to comfort his grieving wife, and so he simply asked what she needed. She told him that she wanted to go away for a few days to a quiet bed-and-breakfast, lie unclothed together, visit, pray, weep, and make love so that she did not feel alone in any way. They reported that being able to physically comfort each other at that time was a vital part of their healing and grieving process.

It is our prayer that you and your spouse would see sex as a gift from God. A gift to be stewarded. A gift to be guarded. A gift to be enjoyed. And a gift to be shared together for God's glory and your good.

---

a Gen. 4:1.
b 1 Cor. 7:2–5.
c 2 Sam. 12:24.

Before proceeding, it is vital for you and your spouse to be honest. Are either of you prone to view sex as god or gross? If so, you are in danger. Are either of you reading this book hoping to convert the other person to gross or god sex? If so, you are in danger.

We were. When we married, I (Mark) tended toward sex as god. I was a newer Christian who had accumulated most of his knowledge about sex from culture, locker-room talk, and sinning sexually with a few young women. Conversely, Grace was raised in a home that was religiously conservative when it came to sex, had sinned sexually, and had been sinned against sexually. She considered sex gross. For her I was too much sexually. For me she was too little sexually. We made very little progress for many years until we had spent considerable time talking through our sexual history and beliefs, working together through many hours in the Bible and Christian books to arrive at a unified view of sex as gift. Once we came to the same place in our thinking about sex, we began to work as allies instead of enemies. Our marriage has never been the same since, and our sex gets better all the time.

When we got married, I (Grace) didn't understand the physical *and* emotional aspects of sex for men. It seemed with his high sex drive that was all Mark wanted from me and that he didn't appreciate anything else I did. His drive seemed to get stronger the less we had sex, and I wondered if it was an idol to him or if that was normal for men. I later realized it was partially a real physical need, not an obsession, since he wasn't masturbating or getting relief some other way, which I am thankful for. I read somewhere that if you have sex more, it actually decreases the necessity for frequent sex over time for most men. I tried that but it didn't seem to change anything for Mark.

There were issues of abuse underlying my lack of desire, so I needed to deal with those first. This was scary for me to embark on, but we were at a breaking point. I asked God to renew my mind, and He began that process through my study of the Song of Solomon, reading Bible-based books on sex and marriage, and having honest conversations with Mark. I asked him to pray for and with me when I was struggling with sex, which built trust and intimacy, and I think it started to break his bitterness since he was finally seeing change. I wasn't feeling as forced to change but more invited to change for God's glory and our mutual enjoyment.

My feeling of being broken started to fade as we talked very honestly about how we could build mutual intimacy. I wanted to see sex as a gift from the Lord, but it didn't come without hard work and obedience to the Holy Spirit's conviction. After working through the past abuse issues, God told me to have sex frequently and He would bring my heart and mind along. I needed to obey Him first and trust Him to change me along the way. This took some time, but God has faithfully given me a new perspective and continues to work with me on more freedom in intimacy. Honest conversations, repentance, obedience to God, a teachable spirit, and praying together against fear and for freedom all lead to healthy intimacy.

If either of you is prone toward sex as god or gross, the apostle Paul exhorted you to "not be conformed to this world, but be transformed by the renewing of your mind."[a] Change begins in the mind. Your biggest sex organ is your brain. Thinking rightly about sex is essential to your enjoyment of sex. It's not okay for you to try to make your spouse think like you. Instead, both of you need to think like God as revealed in His Word by the Holy Spirit.

---

a Rom. 12:2.

7

DISGRACE AND GRACE

The Lord . . . has shown his favor
and taken away my disgrace.

—LUKE 1:25 NIV

O ne night, Mark and I were casually talking about past relationships
and situations in our lives when I found myself describing sexual
abuse that had occurred in my past as if I were explaining how I did
the laundry yesterday—no emotion, seemingly no pain, no pause for tears or
reflection on my words. Mark was crying as I finished the story, and when I
asked what was wrong, he informed me that I had just explained abuse. *What?*
I had so much shame and had stuffed it for so long that I didn't even know it
was abuse until Mark told me it more than fit the definition.

To me, it was just something that happened, and I moved on. It was history, and it didn't affect me in any way. By God's grace to me, that night I
realized that couldn't be farther from the truth. The reality was that it had
been very destructive in my relationship with God, Mark, and friends. I didn't
really trust anyone or let anyone see who I was underneath the Christian girl
wearing a smile. Now, many years after the abuse had taken place, God was
asking me to look it straight in the eye and let Mark be part of the healing
process. I honestly wanted to take back my words and forget the conversation.
It couldn't possibly be helpful to talk about it more, I thought. Was it really
necessary to reexamine that part of my life? Was Mark really safe to talk to
about it, or would his response cause more pain?

Tragically, abuse is far too common for women today. Sexual assault
happens to one in four women and one in six men at some point in their life-
times.[1] Because it is one of the most underreported crimes, those numbers are
likely very low and only 5 to 40 percent of the actual total.[2] Emotional and

123

psychological abuse are also destructive and painful to face. If any of these are part of your past, I encourage you to read on and seek God's grace for you in the healing process.

I had described to Mark a relationship I was in before he and I ever met, with a guy who was a little older than me and who came from a rough family life. I met the guy in church, and I was an emotionally needy, naive girl who didn't have brothers and wasn't informed about boys or protected from the bad ones—admittedly not a good combination. We voluntarily slept together, and I lost my virginity to him. Over time, the guy became controlling, telling me what clothes I couldn't wear in public, because he was very jealous. He controlled when I went out with my friends and who I could hang out with (which basically was rarely and few). He determined my schedule and free time, having me stay with him at his work much of the time. He even organized his life to follow me around and keep an eye on me. It was like having an invisible fence around me, getting stung when going outside the boundaries, and I was ruled by my fears.

Sadly, I thought all this was him taking care of me and saw myself as increasingly unable to make my own decisions. At one point his jealousy turned to rage, and he ran after me, caught me, and threw me up against a wall. I grew more and more afraid of him, too afraid to tell him to leave me alone. Like many other girls, I didn't see this as abuse and thought he would change, but it continued far too long. I was filled with my own guilt from fornicating and told myself if I married him it would cover my sin somehow. So that was my plan until he confessed he had been sleeping with another girl. Somehow that was the one thing that took my fear away long enough to end the relationship, which I now see as my "way of escape" given by God. If in that moment I had chosen to continue being abused, my life would look completely different today.

Because of God's protection as a Father, today I can pray for that guy, not be bitter, and trust that God is changing him too. On this, theologian Miroslav Volf said, "We must name the troubling past truthfully—we must come to clarity about what happened, how we reacted, and how we are reacting to it now—to be freed from its destructive hold on our lives. Granted, truthful naming will not by itself heal memories or wrong suffered; but without truthful naming, all measures we might undertake to heal such memories will remain incomplete."[3]

When someone other than the Holy Spirit controls where you go, whom you see, what you wear, and what you do, it's emotional abuse, and it affects your life deeply. When someone stalks you, is obsessed with you, and threatens you, it's psychological abuse, and it changes you drastically. When someone makes you have sex, and you continually say no verbally or through body language (nonparticipation, pushing away, clenching your body), it's sexual abuse and it affects you spiritually. All this had been a part of my past, but it was bringing death to my present and future life. For Mark it answered more of the questions as to why intimacy in our marriage was stuck and had been so hard to experience together. I couldn't even explain why I would often tell him no to sex, or offer any variety of excuses. I would later realize I was letting fear from my past abuse, instead of conviction of enjoying my husband, rule me. The God-intended beauty of oneness had passed us by, and the lie I had concealed and abuse I had experienced were both at the root.

Defining what constitutes sexual assault is very important. It is a broad term that includes several sexual behaviors against an individual, whether physical, psychological, or verbal. Sexual assault, the current term that has replaced rape legally, is different from state to state in the United States and nation to nation around the world, making it confusing for people who have been harmed by it. In their book *Rid of My Disgrace*, Dr. Justin Holcomb and his wife, Lindsey, who are leaders at our church, have created a thorough and helpful definition:

> There are three parts to our definition of sexual assault: 1) any type of sexual behavior or contact 2) where consent is not freely given or obtained and 3) is accomplished through force, intimidation, violence, coercion, manipulation, threat, deception, or abuse of authority. . . .
>
> When defining sexual assault as any sexual act that is nonconsensual—forced against someone's will—it is important to understand that the "acts" can be physical, verbal, or psychological. . . . Sexual assault occurs along a continuum of power and control ranging from noncontact sexual assault to forced sexual intercourse. Sexual assault includes acts such as nonconsensual sexual intercourse (rape), nonconsensual sodomy (oral or anal sexual acts), child molestation, incest, fondling, exposure, voyeurism, or attempts to commit these acts.[4]

For me, sexual assault caused disgrace. In *Rid of My Disgrace*, the Holcombs wrote,

Disgrace destroys, causes pain, deforms, and wounds. It alienates and iso-lates. Disgrace makes you feel worthless, rejected, unwanted, and repulsive, like a *persona non grata* (a "person without grace"). Disgrace silences and shuns. . . . To your sense of disgrace, God restores, heals, and re-creates through grace. A good short definition of grace is "one-way love." This is the opposite of your experience of assault, which was "one-way violence." To your experience of one-way violence, God brings one-way love. The contrast between the two is staggering.[5]

Martin Luther said, "God receives none but those who are forsaken, restores health to none but those who are sick, gives sight to none but the blind, and life to none but the dead. . . . He has mercy on none but the wretched and gives grace to none but those who are in disgrace."[6] Refuting the lie that we are permanently disgraced and have to earn God's grace in order to be accepted is part of the healing process from experiencing abuse. If we are sick, blind, and have been sinned against, we can't fix ourselves! Only God's free gift of grace gives us emotional health, clear vision of our heavenly Father, and the ability to forgive as He did for us through Jesus.

Making a Choice

We have a choice to make, whether we are faced with our own sin or the sin of others against us. When we become Christians, we make the choice to love and obey God, so we need to ask Him what wisdom looks like for us in each circumstance.

God was giving Mark and me a way of escape and a path to true healing by grace, so what were we going to choose? Again, our marriage covenant was right in front of us. It's not enough to just stay together and not glorify God in our marriage. He requests more because He loves us and has more for us! Were we going to run from Jesus or grow in our faith and run to Him? The pain seemed too much for both of us, and we wondered if it was really possible to trust each other again after all this. First, we had to trust God—we were still going to sin and fail, but He wouldn't.

I had been more concerned about what people would think of me if they really knew about my sins and the sins against me than I was about acting sinfully against God and others. I had lived a double life, a pastor's daughter and wife filled with deception and fear. I wanted to crawl into a hole and never come out. I already questioned that I had any value in God's eyes much of my life; now this seeming flaw was added to the pile. How would I ever get through such a trial? The Psalms promise, "The LORD is close to the broken-hearted and saves those who are crushed in spirit"[a] and 2 Corinthians 12:9 says, "For my power is made perfect in weakness" (NIV). Were those verses really true? I had asked Jesus into my life when I was three years old, but in my thirties I was about to experience how much God truly loves me as a Father and how powerful He is.

We all get to a point where we need to stop running from God in shame and start running to Him for protection and the healing of our souls! Do you find yourself struggling to spend time with Jesus regularly because you feel unlovable and undeserving of His comfort and forgiveness? Does your pride tell you that you need to fix things on your own (not even possible) or pretend they didn't happen to earn His approval? We find it so easy at times to believe the greatest lie—that Jesus' death wasn't enough for us and what we did. I had reached a critical point where I knew it was time to discover the story of Jesus all over again and let it seep into my life.

I had to start by repenting of trying to hide the abuse from God and Mark. That meant asking the Holy Spirit to restore any memories that needed to be brought into the light so I could be cleansed and remade as a child of God. And it meant Jesus' righteousness alone had to replace all my old identity of abused, neglected, dirty, and worthless. I had nothing to give and every-thing to receive from the Lord. This process was painful and didn't happen overnight. It went in phases of hard, really hard, and extremely hard as God faithfully and patiently became my trustworthy Father and Mark learned how to love his "new" wife.

Admittedly the timing seemed extra difficult with another new baby and four other children to care for; I had the best excuse to wait. But once again God wouldn't let me wait anymore. I joined a group of women in our church who had all experienced abuse in different ways, and in the group walked through a twelve-week process of talking through the years of sin against me

a Ps. 34:18 NIV.

and sin I committed against others in response. When I joined the group, it was a bit disheartening to start out with one of the women putting our family on a pedestal as she said, "Oh, you are *that* Grace, Mark's wife, I just love his preaching . . ." *How can I possibly be honest and real now?* I thought. *What will happen to our church and our life if they know about my abuse?*

My leader thankfully addressed the issue with the woman, and every week it was helpful to hear others' stories and have the women respond to mine. I wasn't alone! But I also needed to realize no other "friend" was going to fix this for me. Although I was blessed to have people in my life who loved me very much, our church lacked resources in helping abuse victims. We quickly realized there were large numbers of abuse victims attending our church and began the process of gathering resources to help.[7] Mutual, honest accountability had always felt too vulnerable, but it was part of the process I needed to prayerfully participate in. I needed discernment as the pastor's wife so that I didn't put my husband wrongly in the middle of fire from critics. Along the way, I ran into several obstacles and was tempted to stop and not continue going through the pain, but I wanted to experience freedom and not pretend anymore, so I wasn't going to let anything keep me from it. I finally wanted to put my own sin and shame to death, through Jesus' death on the cross, and experience real joy!

I got on my knees, and God told me to trust Him with everything. He reminded me of Philippians 4:4–9, which had been a life Scripture:

Rejoice in the Lord ALWAYS. Again I will say, rejoice! . . . THE LORD IS AT HAND. Be *anxious* for NOTHING, but in EVERYTHING *by prayer and supplication*, with thanksgiving, *let your requests be made known to God*; and the peace of God, which surpasses all understanding, will guard your hearts and minds through Christ Jesus. Finally, brethren, whatever things are true, whatever things are noble, whatever things are just, whatever things are pure, whatever things are lovely, whatever things are of good report, if there is any virtue and if there is anything praiseworthy—*meditate on these things*. The things which you learned and received and heard and saw in me, these do, and the God of peace will be with you. (Emphasis [small caps and italics] added)

I couldn't walk this path of healing unless I realized the Lord was right there with me, that His peace would guard my heart, and that I needed to rejoice in even the smallest thing when it seemed as if there wasn't anything to celebrate. I was blown away by His specific love for me. He took some of the few memory verses I knew and shined a light on them to give me hope in Him for the hard journey ahead! Again I knew more of my loving Father and experienced His forgiveness and cleansing. Another layer of junk was being removed from my soul.

———

Over a couple of years, and continuing today, I learned to pray and cry out to God, I studied God's character,[8] and I was more honest with Mark than I had ever been. God gave me a few trustworthy women to encourage and exhort me and love me, despite knowing the truth about me. I read recommended books[9] and listened to biblical counselors online.[10] Although I had always thought *all* anger was a sin until I studied righteous anger, I finally experienced righteous anger and prayed against bitterness. I grieved the sin against me and the sin I committed against others and created healthy temporary boundaries with people who weren't able to help me for a season as I processed my own sin and the abuse.

Many tears, many hard conversations, many eye-opening times with the Lord, many idols of my heart were revealed—all for God's glory and my healing. I never thought it was possible, but that is what repentance and redemption feel like. Now I not only know what they mean but have experienced them through Jesus—and will continue to for the rest of my life.

The Masks of an Abused Person

A person who has been abused can become adept at hiding the pain behind a mask. It helps us cope with others and makes us feel safe, but in truth it's really just something that prevents us from actually dealing with the abuse. Now that you know about my abuse and responses, do you understand more clearly whether you have experienced sexual assault or abuse of any kind? How have you tried to cope with it in the midst of your relationships? Do you act out a role or hide behind a mask? I would have never imagined that talking about pain from my past would help me heal, but that is exactly what happened. In talking about it, I was able, by God's grace, to take off the masks I had been wearing, stop playing a role and pretending, and be known. Once I realized that my identity was not determined by what I had done or not done, or what had been done to me, but rather by what Jesus had done for me, I was set free.

To cope with the pain, I initially pretended to be a "good girl," outwardly displaying kindness, patience, smiles, and quick apologies without true repentance. I never seemed to get angry and was constantly serving other people, making them happy, but sacrificing my own family and health. Though I seemed happy, I was emotionally shut down and disengaged at any deep levels. I had to work hard to be passionate about anything and envied women who seemed to be so naturally zealous. As a "good girl" I avoided conflict and wanted peace at all costs, even if it meant enabling a person's sin or sinning myself so as not to offend. On the outside I was cool as a cucumber, while on the inside I was full of shame, devastation, and accusations of the Enemy.

In the first years of ministry, I also wore the mask of "religious girl" at times. After all, I had been a pastor's kid and was expected to be a wise pastor's wife, right? If people needed advice, I would give them a verse or a book to read, not considering how I should apply it first. If people needed help, I would serve them without question, even enabling or allowing people to use me. If people needed a meal, I would make whatever they liked, sometimes making my own kids wait longer for dinner. I steered clear of examining my own heart by staying busy with everyone else's lives. I was moralistic and judgmental, not always verbally, building up my own pride and accomplishments. I felt better about myself when I was serving other people. I didn't like recognition for my service, but if people didn't seem grateful, I was bothered by it.

Another mask I had worn in high school was the "party girl." I liked to have "fun" and numb the pain with alcohol. Some use drugs, food, or being funny all the time as party masks. They may be sarcastic or use jokes to change the subject if the mood gets too serious. Their names are associated with fun, so they are always invited to events and seem to love a crowd. Sadly, it's the perfect place to hide and not be known as an individual.

A mask I didn't wear, but that is common, is "tough girl." She seems in control, confident, unaffected by the world's pressures, and not at all needy. She often leads with making people fear her, and as a result isn't liked by many.

She pretends to embrace being alone, but inwardly wishes for relationship and closeness. Her hard exterior keeps people at arm's length and avoids her getting hurt. She is critical and doesn't trust people, and works hard to be the protector of others. Outside she is hard as a rock but inside is vulnerability and loneliness.

Which mask I wore depended on whom I was with or how I was trying to protect myself. It was an identity crisis because I wasn't rooted in Christ. I was shaped by what others had done to me and what I had done, rather than who God created me in His image to be and what His Son had done for me at the cross. Which mask(s) are you wearing to avoid dealing with the pain of life? I urge you to take off the mask by being honest and allow God to reveal His grace, mercy, and love. All these masks lead to continued hiding of our sin and the sin against us, which is equivalent to "suppress[ing] the truth in unrighteousness," as Romans 1:18 says. He wants to clothe us in truth and His righteousness instead.

Ready to Respond

As I previously mentioned, our church was on a mission to equip people as best and as efficiently as possible to serve the people in our congregation who had suffered abuse. The number of abuse victims was in the hundreds or more, just with those we were aware of at that point. For most churches, this topic is taboo and not discussed, but for us it had to be. Several elders were researching and trying out different programs but to no avail. Most weren't gospel centered or they focused wrongly on helping behavior rather than the person's heart. God cares about our hearts, and we needed something Jesus and Bible focused, so the elders decided to write their own material and train our people.

How does abuse make the victim feel? Abused people may experience many feelings, including anger, shame, fear, confusion, condemnation, despair, anxiety, decreased sex drive, panic attacks, sleep disturbance, denial, guilt, and embarrassment. So what do we do if we have been abused? I strongly agree with the Holcombs, who say, "The only way to move from denial, isolation, and self-protection is to look honestly at the assault that has been done to you. Healing begins when the secret is disclosed and the shackles of silence are broken."[11] I would never have agreed with this before having to do this with my own abuse. As I did, you may think it doesn't seem possible that talking about it with trustworthy people who can help or "reliving" the horror could in any way be healing. Perhaps you don't want to see how much it has affected your life in negative ways. But we each need a new identity so that we don't feel condemned by our sin. Jesus loves us because He *is* love, not because of who we are or pretend to be. He created us, chose us, and has unfailing love for us. We did nothing to deserve His love and can't do anything to lose it. This is an invitation to respond to His love. As you respond, the condemnation will begin to fade.

When a Friend Shares Her History of Abuse

Over the years, I've had conversations with women who completely deny that sexual assault, including by their own fathers, has at all affected their marriages. Such women are prone to say it's in the past and they have moved on. Similar to my own story, some wrongly believe it's best not to tell their husbands about the assault because it will hurt their spouses more to reveal the truth. Had I not experienced the fruit of dealing with the past, I would have counseled them to continue concealing the truth to avoid the pain. In reality, the pain is worse when we live in denial of truth. By God's grace, I get to hear stories of redemption and enjoy my own. We get to actually comfort others with the comfort we have received when we take what we have learned and share it with other women. When a friend tells you about her history of abuse, that is the important first step to walking on the road to redemption. Be a tender listener and safe confidante. Pray for and with her, and ask God for wisdom, truth, and healing in the journey.

Responding in Love

News of my past abuse was all new for Mark, and he was going through a hard time with the church as well. God was working in him too. My poor husband had a wife who was "falling apart" and being put back together slowly. He tried his best to listen and respond lovingly. He asked good but hard questions to get me beyond scratching the surface. Sometimes his responses caused fear all over again, and I wanted to run, but I had to stop believing the lies of the Enemy and trust God to change me and bring Mark along in the process. As he started to see my complete brokenness, he didn't use it to hurt me; he became more tender with me. He felt as if I finally needed him in our marriage, which he hadn't felt before due to my lack of emotion toward him.

Mark had actually been the one to remove me from the abusive relationship when he stepped in as my boyfriend. He protected me from further harm during those years but had somehow become the "bad" guy in my mind after that. I enjoyed being cared for but became afraid of the outcome—intimacy. Now as my husband, he wanted to know the real me and kept praying for what to say and do. He asked me to go to a safe place to stay for a couple of days, where I could read, journal, pray, cry—whatever I needed to do. I initially felt rejection, as if he wanted to get rid of me and not deal with me, but submitted to his request and realized it could be a fruitful time with no distraction. I journaled everything God brought to memory about instances of verbal and sexual abuse, my sin, fears, and lies. I remembered many more situations that I had considered innocent or inconsequential. For example, my workplace in high school was full of men who enjoyed perverse jokes, sexual conversations and innuendos, and inappropriate talk about the nude photos they took of women. Also, because they were short on women's housing at the first college I attended, I lived in the study room of a guys' dorm. The guys invited me to play strip poker (which I always declined), talked disrespectfully about girls, and would try to manipulate me through compliments.

While still away from my husband and kids, even though I wasn't at all a "crier," I sobbed off and on for hours over the pain of abuse and the conviction of my own sin. I caught a glimpse of what the Bible means by being broken before the Lord, but still had a long way to go. In my darkest moment I wrote,

> I feel dead, alone in everything right now (wife, mom, friend). I am numb and need you to meet with me and change me, but I'm scared to go forward. I'm stalled because I fear other things instead of you. Lord, please pull me out of the mire of my sin and stubbornness. Create in me a clean heart and renew a right spirit within me. Only make me alive if it is IN YOU. I can't and don't want to pretend anymore. I don't want to be dead to you, but dead to myself (sin) instead.

Another journal entry said, "Knowing the truth explains the pain, and is ultimately worth the further pain it causes on the way to freedom in Christ."

God had given me enough faith and hope, even though I didn't know the future, to trust Him to guide me.

More healing came as Mark and I sat many nights just talking and trying to get back our friendship that we had let slip away. We were honest, trying to speak lovingly but sometimes hurting each other with words of bitterness or pain. We kept reminding each other of our covenant and how we didn't want to just throw away all the years we had been together. When we got stuck, we sought wise counsel, including a few sessions with a Christian counselor, and we followed the counsel. We knew God was big enough to heal us both, but had no idea what that was going to look like. We prayed together, read books and talked about them together, went on date nights to just have fun together, and slowly started to rebuild all aspects of friendship and intimacy.

If you are walking through this process, you might go through times of deep sorrow and righteous anger about the sin against you and the sin you've responded with toward others. You might also feel selfish or awkward having so much focus on yourself, or as if you will always keep seeing more and more layers of junk to work through. This should eventually lead to peace, forgiveness, and trust in God's healing hand. Your spouse might not know how to respond at all, so you need to express what you need from him or her as patiently as possible. Try not to be demanding and be prayerful in your conversations together. Sometimes couples need to have a pastor or biblical counselor walk them through how to respond to each other lovingly. It is a process of building trust and it might feel as if you are starting all over again. When you feel like giving up or it's too hard, pray for wisdom and push through to the other side of the pain. Be willing to rely on God in new ways. He is faithful!

A Friend in Need

I remember calling a friend and crying. "I can't do this. It's too hard and painful. I can't stop crying and just want it to stop!" She listened, prayed with me, encouraged me to listen to God through reading the Bible and praying—which seemed too simple and obvious in that moment—and said she loved me and would be there for me. She said she couldn't fix anything but knew

God was working, and I needed to depend on Him in new ways. Somehow she knew just what to say at that moment. Unfortunately, many people don't know how to respond to abuse victims, and they can do more damage with a shaming response. It is important to listen, not place blame on the person, and pray for and with them, asking God for words.

If you don't know what to say, don't just fill the space with your own words or leading questions; rather, tell them you are very sorry for their pain and, if they are ready, try to help them find someone trustworthy to get counsel from and get them biblical resources. (Mike Wilkerson's book *Redemption* and Justin and Lindsey Holcomb's book *Rid of My Disgrace* are excellent.) You could even offer to go with them as a support. Godly church community during this healing process is essential. It is also important to make God the first person to "go to" when you are confused, hurting, lonely, in need of wisdom, whatever your trial, because He knows what you truly need and is faithful to answer. As the book of James says, "If any of you lacks wisdom, let him ask of God, who gives to all liberally and without reproach, and it will be given to him. But let him ask in faith, with no doubting, for he who doubts is like a wave of the sea driven and tossed by the wind. For let not that man suppose that he will receive anything from the Lord; he is a double-minded man, unstable in all his ways."[a] When God gives you that wisdom, don't allow your fears to keep you from obeying Him.

The process of what theologians call "expiation," cleansing from the stain of sin on our souls, needs to take place for the victim to feel clean and whole again. Many abuse victims, specifically women, didn't have fathers who protected them or gave them wisdom about guys. If girls are allowed to date just any boy who shows interest, not given healthy boundaries with them, and not told about the way guys in this world think, girls are bound to get hurt by them, as statistics show. Sadly, I wasn't given this protection, either, but I also made the choice to have a relationship and sex. I wasn't honest about the danger I was in because I didn't have a heart-level relationship with my dad and was ashamed for him to see my sin. While my dad committed the sin of omission—not doing what he should have done to protect me—the guy and I committed the sin of commission, by having sex outside marriage. At first it

---

a James 1:5–8.

was voluntary, and later he assaulted me. Both types of sin are hurtful, both physically and emotionally.

In no way did I deserve to be abused; that was fully the guy's sin, but I needed to see my initial sin and where it led. It changed the course of my life, took my dignity, my joy, my virginity, and separated me from God and Mark because of the overwhelming shame. My judgment was clouded once I had sex with someone outside a marriage relationship. The abuse made me feel dirty and defiled, and the lie that I had no value became even more believable. This prevented me from getting help and kept Mark from really knowing me because I didn't allow him to get close. When God peeled back the layers of shame, I could see clearly the death and destruction caused by my sin and the sins against me.

We are all made dirty and defiled through the sins we commit and the sins committed against us. So, how do we "get clean"? Because of Jesus' death on the cross, if you are a Christian, God sees you not by what you have done or by what has been done to you, but solely by what Jesus has done for you. You are a daughter of Christ, and He already did all the work to make you clean. He takes your shame and filth and replaces it with His grace and righteousness. Isn't that *incredible*? And we don't even do anything to deserve it. You just need to accept Him and believe His promises.

Serving and Protecting Your Children

How would I want my own daughters to be cared for? When I think of the possibility of my own daughters experiencing such things as I have, I am devastated. Mark and I want to do all we can to protect and inform them so that pain can be avoided and their legacies can be different. Being preventive as a parent is very important. Resources such as "Kids Need to Know"[12] booklets and training give helpful discussions and terms you can use with all ages of kids. Not only are many children sexually abused; most are abused by children and adults they know. Tragically, many parents think it is rare and would never happen to their kids. They trust people without even knowing them and end up leaving their children vulnerable.

Safety is an urgent issue and one that parents can overlook for the sake of convenience. It takes time to get to know and trust whom your kids play with or the family members present. Often parents just want to drop the kids off to get a break, not considering the possibilities of how their children's lives could be altered if they are abused. As parents, we need to be teaching our children healthy boundaries with their bodies (private parts are what a swim suit covers); giving them words to use if they need to report abuse; explaining the difference between good secrets like surprise parties and bad secrets that a child is told never to tell; helping them not be afraid to say stop or no if someone is making them uncomfortable; believing them (young children rarely lie about sexual abuse); and assuring them they won't get in trouble if they tell about someone harming them.

We also need to be regularly asking safety questions when our kids have been out of our care: What did you do at your friend's house? What kind of things did you talk about? Was there anything that you really enjoyed or that made you uncomfortable? Were brothers or sisters or anyone else in the home? If we take time to have regular conversations with our children, we will more easily be able to educate them and detect if they have been harmed or are in danger.

If your child has already been abused, you need to be available to talk about it and find a biblical counselor who can point your child to Jesus and show you how to walk alongside through the healing process. In retrospect, had I learned these things as a child, my sexual assault as a teen may have been prevented.

It's About Jesus

First John 1:7–9 says: "But if we walk in the light as He is in the light, we have fellowship with one another, and the blood of Jesus His Son cleanses us from all sin. If we say that we have no sin, we deceive ourselves, and the truth is not in us. If we confess our sins, He is faithful and just to forgive us our sins and to cleanse us from all unrighteousness."

I needed to confess, journal, and talk with Jesus, Mark, and godly, safe, wise Christian women about the sins I committed and the sins committed against me. This would keep me from hiding in shame and teach me to walk in the light. As daughters of Eve, we all have the propensity to put on fig leaves to cover our sin, but God calls us out so we can have honest fellowship with Him and others.

A few years into this, I now think redemption is always an opportunity in front of me, and my fears and "victim identity" are becoming a part of my past. There has been so much fruit that has come from the pain of healing that it has caused me to have more faith and hope in Jesus than ever before. I have shared my story and God's faithfulness with many women who struggle with sexual assault. If God can use anything in my story to help other women in their marriages, I will share whatever He asks. It doesn't mean it isn't still painful at times, especially to hear other stories, but I'm so thankful that God has removed my shame and has replaced it with His righteousness! I don't have to worry about what other people might say about me; rather, I get to tell people about Jesus! It's about Jesus, not me.

8

THE PORN PATH

Whoever looks at a woman to lust for her has already
committed adultery with her in his heart.

—MATTHEW 5:28

I (Mark) don't remember many days of my childhood, but one particular day when I was maybe nine or ten years old is embedded in my mind.

I was using a bathroom in a home, and there was a sink with drawers right next to the toilet. I needed something, probably a Band-Aid, so I pulled open one of the drawers. In it was a glossy magazine with a beautiful woman on the front. I took the magazine out of the drawer. Page after page had photos of beautiful, unclothed women. At that moment, I simultaneously felt curiosity, excitement, discomfort, and shame. I had no idea what the magazine was, suspected it was something forbidden, but found it enticing.

Shortly thereafter I became aware, while hanging out with the boys in my neighborhood, that most of their dads had similar magazines. The boys would steal the magazines and then add them to a collection in a fort they had built in the neighborhood woods. To get to the fort took some skill. It was hidden in the back corner of a dense woods and was only accessible from a narrow, worn path. Until you learned where the path was, you would be unlikely to find it. But once you found it, it seemed easy to find and follow.

Little did the young boys who ventured down the path know, but they were carving an entirely different path in their brains as well. Writing on the issue of pornography, William M. Struthers, a Christian biopsychologist who is specially trained to give the physical and spiritual reasons for pornography addiction, provided in his book *Wired for Intimacy* an insightful look into the physical consequences of porn, in addition to the spiritual. Christians have already written many books from a spiritual perspective, and his book is meant to fill an ignored gap in Christian circles by providing an integrated physical, psychological, and biblical perspective. Struthers said that as we

> fall deeper into the mental habit of fixating on these images, the exposure to them creates neural pathways. Like a path is created in the woods with each successive hiker, so do the neural paths set the course for the next time an erotic image is viewed. Over time these neural paths become wider as they are repeatedly traveled with each exposure to pornography. They become the automatic pathway through which interactions with woman are routed. . . . They have unknowingly created a neurological circuit that imprisons their ability to see women [and men] rightly as created in God's image.[1]

Mirror neurons are one part of the brain that pornography affects. Mirror neurons are "motor system cells that activate when you see a behavior."[2] They are in action when you see someone frightened and you, too, respond with fear. Similarly, in viewing pornography, mirror neurons cause people to "vicariously" participate in the pornography through viewing it, including watching the woman's face during the sex act, which is particularly enticing for many men.[3]

One study showed that human orgasm affects the same parts of the brain that heroin and cocaine do. "Because of this activity, many have referred to being "addicted" to sex. The orbitofrontal cortex is our emotional modulatory system. This is our decision-making system. To be addicted to something is to release dopamine, which causes you to want it and to make the decision to pursue it. That's our addiction pathway."[4]

Viewing pornography while masturbating traces a similar path. Struthers wrote,

> When sexual images come through the visual system they stimulate sexual arousal. When there is a male performer, they can (via the mirror neurons) vicariously participate in the sexual act. If they arouse themselves and masturbate to pornography, they now begin to set in place a neurological habit. The images, arousal, masturbatory act and ejaculation are all associated with one another.
>
> This is how a pornography addiction and sexual compulsion is built from scratch. It involves the visual system (looking at porn), the motor

system (masturbating), the sensory system (genital stimulation) and neurological effects of orgasm (sexual euphoria from opiates, addictive dopamine in the nucleus accumbens and reduced fear in the amygdale). They have now begun to store this pattern as a reinforced neurological habit.[5]

This is, at least in part, because oxytocin and vasopressin are released slowly during sexual activity, and released in much larger quantities in conjunction with an orgasm. These chemicals so heighten pleasure for a man that they essentially bind him to whatever caused it.[6] As an example, two-thirds of men who frequent prostitutes use the same prostitute rather than multiple women for a variety of experiences, perhaps because they have chemically caused themselves to desire that one person physically above all others.[7]

The natural chemical "high," what some call a "biochemical love potion," resulting from sex and orgasm was designed by God to bind a husband and wife together. In the best sense of the word, God intends for a devoted married couple to be "addicted" to each other, bound together in every way. Tragically, when the source of this binding is someone or something other than one's spouse, the person becomes so habituated to the pleasures it brings that it leads to an addiction. This explains why, for so many men, pornography becomes a neurological pathway to sinful masturbation and addiction that becomes increasingly difficult to escape as each new "high" causes the path to become a deep rut.

This also explains why God intends sexual pleasure to be experienced solely within marriage. God is good, and His commands are good. When He forbids sex outside marriage, He is not being prudish, outdated, or prohibiting our joy.

First Timothy 3:2 says, "A bishop [Christian leader] then must be blameless, the husband of one wife [literally a "one-woman man"]." Since Hebrews 13:7 instructs God's people to follow the life example of their leaders, the normative pattern of the church is people whose eyes and desires are directed solely toward their spouses. Similarly, as biology catches up with theology, Job 31:1 makes incredible sense:

> I have made a covenant with my eyes;
> Why then should I look upon a young woman?

Those who fail to heed the wise warnings of Scripture run the risk of ending up like the musician John Mayer, who, despite having dated and slept with some of the most beautiful women in the world, still prefers porn to an actual woman. Here is a segment of his *Playboy* interview that is admittedly disturbing but serves as an honest warning:

> **MAYER:** Internet pornography has absolutely changed my generation's expectations.
>
> **PLAYBOY:** You seem very fond of pornography.
>
> **MAYER:** When I watch porn, if it's not hot enough, I'll make up backstories in my mind . . . This is my problem now: Rather than meet somebody new, I would rather go home and replay the amazing experiences I've already had . . . What that explains is that I'm more comfortable in my imagination than I am in actual human discovery.[8]

Porn

Defining pornography is terribly difficult, as evidenced by the inability of our nation's Supreme Court to clearly articulate exactly what it is. For the purposes of this book, we do not necessarily include as pornographic such things as nude works of art or a romantic scene in a movie without nudity, while also acknowledging that some people can use such things for sinful lust. We do include as pornography such things as porno movies, magazines, Web sites, online sexual chat, romance novels, phone sex with paid operators, explicit movies, lingerie catalogs, and even the swimsuit issues of sports magazines, and the increasingly base men's and women's magazines. They show more skin than pornographic magazines did just a few generations ago, for example, such as when *Playboy* debuted in 1953. In essence, yesterday's porn is today's mainstream pop culture.

In our increasingly brazen and desensitized culture, we have to be careful not to define pornography in terms of only harder forms while neglecting the softer forms. As an example, on an international flight we took, movies with full nudity and sex scenes played on the headrest televisions around us while bored young children looked on. In our home, we have Net nanny software on the family computer, which remains in the kitchen in plain sight, in the most trafficked part of the house. Our family television is also in the most visible area of the home in an effort to help us monitor what our children watch. We do not have any cable movie channels because they contain so many movies and shows with nudity. We make every effort not to watch any films with sexual nudity, and we have shows with certain ratings and content banned from our television through a security code.

Tragically, porn has now become a mainstream aspect of pop culture. Many music videos are little more than soft-core porn, especially in the rap genre, where women are spoken of and shown in the most debasing of terms. The popular video game *Grand Theft Auto IV* contains one scene where the main character, Niko, visits a prostitute, and as she walks away, he proceeds to gun her down. Many reality television shows now include porn stars doing outlandish things.[9] Porn such as *Girls Gone Wild* has propelled the lie to a generation of college-aged women that volunteering to act like a porn star is simply part of being a young woman. And it seems the quickest path to stardom is for women to make a porn film. This explains why everyone from Kim Kardashian to Paris Hilton and Pam Anderson have done so.

Most experts agree there are four basic aspects to virtually all heterosexual pornography, which constitutes the majority of porn:

1. The message is consistent that all women want sex from all men all the time in all kinds of bizarre ways and are essentially nymphomaniacs.
2. Women really enjoy whatever any man does to them sexually.
3. Any woman who does not meet the stereotype of points 1 and 2 can quickly be changed through a bit of force or intimidation.
4. The woman is dominated and degraded by the man in a way that exploits her as essentially a tool for the pleasure of the man and not really a person, but rather, parts.

Porn is not about love, romance, empathy, respect, covenant, sacrifice, and fidelity. This explains why porn rarely, if ever, includes men and women holding hands, kissing, snuggling, going on dates, and the like, because that would suggest love and relationship, which porn is in no way about.

Much like a sexual predator who grooms the young and naive, pop culture with its increasing pornification is grooming young people for sexual sin and sexual assault. Subsequently, younger people are increasingly likely to consider that which is pornographic to be normative sexuality. One particularly troubling example of this is Academy Award nominee Laurence Fishburne's eighteen-year-old daughter. Being a famous actor in movies and on television, he could have seemingly helped her begin a career in mainstream non-adult entertainment. Instead, she made her own porno film and sold the distribution rights to one of the largest porn makers, Vivid Entertainment. Her father was reportedly mortified, but she said, "I started thinking about it . . . when I was 16. . . . I knew they [Vivid] had released Kim Kardashian, Paris Hilton and Pamela Anderson [sex tapes]."[10]

Our point? Our culture is becoming increasingly sexualized, and it has taken forty years to go from one dirty magazine under the counter at the local convenience store to today where it is expected that junior high boys have at least one nude shot of their junior high girlfriend on their cell phone—a tragically common practice.

Lust

The purpose of pornography is clearly lust. And throughout both the Old and New Testaments, God repeatedly condemns—as a grievous evil—lust for anyone but your spouse.[a] The act of desiring the unclothed body of a person is not a sin. The issue is *which* person's unclothed body you are lusting after. If it is your spouse's, then you are simply making the Song of Songs sing again to God's glory and your mutual joy. If it is not your spouse's, then you are committing the sin of coveting. The Ten Commandments are clear that we should not commit adultery,[b] including the lustful mental adultery of coveting our neighbor's spouse.[c]

---

a E.g., Prov. 6:25; Job 31:1; Matt. 5:28; Col. 3:5; 1 Thess. 4:5; 1 Peter 4:3.
b Ex. 20:14.
c Ex. 20:17.

Likewise, Jesus taught that sexual sins are committed not only in acts we commit, but also in our lustful thoughts. For example, in Matthew 5:27–28, Jesus said, "You have heard that it was said . . . , 'You shall not commit adultery.' But I say to you that whoever looks at a woman to lust for her has already committed adultery with her in his heart." Also, in Mark 7:21–23, Jesus said, "For from within, out of the heart of men, proceed evil thoughts, adulteries, fornications, murders, thefts, covetousness, wickedness, deceit, lewdness, an evil eye, blasphemy, pride, foolishness. All these evil things come from within and defile a man."

In the lust category, along with sexual nudity and pornography, we also include women's romance novels. They commonly entice sinful lust and cause women to fantasize about sexual sin with all the alluring power of visual pornography for men. This kind of sinful lustful fantasizing extends to such things as the *Twilight* phenomenon, where older women, many of them mothers, openly fantasize about sexual desires they had for the young actors in the film.

Even mainstream women's magazines contribute to the objectification and degradation of sex. *Cosmo*, as well as an entire industry of other women's magazines lining the rack of your local grocery store, fills its covers with pornographic article headlines shouting to the world that lust is a good thing. And their pages are filled with detailed instructions teaching a young woman how to look and act like a porn star so as to attract a boyfriend, outperform his previous girlfriends in bed, and be as hot as his favorite porn fantasies. The goal is to keep him well satisfied and in the relationship as if he were a god to be worshipped.

This cycle of men and women viewing and then acting out leads to an increasingly soulless and dangerous sexuality for both men and women. Dr. Drew, a well-known therapist, has written about what causes this kind of behavior in his book *The Mirror Effect*.[11]

Dr. Drew is perhaps the most famous counselor in the world with his VH-1 reality television shows *Sober House* and *Sex Rehab with Dr. Drew*. He is perhaps best known for his long-running radio show, *Loveline*, where he takes calls from sexually troubled, assaulted, and deviant people. I (Mark) have cohosted the show with Dr. Drew, and was told I was the first pastor to do so.

In what he calls "the mirror effect," Drew says that we are suffering from a culture of celebrity narcissism. To gain and retain attention, celebrity narcissists have to continually act out in extreme, dangerous, and self-destructive behavior. This includes such things as body image (extreme weight loss, excessive plastic surgery, the relentless pursuit of being sexy or beautiful), hypersexuality, substance abuse and addiction, dangerous and violent behavior, and self-harm, including cutting and suicide attempts.[12]

As a pastor, I recognize that in theological terms, narcissists want to be the center of attention, like a god, and have people worship them by paying attention to them, buying the products they promote, and emulating their behavior. Aiding them in this pursuit is everything from reality television shows, daytime talk shows, social media outlets (blogs, Facebook, Twitter, YouTube, etc.) and a host of magazines (*People*, *Entertainment Weekly*, etc.), television shows (*TMZ*, *Entertainment Tonight*, etc.), and Web sites tracking the every move of celebrities. Their fans then emulate the extreme behavior of celebrities because the more they are exposed to it, the more normative or even desirable they believe it is. Simply, celebrities model, and their fans mirror.

The mirror effect explains why, as pornography has become increasingly more culturally accepted and emulated, it has also escalated and become more extreme with an entire category for that purpose, called "gonzo porn." The National Online Resource Center on Violence Against Women reported, "As pornography has become more acceptable, both legally and culturally, the level of brutality toward, and degradation of, women has intensified."[13]

Proverbs 27:20 says,

> Hell [Sheol or Death] and Destruction [Abaddon] are never full;
> So the eyes of man are never satisfied.

If we apply this principle to pornographic lust, it becomes apparent that porn and sexual sin are not going to satisfy your lust but rather inflame it for more. Lusting eyes may begin with a magazine, Web site, or video and continue to view more magazines, Web sites, or videos until they become bored. Then the person descends into strip clubs, prostitutes, or acting out with people, which eventually become boring and lead to orgies, voyeurism, exhibitionism, pedophilia, and wherever else a crooked human heart can venture. It may be hard to believe, but a stark example is craigslist, which includes a few thousand bizarre sexual requests posted for our city of Seattle alone every day under "casual encounters." Don't kid yourself. Sin is an on ramp to death. If you get on it and don't repent (turn around) and exit, you will find the landscape getting darker, grosser, filthier, and deadlier. One prominent feminist wrote after surveying the top rented porn movies that at least one act of verbal and/or physical abuse of women occurred in 90 percent of scenes, with an average of twelve acts of aggression against women per scene.

In one of many interviews conducted for this book with women who were formerly strippers, prostitutes, and porn stars, I spoke with a woman who was a prostitute for many years before becoming a Christian and leaving that life. She recounted the painful connection between pornography and prostitution and said that young women, often in their midteens, being broken in by her pimp would first be raped, then locked in a room to watch porn for days on end to learn what to do to clients. The prostitute reported that nearly every time she showed up to have sex with a client during her many years in the business, he was watching porn and demanded she do for him what he was watching on film. Perhaps most chilling are some excerpts from serial killer Ted Bundy. He roamed the streets I rode my bike on as a kid, picking up women from my neighborhood to murder. In an interview conducted by James Dobson hours before he was executed, Bundy said,

> I grew up in a wonderful home with two dedicated and loving parents, as one of 5 brothers and sisters. We, as children, were the focus of my parents' lives. We regularly attended church. My parents did not drink or smoke or gamble. There was no physical abuse or fighting in the home. . . . [It] was a fine, solid Christian home. . . . I want to emphasize this. The most damaging kind of pornography—and I'm talking from hard, real, personal experience—is that that involves violence and sexual violence. The wedding of those two forces—as I know only too well—brings about behavior that is too terrible to describe. . . . Once you become addicted to it, and I look at this as a kind of addiction, you look for more potent, more explicit, more graphic kinds of material. Like an addiction, you keep craving something which is harder and gives you a greater sense of excitement, until you reach the point where the pornography only goes so far—that jumping off point where you begin to think maybe actually doing it will give you that which is just beyond reading about it and looking at it.[14]

Clearly, while not everyone who looks at porn will end up doing such evil things as Ted Bundy, they will do evil things even if less intently or frequently. To use an old Puritan illustration, porn is simply bait on a hook intended to lure you in. If you bite, the hook will sink into your mouth. You will get dragged into death. Some are dragged quickly, as they do not thrash on the line and fight back. Others are dragged slowly, as they do thrash on the line and fight back with such things as guilt and moralism. But unless the line is entirely cut through repentance and the grace of God, the pulling of death is unstoppable. You don't control porn. Porn controls you.

One of the most powerful lies in support of pornography is that it does not harm anyone. But that is a demonic lie.

Porn hurts God. Every human being is made in the image and likeness of God. Every human being is known, loved, and observed by God. When people are abused, defiled, and objectified, God is grieved in His heart. None of these evil and vile things are done in secret and private. Even if no one is present, God is there. God is seeing all that is happening, and His heart is breaking. That He has revealed Himself to us as Father means He feels infinitely and perfectly exactly what we would if it were our children involved.

Porn harms viewers, rewiring them so as to have their sexuality defined by a sick industry seeking to addict them, take their money, and destroy any intimacy with or connection to their spouses. Do not be fooled: porn is not about sex; it's all about money. Like a drug dealer who gives away free samples of heroin, the porn industry continually bombards us with temptation in an effort to get us hooked and make them rich.

Porn ultimately leads to the objectification of women. "Pornography shapes and rewires in such a way that we become unable to see women as we should. We no longer direct our sexual drives in appropriate ways."[15] When porn is in a marriage, even the residue from past use that has stopped, sexual intimacy is replaced with sexual technique and the goal becomes performing rather than loving. Porn consumption also anesthetizes men to real women and meaningful relationships. Naomi Wolf, a feminist, provocatively discussed the influence of porn upon men:

> For most of human history, erotic images have been reflections of, or celebrations of, or substitutes for, real naked women. For the first time in history,

the images' power and allure have supplanted that of real naked women. Today, real naked women are just bad porn.[16]

Porn also harms women. Like the rewiring and corrupting of men, porn does the same for women who consume it. Porn harms the relationship between a man and a woman, as they are prone toward selfishness and laziness, not doing the hard work of having a loving covenant, but instead just watching porn and masturbating alone. Porn also degrades women and encourages men to do so. Seeking to emulate what they or their husbands view in porn compels women to push their bodies beyond God's creation design. There is nothing loving, beautiful, cherishing, or honoring of women presented in porn.

Simply, porn is a form of prostitution, and God repeatedly, emphatically, and clearly forbids us to participate in prostitution, whether the body is seen as a commodity to be paid for with a good time or good image.[a] People who fail to acknowledge that free porn on the Internet is also a form of prostitution are in denial. No porn is free. "Julie," a former porn starlet interviewed for this book explained that her "free" porn pages on the Internet actually generated revenue from sponsors and advertisers every time her pages were clicked, thereby contributing financially to the sick industry.

Julie's life was a tragic one for many years. She grew up in a divorced family with a highly religious father who was an unstable and highly emotional alcoholic prone to rage. He was also a pastor. She was repeatedly sexually assaulted starting around the age of four by both children and adults. Her mother was not a Christian and started buying her birth control as a teenager. Julie started sleeping with boys in her teens, starving to be loved and in a relationship. At the age of eighteen she was kicked out of her family home, after which she moved in with a boyfriend who pressured her to start watching porn with him and doing what the women in the movies did. That relationship turned abusive and dissolved.

She started modeling after moving from a small town to a big city. And after repeatedly being denied work for refusing to do nudes, she gave in. Before long she was doing full nudes, and then soft porn. She started dating a fellow model and porn actor. He was a serious porn addict and bisexual who raped

---

a Prov. 23:26–27; 1 Cor. 6:15–16.

and beat her frequently. She weighed less than 100 pounds, he weighed over 220 pounds. She started doing drugs to self medicate and tried to kill herself on more than one occasion.

Julie's porn career took off, and she was a cover girl and centerfold for the most popular porn magazines, appeared in multiple porn films, and made hundreds of thousands of dollars a year through her pornographic web site. She does not remember much of the filming as, like the rapes, she disassociated and mentally checked out. She reported often leaving a filming set bawling her eyes out in shame vowing never to return, yet she always did.

Over the years, she bounced from abusive relationship to abusive relationship, dating men as much as twenty years older than her. She has no idea how many times she has been raped or how many abortions she has had.

This little girl who grew up in a small Baptist church, loved singing songs to Jesus, came forward for an altar call at age eleven and was baptized. Today, she is back in the arms of Jesus and involved in a wonderful church. She has been diagnosed as bipolar 1 with manic episodes that include her experiencing severe hallucinations and panic attacks. Ongoing counseling and medication has helped her, but she still cannot hold a job as the stress is too much for her to bear. She volunteers her time for ministry—helping women exiting the sex industry.

Julie is also fighting to get all the porn she has filmed over the years taken off the Internet and store shelves to no avail. Practically, this means some of her brothers and sisters in Christ reading this chapter may have recently watched it when they should have been weeping. Because she is their sister.

You can see that porn has hurt women in terrible ways. It also harms children.

Parents who have porn in their home run the risk of exposing their own children to their poison, with life-changing damage ensuing. Parents who would not allow illegal drugs or dangerous poison into their home nonetheless fail to see the same dangers in porn. But "just as food is consumed and digested by the body, pornography is consumed by the senses and digested by the brain. . . . However, there is no process for 'waste' products associated with pornography to be removed. Pornography and our response to it alter our brain in a way that is difficult to undo. Pornography is the consumption of sexual poison that becomes part of the fabric of the mind."[17]

Porn also hurts daughters. Through our ministry relationships, we know many women whose fathers ceased meaningful interaction with them once they entered puberty. Because their fathers were habituated through porn to be sexually attracted to young women, once their own daughters began to look like the images they lusted after, the fathers became uncomfortable around them. Subsequently, such things as appropriate affection (for example, a kiss on the head or sitting together to watch a movie) ceased, making the young woman think there was something wrong with her that made her father reject her. Furthermore, this kind of confusing rejection leaves a daughter more vulnerable to the approval and affection of dangerous boys seeking to replace her father as the main male in her life in exchange for sex.

Rather than being ashamed as they ought to, some fathers fuel their own sinful lusts toward their daughters and their daughters' friends.

Another troubling effect, as porn use increases among women, is the rise of the "cougar" phenomenon. This is where older women sexually desire and pursue younger men, sometimes roughly the same age as their own children.

Porn and the lust it inflames include child pornography. As far back as 2002, the U.S. Customs Service estimated that there were already more than one hundred thousand Web sites offering child pornography—which is illegal worldwide.[18]

The line between child pornography and adult pornography is blurring, which likely means that sexual abuse of children, already an epidemic, will be on the rise. In 2002 the United States Supreme Court narrowed the definition for child pornography from "any visual depiction that appears to be of a minor engaging in sexually explicit conduct" to be "only those images in which an actual person under the age of eighteen (rather than one that simply appears to be) is involved in the making of the porn."[19] This paved the way for pornographers to intentionally make women look younger and childlike, like putting them in pigtails and schoolgirl outfits, as well as use computer-generated images of children in porn. After all, if the actors look like kids, it's legal so long as they are not kids.

One feminist scholar said, "The average length of time between downloading the first child porn and sexually assaulting a child was one year. Most men told me that before becoming addicted to Internet porn, they had not been sexually interested in children."[20] Perpetrators often use child porn as a "manual" to teach young children how to perform sex acts.

This chapter may have been as brutal for you to read as it has been brutal for us to write. We have sought to sand the varnish off porn and sinful lust so as to see it for what it truly is—a horrific evil with no redeeming value. As horrific as these evils are, people enslaved by them are not beyond the redeeming grace of God made available through Jesus Christ. In closing, we offer some practical advice for those wanting to be free of porn and sinful lust, as well as those spouses who love them.

You must be honest with yourself. Most people we have counseled are not fully honest regarding their sexual sin. We would strongly encourage you to prayerfully journal your entire sexual history, including everything you have seen, done, and had done to you sexually. Do not deny the truth because it is embarrassing. Do not minimize the truth as if it were no big deal. Do not normalize the truth as if it were okay because it is so common. Do not rationalize the truth with excuses like "It's not as bad as adultery" or "I've got it under control." Do not celebrate it as a freedom when it is in fact slavery.

You must be honest with God. It is vital that you spend however many hours it takes with God prayerfully, tearfully, and earnestly talking about the painful details of your sexual history. Equally vital is asking Him for specific help in areas where you have been most wounded or tempted or both. The truth is, God has been present every moment of your life and already knows everything. Your speaking with Him is for your healing and the maturing of your relationship with Him.

You must be honest with your spouse. Your spouse deserves to know who you are and also has to have an accurate account of how to help you and exactly what you are dealing with. This will be difficult for him or her to hear, so prepare your spouse in advance and schedule an entire day or two for the purpose of coming clean. Your spouse will need to hear you sincerely repent of things you have done, report what has been done to you, and also be told about areas you are struggling in and where you need to be held accountable. How much detail you share is important. If you share too much, he or she could be haunted for life. If you share too little, your spouse will not really know the truth and may allow his or her imagination to make things worse than they are. If you are parents, do not have your children nearby. Have a biblical counselor or pastor chosen to meet with for continued help. Allow your spouse to have righteous anger over your sin against him or her.

You must put your sexual sin to death by the grace of God. First John 3:9 teaches that "whoever has been born of God does not sin [make a practice of sinning], for His seed remains in him; and he cannot sin, because he has been born of God." While none of us can become perfect in this life,[a] God does promise that Christians can put their sin, including sexual sin, to death because Jesus died for it. In 1 Corinthians 6:9–10, Paul said, "Do you not know that the unrighteous will not inherit the kingdom of God? Do not be deceived. Neither fornicators, nor idolaters . . . will inherit the kingdom of God."

Sure, the naked people you like looking at are hot . . . but so is hell. Titus 2:11–12 says, "For the grace of God that brings salvation has appeared to all men, teaching us that, denying ungodliness and worldly lusts, we should live soberly, righteously, and godly in the present age."

You must submit to God the Holy Spirit. The same presence and power of God the Holy Spirit who enabled Jesus Christ to resist every temptation, resides in every Christian. By His power, you can overcome sexual sin. This includes heeding His conviction, reading the Bible He inspired, attending a church that follows Him, and living in community with Spirit-filled believers. First Thessalonians 4:3–8 says,

> For this is the will of God, your sanctification: that you should abstain from sexual immorality; that each of you should know how to possess his own vessel in sanctification and honor, not in passion of lust, like the Gentiles who do not know God; . . . For God did not call us to uncleanness, but in holiness. Therefore he who rejects this does not reject man, but God, who has also given us His Holy Spirit.

It is the Holy Spirit who gives us desires that are deeper and stronger than sinful desires. Thus, a holy life is the most passionate life that does not settle for petty things like sexual sin but rather passionately pursues the glory of God in all things. Galatians 5:16–24 says,

> Walk in the Spirit, and you shall not fulfill the lust of the flesh . . . adultery, fornication, uncleanness, lewdness, idolatry . . . revelries, and the like . . .

---

a 1 John 1:8.

those who practice such things will not inherit the kingdom of God. But the fruit of the Spirit is love, joy, peace, longsuffering, kindness, goodness, faithfulness, gentleness, self-control; against such there is no law. And those who are Christ's have crucified the flesh with its passions and desires.

You must practice sexual contentment. Proverbs 5:18–19 says,

> Let your fountain be blessed,
>> And rejoice with the wife of your youth.
>> As a loving deer and a graceful doe,
>> Let her breasts satisfy you at all times;
>> And always be enraptured with her love.

Sex is a part of your life, but it is not your life. If you allow sex to become your life, you will compare your spouse's appearance and performance to other people in general, and sinful people in particular, thereby becoming dissatisfied. This opens the door to temptation. To close the door, you must frequently seek evidences of God's grace to you through your spouse. Spend more time thanking God for what you have from your spouse than you do picking at what she or he does not have or give, and your attraction toward and satisfaction with your spouse will increase.

You must carve a new path and avoid old ruts. If your history includes such things as porn, the worst thing you can do is bring along your spouse on your path to death by having her or him watch porn with you, tolerate you watching porn alone, or relusting porn images in your mind when together. Instead, the two of you need to carve a new path together. Some men I (Mark) have counseled have such a porn rut hardwired in their brains that they cannot even maintain an erection with their wives unless porn is involved, also known as "porn impotence." A couple wanting to get beyond sin to oneness needs to work together in the forging of a new neural pathway through holy sex. William J. Struthers, an expert on this, said,

> Each time that an unhealthy sexual pattern is repeated, a neurological, emotional and spiritual erosion carves out a channel that will eventually develop into a canyon from which there is no escape.

But if this corrupted pathway can be avoided, a new pathway can be formed. We can establish a healthy sexual pattern where the flow is redirected toward holiness rather than corrupted intimacy. By intentionally redirecting neurochemical flow, the path toward right thinking becomes the preferred path and is established as the mental habit.[21]

To work together, if either or both of you have carved paths toward death, you need to fight against sin and for holiness. There are a number of weapons available for this battle.[22]

You must think in terms of legacy. More than just a good time, you should seek a good legacy. Who do you want your sons and daughters, grandsons and granddaughters to marry? How do you want them to treat others and be treated sexually? How you behave today sets in motion a future for sexual freedom or slavery, life or death—a future not only for your life but also for the generations that will follow in your wake. Keeping this in mind will help your theology conquer your biology for the sake of your legacy.

Grace has still never seen what most of us consider pornography, and we pray the same for each of our children. If you are like Grace and are without any pornographic exposure, we implore you to continue to avoid it. Thankfully, I was never addicted to pornography, and it has not been an issue in our relationship. For those who, like me, have seen porn, we encourage you to do whatever is necessary to put that sin to death and walk in the freedom and forgiveness that Jesus gives.

9

SELFISH LOVERS AND SERVANT LOVERS

Whoever desires to become great among you shall be your servant.

—MARK 10:43

Their honeymoon was quite a disappointment.

He was very excited to finally be married and have regular sexual intercourse. She was a virgin on their wedding night and had grown up in a fairly religious home where sex was viewed as moderately gross. She had some anxiety regarding their first night together that made her body tense up as they attempted to consummate their marriage. As a result, they were unable to experience intercourse and without putting in too much effort to overcome their obstacle, she instead gave him a helping hand before falling asleep.

He was very disappointed but assumed that in time things would improve. Sadly, they did not. The first months of their marriage were spent with her rarely, if ever, initiating sexually. He felt embarrassed that his wife had so little sexual interest in him, and was further embarrassed that they had intercourse so infrequently that she usually experienced discomfort, as her body had not adjusted to being sexually active. And the helping hands continued—for years.

Eventually she wanted to have a baby. Suddenly she did begin initiating sexually and could be intimate. But it was only when her fertility chart said she was ovulating, which made him feel more as if he were being used for medical purposes than loved for marital purposes. When we met, she seemed surprised to hear that she was selfish.

Are you best described as a servant or as selfish?[1]

We live in an age that is dominated by a service economy. We pay people to serve us. The richer, and more powerful and famous we become, the more we are able to be served and the less required to serve. In summary, our aim is to be served and not to serve.

Jesus Christ's life on earth was countercultural in that He did not use His position, power, or prestige to be served. Instead, He came to serve. Jesus actually said He "did not come to be served, but to serve."[a] The greatest person who has ever lived is the greatest servant. Furthermore, He taught us how to be great. The Bible records a curious series of events where disciples of Jesus wanted to know how to be the greatest. Rather than rebuking them, Jesus taught them, saying, "If anyone desires to be first, he shall be last of all and servant of all."[b] Jesus also said, "Whoever desires to become great among you shall be your servant."[c]

The principle of valuing servants and welcoming the lowly position of servant is vital for all of life. But perhaps being a servant is most important in marriage.

The biggest barrier to embracing our roles as humble servants is pride. Without humility we simply cannot serve in an ongoing and loving manner. The Bible says that pride is an enemy and that humility is a friend that allows us to live for God's glory and thereby love and serve others rather than use and abuse them.

Pride is the default mode of the human heart. As sinners, we are prone toward pride. It is a besetting sin and the root of all sin that we must continually seek to be conscious and repentant of. No one can claim they are humble, but as one author says, "I'm a proud man pursuing humility by the grace of God. No one can ever truly say he is humble, but we can at best only say we are proud people pursuing humility by the grace of God."[2]

Throughout the Bible, pride is dealt with in the sternest of terms. God's emotion toward pride is "hate."[d] God's action toward the proud is punishment[e] that includes "destruction" and "a fall."[f] This explains why God said to clothe

---

a Mark 10:45.
b Mark 9:35.
c Mark 10:43.
d Prov. 6:16–17; 8:13.
e Prov. 16:5.
f Prov. 16:18.

ourselves with humility toward each other, for "God resists the proud, but gives grace to the humble."[a]

Looking to Jesus we see the clear connection between humility and being a servant. Philippians 2:3–8 says,

> In lowliness of mind let each esteem others better than himself. Let each of you look out not only for his own interests, but also for the interests of others. Let this mind be in you which was also in Christ Jesus, who, being in the form of God, did not consider it robbery to be equal with God, but made Himself of no reputation, taking the form of a bondservant, *and* coming in the likeness of men. And being found in appearance as a man, He humbled Himself.

How have you humbled yourself to be a servant to your spouse? How has your spouse humbled herself or himself to be a servant to you? How have you refused to humbly serve your spouse? How has your spouse refused to humbly serve you?

If we do not choose humility, God will choose humiliation for us. So we must willfully, earnestly, and continually humble ourselves. We do this five ways in our marriages. First, we consider our spouses and their needs and desires above our own. Second, we are willing to do the thankless menial things that marriage requires as an act of love to our spouses and worship to our God. Third, we humbly receive instruction and correction from the Scriptures, Holy Spirit, godly spiritual leaders, godly friends, and our spouses. Fourth, we humbly seek to encourage and nurture the humble service we see in our spouses more continually and passionately than we criticize their faults, flaws, and failures. And fifth, we continually remember the humble servant Jesus was and is for us while asking the Holy Spirit to make us increasingly more like our humble Servant.

Selfishness begins in childhood. The more our parents coddle, accommodate, and center their lives around us, the more selfish we become. For those who were an only child, this propensity toward selfishness is often higher, as they did not have to share their toys, room, and life with siblings who inconvenienced

---

a James 4:6; 1 Peter. 5:5.

them. And selfishness is often mastered during singleness. Then we marry, expecting our spouses to serve us humbly, only to find they were expecting the same thing. Conflict ensues along with disappointment and frustration.

The pattern of selfishness is so deeply woven into the fabric of our lives that it takes years of marriage to even begin to deal with the problem and move from "me" to "we." The experts tell us that no less than 50 percent of all marriages end in divorce by year seven.[3] If you have ever heard of the seven-year itch, it is apparently true. While there can be biblical grounds for divorce, the painful truth is that most marriages end simply because of selfishness on the part of one or both spouses. Selfish people who divorce without dealing with their selfishness then remarry only to repeat the first seven years of selfishness with another person and are more likely to divorce yet again. Why? Because a selfish person who changes spouses has not changed his heart.

It takes between nine and fourteen years for a couple to become not entirely unselfish, but rather less selfish, and begin to shift from "me" to "we."[4] Couples who hang in there by God's grace through those early first years report having greater levels of marital happiness. And couples married thirty-five years report the same level of marital happiness as a newly married couple. Why? Marriage is for our holiness before our happiness. Your spouse is the most sanctifying, and often most frustrating, relationship you will have. God will use our spouses to expose our selfishness and make us to be increasingly more humble servants like Jesus Christ.

Our selfishness often shows up in the little things. The Song of Songs 2:15 refers to such things as "the little foxes that spoil the vines." In a vineyard there is the potential for beauty, wonder, and life. But, the vineyard must be cultivated, weeds must be pulled, and foxes must be kept out. A Christian winemaker in Napa Valley explained that it takes many years, even decades, of tender care to raise a mature and fruitful vine. She said that keeping large animals out of her vineyard was easier than keeping out small animals that could sneak in. In particular, she said, small animals like foxes were particularly dangerous because they gnawed on the root of healthy vines, thereby killing the entire plant and robbing its harvest after years of investment. The key to a harvest of fruitfulness, fidelity, oneness, love, and joy is to catch the little foxes that creep into your marital vineyard. Most often these are seemingly small differences that become battle lines in a raging war.

Foxes in our vineyard for me (Grace) include name-calling, strong language, having an all-or-nothing attitude, using discouraging words, being preoccupied on the computer or phone while we are talking, and being unthankful. Mark is working on having better self-control, waiting and praying before responding, asking questions before making assumptions, listening more often, and being more grateful for the "little" things I do.

I (Mark) like to be early whenever I am going somewhere, and I have an uncanny ability to always know what time it is and exactly how long it takes to get something accomplished. My life moves along very efficiently and orderly with enough time to spare that if something happens or I am running late, I will still be on time.

For me (Grace), this is difficult. I have spent much of my life running late and not seeing it as inconsiderate. I have tried everything I can think of, including setting every watch and clock ahead in an effort to trick myself into being on time. Until I saw it as a sin issue, the methods were unfruitful. If I want this issue to change, I have to constantly plan to be early, and not try to squeeze one more thing in before I walk out the door.

I (Mark) have spent many cumulative hours of my life sitting in the car, waiting for Grace to run out the door and jump in so that I could speed off. Every second that I sit there, I am prone to get one degree warmer until I am boiling with frustration when she opens her door. And my attitude affects our children, who, sensing my frustration while sitting in the car with me, are prone to start speaking ill of their mother—especially the children who are more like me. To be a good servant, I am continually learning how to help Grace be aware of the time and when we need to go, taking the work of getting the kids ready and out the door off her plate, and working with her as an ally instead of being frustrated with her as an enemy in an effort to keep this fox out of our vineyard.

What foxes are in your vineyard? How can you lovingly serve each other to work together to keep the foxes out of your vineyard?

Husbands and wives live on a continuum from selfish to servant both in and out of the bedroom. If a marriage is between two selfish people, it will be cold and functional. If a marriage is between a selfish person and a servant, the marriage will be selfish and abusive. If a marriage is between two servants, it will be increasingly uniting and satisfying both in and out of the bedroom.

Perhaps the sharpest dagger to the heart of sexual selfishness is 1 Corinthians 7:3–5, in which God through Paul said,

> Let the husband render to his wife the affection due her, and likewise also the wife to her husband. The wife does not have authority over her own body, but the husband does. And likewise the husband does not have authority over his own body, but the wife does. Do not deprive one another except with consent for a time, that you may give yourselves to fasting and prayer; and come together again so that Satan does not tempt you because of your lack of self-control.

The biblical pattern for Christian marriage is free and frequent sex. The exception is when the couple agree that for valid reasons and a needed season they will abstain from free and frequent sexual activity to prayerfully devote themselves to a critical matter in the marriage. Examples include such things as spouses suffering from injuries or illnesses to such a degree that they cannot be intimate, or the tragic event of an adultery from which the couple is seeking to reconcile but are emotionally raw.

When there are not extenuating circumstances governing seasons of sexual abstention, there is an opening for Satan to tempt the husband or wife or both. Such temptations include bitterness, sinful lust, and emotional or physical adultery. While such sinful actions are never excusable, it is nevertheless true that wisdom dictates we do all we can to serve our spouses and reduce the opportunities the Enemy has to attack our marriages. For a stark picture of what this looks like, the next time you and your spouse are lying in bed angry, bitter, and physically distant, with your backs turned toward each other, imagine Satan himself sleeping in the open space between the two of you.

One of the most common questions we receive from couples is, "How often should we have sex of some kind?" In asking this question, some couples are wanting to find out what is normal and how they stack up in comparison. Other couples ask this question because they are at an impasse, and one spouse thinks the other is a sex fiend and the other thinks that spouse is a cold fish. The Bible does not give the number of times in an average week a typical couple should have sex. More than four hundred years ago, the Protestant Reformer Martin Luther counseled married couples to have sex "twice a week, hundred four a year."[5] What we can tell you is that most surveys and reports state that the number varies by age, as elderly couples have less sex than younger couples. Studies reveal that decreased sexual activity and interest begins in the first two years of marriage.[6]

Married couples in the United States are mostly having sex on a weekly basis when people of all ages are factored together, with the older couples having less sex than younger ones. Protestants and Catholic couples reflect similar percentages of sexual frequency, with fundamentalist Protestant couples being the most sexually active, followed by moderate, then liberal orientations.[7] Those curious about more specific data regarding sexual frequency among married couples will find that information in appendix V in the e-book and also on our website, www.pastormark.tv.

Accurate data on married sexual behavior by religious orientation is nearly impossible to obtain because the research has simply not been done. The most comprehensive study in the last twenty years—conducted in 1994—showed that evangelical Protestant adults reported the highest frequency of sex, the highest levels of satisfaction with sex, and the lowest frequency of oral and anal sex. Moreover, they were more likely to have had only one sex partner in the previous year.[8]

The younger a couple, as a general rule, the more sex they have. One study reported that couples under the age of twenty-four had a mean frequency of sex about 132 times a year, which is about 11 times per month, or once every 2–3 days.[9] Another more recent report said, "Married people under thirty have sex about 111 times a year" which is about 9 times a month, or 2–3 times a week.[10] The report goes on to say, "Married men and women, on average, have sex with their spouse 58 times a year, a little more than once a week."[11] The number of what is average sexual frequency for a married couple is greatly affected downward by the fact that "about 15 percent of married couples have not had sex with their spouse in the last six months to one year."[12]

According to a 2003 *Newsweek* study, between 15 and 20 percent of couples are living in a sexless marriage—meaning they have sex no more than ten times a year.[13] We have spoken to Christian couples who have not had sex for as many as twenty years. This includes pastors and their spouses, because sadly, in Christianity there are consequences for going too far (adultery) but none for not going far enough (abstaining). Even the Puritans understood this fact. In Boston there was a case among the Puritans in which a man was excommunicated because he refused to have sex with his wife for two years.[14]

The issue of sexual frequency is a point of pain and contention in many marriages. It is our strong recommendation that if a married couple are going to err, it would be wisest to err on the side of too much rather than too little sex.

In our own marriage, this was a serious issue for many years. I (Mark) have never been clinically diagnosed, but it seems obvious that I've had bouts of depression. One of the reasons many other men and I fail to understand when we are depressed is that most books and research on the subject are for women. Both men and women get depressed, but they can express their depression differently.[15] Whereas women often feel their depression and become sad, men more commonly act out their depression in behaviors such as being grumpy, irritable, sullen, discouraged, annoyed, mad, withdrawn, cold, and aloof.

Archibald Hart, a clinical psychologist and a leading Christian expert on male depression, lists "testosterone-induced depressions" as the first hidden cause of male depression.[16] He explained,

> I have seen it mostly in men who have a high sex drive (and therefore high testosterone levels with a need for more frequent sexual outlet than average). When a sexual outlet is denied, and by this I mean a reduced frequency of orgasm, such males become irritable and aggressive and develop a set of behaviors that can best be described as "sulking" or "moodiness." The male goes silent and withdraws from his partner and acts out his anger in either active or passive ways, depending upon his personality. . . . This unique form of depression sets in fairly quickly whenever sexual activity diminishes. In other men, whose sex drive is not quite as strong, it seems to take longer, but sooner or later depression sets in. . . . Sexual release seems to restore the balance, quietening the testosterone's tantrum, and thus relieving the depression and anger.[17]

Men, you may be tempted to use this information in the wrong way. It's not a weapon to be used to induce your wife to have more sex with you. Don't try to manipulate her by holding it over her head as a threat, saying you'll get more depressed if she doesn't make herself more available to you sexually. Rather, know that the healthier your love life with your wife is, the better you'll likely feel, so it's vital that you put in the time and effort to make your sex life the best it can be. Remember, too, that there are many causes for depression, so if you think you may be depressed, the first thing you should consider is a trip to your doctor. I did not seek professional help, and my hope is that if you're depressed often, you don't try to solve it yourself.

As with many things in marriage, communication is key. When I came to the conclusion that the cure for a lot of my moodiness was having more frequent sex with my wife, I simply told her. Yes, it's that simple. For years, when I would endure depression, I tried to talk to Grace about it. Her natural inclination was to want to have long talks about our feelings toward each other, and I know that connecting with her like this is important. But sometimes I was just too frustrated and ended up blowing up and hurting her feelings. The truth was I wanted to have more frequent sex with my wife, and we needed to discuss how that could happen.

To make matters worse, seemingly every book I read by Christians on sex and marriage sounded unfair. Nearly every one said the husband had to work very hard to understand his wife, to relate to her, and when he did that to her satisfaction, then, maybe, she would have sex with him as a sort of reward. After many years, I finally told Grace that I needed more sex. I asked if we could have sex more days of the week and try a variety of positions. She'd be the one to decide exactly how we would be together. Grace said that helped her think about our intimacy throughout the course of the day, which helped prepare her mind and body. To our mutual delight, we discovered that both of us felt closer, more loved and understood, and were more patient with each other if we were together regularly in some way. And whether my depression was testosterone-induced or not, I just generally felt happier.

For a wife, sex comes out of a healthy relationship, whereas, for a husband it leads to one. I (Grace) loved Mark but also needed to obey God and be sensitive to my husband's physical needs. I had allowed fear from my past experiences to enter into our marriage and cause distance with Mark. I began to pray that God would help me overcome my fears and give me the passion for my husband that I truly wanted to express. Over time, as I obeyed God, those prayers were answered, and my desire to be with my husband grew along with my enjoyment of our intimacy.

We want to state this carefully: a spouse who is evil, distant, cruel, unloving, or abusive should not use this information to demand more sex from his wife without first dealing with his sin. But if your spouse is not getting enough sex, maybe you don't need marriage counseling and long, deep conversations as much as you need to try regular sex. You may discover that your spouse will actually be more open to reading books like this with you, discussing matters of the heart, and even going in for marriage counseling.

Ways We Are Selfish Lovers

It is important to identify the ways we are selfish lovers and then work to eliminate them.

- *Rarely have sex.* We can simply decide to rarely, if ever, have sex. This is often done through simply and repeatedly denying our spouses' advances, which shames and humiliates them, causing them to feel unloved, unwanted, and undesired. Eventually they will simply stop seeking to be intimate with us.
- *Take too little time and too little effort.* We can do as little as possible sexually. By exerting minimal effort, passion, or interest, we can be sure to discourage our spouses from seeking to be intimate with us frequently. People have explained this as a gross feeling, where their spouses simply lie there, looking away disinterested and disconnected, making them feel as if they are basically using their spouses' bodies. Wives have explained this in terms of husbands who do not patiently take their time to prepare them for lovemaking, but instead lazily rush right into penetration, thereby causing their wives discomfort. Guys, it takes the average woman anywhere from ten to thirty minutes to move from foreplay to orgasm, although forty-five minutes is not unusual. For both spouses to have pleasure, time and effort are required.
- *Only have sex when we both feel like it at the same time.* Can you imagine if everything in your marriage was governed by this same thinking, so that, for example, you only ate together or spoke together when you both felt like it at the exact same time? Sadly, we have heard this illogic from even pastors and their wives. Servant lovers are willing to serve their spouses even when they are not in the mood, and know that on another occasion their servant lovers will do the same for them. Furthermore, humble

servant lovers know that as they serve their spouses, God often awakens their desires, puts them in the mood, and blesses their obedience.

- *Rarely initiate.* In a contentious marriage one spouse is always on sexual offense and the other on sexual defense. This means that one person never initiates talk about sex or activities of sex and is continually on the defensive. The other spouse is then forced to always take the sexual initiative, which makes him or her feel controlled and manipulated in addition to neglected and unwanted, which is discouraging.

- *Let ourselves go—become undesirable.* We can become unattractive or undesirable by failing to bathe, groom, or thoughtfully clothe ourselves. We have spoken to spouses who intentionally gain considerable weight, stop regularly showering, brushing their teeth, and cutting their nails because they were intentionally seeking to repel their spouses sexually. They began wearing pajamas more suited for sledding than lovemaking or changed their clothes into stained sweats and oversized T-shirts.

- *Commit sexual sabotage.* We can conveniently get out of the habit of going to bed at the same time. Or at bedtime we can pick a fight or present a displeasing attitude that makes it unlikely sex will ensue. If this happens often, you can probably assume it is not a coincidence, but rather an intentional ploy to avoid sex.

- *Make our spouses earn sex.* We can control and manipulate our spouses with sex. If they do something we want, then we give them sex. If they do not do something we want, or do something we dislike, we punish them by withholding sex. This kind of sexual relationship is more akin to prostitution than marriage. In essence, our spouses have to earn sex and pay for it in some way.

- *Share our beds with children and pets.* We can allow our children, and even our pets, into our beds. One couple we know had a very unimpressive sex life in large part because their enormous dog slept in their bed under the covers between them. Kids, of course, sometimes have bad dreams and climb into their parents' bed for comfort, but to regularly allow them equal access with your spouse is not healthful for the kids or the marriage.

- *Have separate beds or bedrooms.* We can have separate beds, or even separate bedrooms, as is the new trend among wealthy couples building their custom dream homes complete with his-and-hers bedrooms, closets, and showers. Contrary to old television shows like *I Love Lucy*, where Ricky and Lucy slept in separate beds, a married couple is supposed to sleep in the same bed. Hebrews 13:4 speaks of "the marriage bed" and not "beds." To be fair, some studies have reported that husbands sleep better when in bed with their wives, whereas wives sleep worse with their husbands, often because of their snoring.[18] But a humble servant lover figures out how to have sleeping conditions (temperature, covers, lighting, etc.) that work for both of them, and go in for medical treatment as necessary to stop sounding like a helicopter or a herd of buffalo while sleeping.

Reasons Why We Are Selfish Lovers

An important question to ask is why we tend to be selfish lovers. While each of these answers may be painful, they merit loving patience and attendance to overcome. Some are simply sins that need to be quickly put to death before they kill the oneness and nakedness without shame that God intends for your marriage. Sometimes identifying these underlying factors can help us deal with the cause of our problems. Some are simply a normal part of life but need to be dealt with nonetheless, or they can lead to selfishness.

- *Difficult seasons.* Some seasons of life can be difficult ones for normal lovemaking and need to be discussed and navigated lovingly and wisely. For example, if your wife is unable to be intimate because of a difficult pregnancy that has her on bed rest, or one of you is suffering from an injury or illness, then there needs to be compromise and loving understanding to do all you can, knowing that you cannot do all that you would like.
- *Secret sins.* Sins that have not been confessed to our spouses invariably harm intimacy and oneness. This includes sins of our past as well as sins of the present. These could include mental sins, such as pornography or lustful fantasizing; emotional sin, such as adultery of the heart; or actual physical adultery. Is there anything you have not told your spouse and need to confess?

- *Sins committed against us in the past.* Past sin committed against us—particularly abuse that includes, but is not limited to, sexual abuse—can be a great inhibitor of fully and frequently enjoying sex with our spouses. Is there anything you need to disclose to your spouse and get some professional help to work through?
- *Inappropriate sharing with others.* Gossip about sexual frustration with our spouses instead of speaking solely with them is a common sin that contributes to sexual denial. While it is not sinful for spouses to speak with someone about their marital and sexual frustrations, you must adhere to some conditions. You must not speak to someone instead of your spouse but only *in addition to* your spouse; otherwise no progress can be made in the marriage. This person must be someone your spouse agrees is godly and trustworthy enough to discuss intimate life details with. He or she cannot be a relative, as one of the worst things you can do is drag your extended family into your bedroom. The person cannot be someone of the opposite sex, because the risk of at least emotional and spiritual adultery is incredibly high. Have you been discussing your spouse with someone he or she is unaware of, or have you discussed with someone else things you have not discussed with your spouse?
- *Fatigue.* Exhaustion is a common reason for infrequent lovemaking. While life can indeed be stressful and take all of your energy, it's vital that we do all we can to save some of ourselves for our spouses. Be willing to try having sex with your spouse at a time when you have better energy, be it the morning, afternoon, or evening. Are there things you're doing that you can intentionally cut back on to save energy for your husband or wife? Can you step out of your busyness for a while, splash some water on your face, and cuddle up for an hour? Make your sex life a priority and a matter of prayer.

    Men, we can also help our wives by serving them, especially if they are working outside the home or have children who can take forever to get down for bed. This may include, if finances permit, a housekeeper or other help to free up some of your wife's energy. And if your spouse is willing to be together but very tired, you can be the one who does much of the work in lovemaking on those occasions.
- *Lack of pleasure.* A lack of enjoyment causes some couples not to be

intimate often. Sometimes the answer is for the lovers to get better at their craft and for them to relax, help out, and allow themselves to enjoy it. This includes using water-based lubricants to combat dryness, studying sexual anatomy, and researching sexual techniques and positions in nonpornographic resources.[19] In other cases medical attention needs to be sought to see if there is a medical or hormonal problem. Yes, it may seem embarrassing, but a humble servant is willing to work through that.

- *Insecurity.* Lack of confidence with their bodies explains why some couples do not have sex very often. This is perhaps most often true of wives and can be a very sensitive issue. Our spouses can go a long way toward encouraging us, so ongoing verbal flirtation and affirmation can be a huge help. Furthermore, we can also make an effort to remain in good health, groom ourselves well, and dress ourselves attractively. What is devastating is mean-spirited criticism, backhanded comments, jesting that is not funny, and comparing our spouses to other people, which is the sin of coveting. As we said earlier in the book, our spouses are to be our standards of beauty. All of us have things we would like to change, but culture cannot set our standards of beauty. We need to present ourselves as attractive to our spouses in word, deed, and body. Your spouse will likely be more able to overlook your "flaws" if rather than focusing on them or being unduly self-conscious about them, you act with some sexual confidence and boldness.

- *Wrong perspective of the body.* A medical and not sexual view of the body accounts for infrequent sex in some marriages. If one or both of you view your bodies primarily in medical and clinical terms, then it may be difficult for you to also enjoy and explore your body and your spouse's body sexually.

- *Boredom.* Monotony accounts for many a lackluster sex life. Without a bit of passion, exploration, and variation, sex with the same person the same way every day for decades is going to become boring. So a humble servant does research and finds new ways to take some risks, get out of the sexual rut, and increase the adventure. Honestly, are you bored with your sex life?

Being Visually Generous

People who are visual are keenly observant of what they see, and their minds function like cameras, continually taking snapshots and filing images away in their memory. Nearly all men are visual, to differing degrees. About 25 percent of women are visual. In an effort to serve as a "translator" for women, one Christian wife and researcher wrote a book explaining to wives how their husbands are different from them.[20] She devoted an entire chapter of her book to explaining people who are visual.[21]

Visual people cannot help but notice a beautiful person, but it does not mean they prefer someone else to their spouses. They involuntarily file snapshots of beautiful people, and their files are filled with images stretching back to childhood, which can show up without warning. Our world continually assaults our eyes with sexually beautiful images. As an example, men derive physical pleasure from the simple act of seeing a beautiful woman, which explains why companies continually put beautiful women in ads with their products.

If you are visual, or married to someone who is, this fact can be discouraging. But temptation and sin are different. Hebrews 4:15 speaks of the temptation of the sinless Jesus Christ: "For we do not have a High Priest who cannot sympathize with our weaknesses, but was in all points tempted as we are, yet without sin." Temptation is not a sin. Rather, it is an opportunity to sin, and also an opportunity to bring "every thought into captivity to the obedience of Christ."[a] This means that visual spouses are in a very real battle every moment of every day.

But it is important to know that this fact can be a great ally to our marriages. Be a visually generous spouse, using your spouse's visual propensity to your advantage and your spouse's pleasure. Instead of fighting with your spouse, fight for him or her, and provide lots of redeemed images. Make love with the lights on, or by candlelight. Sleep together naked. Undress in front of your spouse. Bathe in front of your spouse. "Flash" your spouse around the house. Pull the curtains and hang out in your house naked. Dress in clothes that fit and flatter your figure or build. Have a mirror hung near your bed. And keeping an eye on weight and working toward wellness is always appreciated.

---

a 2 Cor. 10:5.

A loving spouse does not expect perfection, but does appreciate a sincere effort made by a wife or husband who seeks to eat well and exercise.

But some will ask, is this something the Bible teaches? Yes.

In the Song of Songs there is an ancient, roughly three-thousand-year-old report of a wise wife being incredibly visually generous with her husband. In the NIV, the most erotic section of the entire Bible begins speaking of the "dance of Mahanaim." One theologian said, "She will now dance nakedly and seductively."[22] The dance of Mahanaim is most likely an exotic private striptease she performed for her husband. Mahanaim is the town at which a host of angels met Jacob, which may mean the husband is telling his lovely wife that she is like an angel to him.[23] Aggressive and confident, she enticed her husband by using all her beauty and charm to allure him. Her boldness may have come from him constantly verbalizing his attraction to her, which has allowed her to see herself through his eyes. (The following verses are from Song of Songs 6:13–7:13 NIV.)

How beautiful your sandaled feet, O prince's daughter!

As she serves him visually, the husband encourages her verbally as she dances naked before him. Solomon speaks frankly about all her body, proving that all the body is to be explored and enjoyed by one's spouse. Open-toed sandals were regarded as very erotic, and he recognizes her beautiful and graceful feet as he watches his wife dance before him. From her feet he continues his description of his wife from toe to head, calling her his princess.

Your graceful legs are like jewels, the work of an artist's hands.

He speaks of the beauty of her inner thighs as crafted works of art as she dances before him.

Your navel is a rounded goblet that never lacks blended wine.

Sadly, it seems those who translated this verse from the original poetic Hebrew into English were more timid than God, choosing the word *navel*. *The New Century Bible Commentary* says, "If the order of bodily parts, from bottom to top, is followed consistently, the navel is in the wrong position between thighs and belly: it comes above those. The part of the girl's body mentioned here is therefore more likely to be the vagina or vulva than the navel."[24] One Old Testament scholar said, "It is generally translated as 'vulva.' The description . . . 'never lacks mixed wine' speaks of it as a source of sexual pleasure and moistness."[25] The president of a Southern Baptist seminary said, "Verse 2 is badly translated, in my judgment, in virtually every English version. The problem is with the word 'navel.' . . . the word almost certainly is a reference to the innermost sexual parts of the woman, her vagina (vulva)."[26] Another widely respected Old Testament scholar said, "This indirect reference to the vulva is in keeping with the poet's strategy of tasteful, though erotic allusions to the woman's body. Whether literally navel or vulva, the image evokes a comparison that is based on taste. The description of the woman's aperture as containing wine implies the man's desire to drink from the sensual bowl. Thus, this may be a subtle and tasteful allusion to the intimacies of oral sex."[27]

Your waist is a mound of wheat encircled by lilies.

Her navel and stomach are a rich, bronzed color with a sweet scent.

Your breasts are like two fawns, like twin fawns of a gazelle.

"Two fawns" conjures images of playfulness that prompt a desire to pet and play with them, much like two fun baby deer one would encounter in a petting zoo.

Your neck is like an ivory tower.

Her neck was long and smooth.

Your eyes are the pools of Heshbon by the gate of Bath Rabbim.

This city was known for its calm and beautiful pools, indicating the peace and stillness in her eyes.

Your nose is like the tower of Lebanon looking toward Damascus.

She had a very prominent nose. But he loves her big nose and rejoices in it, as she is his standard of beauty.

Your head crowns you like Mount Carmel.

Mount Carmel sat beautifully atop rich fertile plains. Likewise, her head crowned her body.

Your hair is like royal tapestry; the king is held captive by its tresses.

He found her hair to be beautiful and alluring. As the Bible says, a woman's hair is her "crown" and "glory," which helps explain why it is important to many husbands.

How beautiful you are and how pleasing, my love, with your delights!

He delights in his wife's sexual abilities and body.

*Your stature is like that of the palm, and your breasts like
   clusters of fruit.
I said, "I will climb the palm tree; I will take hold of its fruit."*

To fertilize a female palm tree, someone would need to climb the male palm tree to get some of its pollen-bearing flowers. He would then climb the female tree and tie the pollen-bearing flowers to the female tree. To "climb a palm tree" literally meant to fertilize it; likewise, the husband is clearly saying that he desires to make love to his wife. Although he has enjoyed seeing her strip for him, he can no longer merely watch her body and wants to enjoy it sexually.

May your breasts be like the clusters of grapes on the vine, the fragrance of your breath like apples, and your mouth like the best wine.

Grapes swell and become increasingly round and full when ripe, like a woman's breasts when sexually aroused. Then he refers to the sweet smell of her breath. Her kisses are his favorite flavor. Like wine, her lovemaking is strong, smooth, savory, and satisfying.

May the wine go straight to my beloved, flowing gently over lips and teeth.

Now speaking, the wife celebrates her lovemaking ability to satisfy her husband. They share a glass of wine along with their bodies.

I belong to my beloved, and his desire is for me.

The wife delights in belonging to her husband alone, and celebrates that all his sexual passion is solely for her. In this, we see that a wife's freedom is the result of the husband's fidelity. While the point is debated, it seems that this statement is made before the multiple wives and concubines ruined the love and oneness they had together. This goes to show that even a great beginning can have a bad ending if you do not tend to your relationship with God and your spouse.

Come, my beloved, let us go to the countryside, let us spend the night in the villages.

After being sexually intimate, the couple lies together unclothed to snuggle and talk. This kind of ongoing connection and intimacy following sex is incredibly important for a married couple. While chatting, the wife tells her husband that she wants to get some time away for a romantic vacation in the countryside. She does so in a way that is inviting rather than nagging.

> *Let us go early to the vineyards to see if the vines have budded, if their blossoms have opened, and if the pomegranates are in bloom—there I will give you my love.*

She reminds him that spring is upon them and that there is much beauty to enjoy in the country. Creatively and aggressively, she also promises to make love to her husband in the warm outdoors as she continues to grow in her sexual freedom and confidence.

> *The mandrakes send out their fragrance, and at our door is every delicacy, both new and old, that I have stored up for you, my beloved.*

Mandrakes were considered an aphrodisiac in the ancient world. The wife here announces to her husband as they lie unclothed in bed that on their getaway to the country, she intends to have sex with him in old ways that they enjoy, and also in new ways that they have not yet tried.

This nice God-fearing woman who married as a virgin speaks first in the series of love songs that comprise the Song of Songs. She also speaks last, and she speaks most. She initiates sex frequently, she talks about sex frankly, and she enjoys sex freely.

Consider for a moment how radically free she is. Not only is the account of her talking to, stripping for, and being with her husband three thousand years old, but it is written in a conservative Eastern cultural context for devout Jews. Many wives wonder if they would be tramps to act in such a way. If it is with their husbands, then they are simply being wives to God's glory and their joy. The issue is not what is done, but with whom it is done. The Bible reveals that even stripping, though not required, can be redeemed within marriage. And we see from the husband's words that being verbally generous, encouraging, and thankful creates a zone of safety in which a spouse can safely risk being a visually generous servant lover.

Lastly, how about you? In reading this chapter, what one or more things has God showed you that you need to change in yourself? What things has God showed you to prayerfully and lovingly encourage in your spouse?

10

CAN WE ____?

All things are lawful for me, but all things are not helpful.
All things are lawful for me, but I will not be brought
under the power of any.

—1 CORINTHIANS 6:12

C an we _____?

Having taught the content of this book around the world, we have been asked thousands of sex-related questions.

Before we answer the most common and controversial questions, a bit of preface will be helpful. If you are older, from a highly conservative religious background, live far away from a major city, do not spend much time on the Internet, or do not have cable television, the odds are that you will want to read this chapter while sitting down, with the medics ready on speed dial.

If you are one of those people who do not know that the world has changed sexually, read this chapter not to argue or fight, but rather to learn about how to be a good missionary in this sexualized culture, able to answer people's questions without blushing. For parents, grandparents, and those in caring professions such as teachers, pastors, ministry leaders, and counselors, this task is all the more urgent.

The questions today are different, and if people don't get answers from pastors and parents, they will find them in dark, depraved places. The truth is that almost every married couple has a list of questions regarding what they can and cannot do. You likely have a list of those questions too. Some of them will, hopefully, be answered in this book.

In the Bible there was a church in a major city called Corinth. They had many questions about cross-dressing, cohabitation, homosexuality, fornication—which was nicknamed "Corinthianizing"—adultery, and whether or not it was okay for one guy to be sleeping with his stepmother. Corinth was so filled with prostitution that prostitutes were nicknamed "Corinthian girls," and there was even "spiritual" prostitution, as the local temple of Aphrodite employed as many as one thousand male and female homosexual and heterosexual prostitutes as part of their pagan "ministry." This was so common that even some Christians in the church were employing prostitutes.[a] So they wrote a letter to the apostle Paul with a list of their questions, and he responded to them in the letter we know as 1 Corinthians.[b]

Paul answered their questions, but he also went further. In addition to teaching them what to think, he taught them how to think. In 1 Corinthians 6:12, amid his teaching on sex, Paul said, "All things are lawful for me, but all things are not helpful. All things are lawful for me, but I will not be brought under the power of any."

This simple taxonomy is brilliantly helpful because it is simultaneously simple enough to remember and broad enough to apply to every sexual question. In this chapter we will ask the following questions in relation to specific sexual questions:

Question 1: *Is it lawful?* With this question we seek to ascertain whether or not something is in violation of the laws of the government in the culture or the laws of God in Scripture.

Question 2: *Is it helpful?* With this question we seek to ascertain whether or not something pulls a couple together as one or pushes them apart as two. If a sex act includes humiliation, degradation, violation of conscience, pain, or harm, then it is not beneficial for the marriage. If a sex act includes one of the six purposes of sex that we established in a previous chapter, then it may be helpful:

1. pleasure
2. children
3. oneness
4. knowledge
5. protection
6. comfort

---

a 1 Cor. 6:15–16.
b See 1 Cor. 6:12, 13; 8:1, 5; 10:23.

Question 3: *Is it enslaving?* With this question we seek to ascertain whether or not an act could become obsessive, out of control, or addictive in an unhealthy and concerning way—what the Bible calls slavery. When most people think of slavery, they consider only imposed slavery when someone is overtaken against his or her will. But there is another form of slavery that is even more common—chosen slavery. Chosen slavery is when a person freely chooses the slave master that rules over him, controls him, and harms him. The most common forms of chosen slavery are drug abuse, alcohol, gambling, shopping, food, and sex. People addicted to these kinds of things are in fact slaves who have simply chosen which shackles to put their hands into.

In the late 1970s, Patrick Carnes, a psychologist and researcher, was instrumental in the initial identification and treatment of sexual addiction as a condition. Carnes's list of criteria for sexual addiction is helpful for people to consider against their own lives and the lives of those they know who are potentially sexually enslaved:

- A pattern of out-of-control behavior
- Severe consequences because of sexual behavior
- Inability to stop despite negative consequences
- Severe mood changes around sexual behavior
- Persistent pursuit of high-risk behaviors
- Ongoing effort to stop or limit behaviors
- Inordinate amounts of time spent on sexual matters
- Increasing amounts of sexual experiences
- Sexual obsession and fantasy as a primary coping tool[1]

Sex addicts have no comprehension of the risks they are taking and have completely lost both perspective and control. To deal with the pain, the addict may resort to other addictions, such as alcoholism, eating disorders, and abusive drugs. Many times suicide is a constant thought. Or the addicts will punish themselves by engaging in sexual acts that are degrading.

Clinically speaking, sexual addiction has many different forms: compulsive masturbation, sex with prostitutes, anonymous sex with multiple partners, multiple affairs outside a committed relationship, habitual exhibitionism, habitual voyeurism, inappropriate sexual touching, repeated sexual abuse of children, and episodes of rape. Of all forms of sexual addiction, none is more harmful to both the addict and the victim than childhood sexual abuse. The beginnings of sexual addiction are usually rooted in adolescence or childhood. More than 80 percent of sexual addicts were abused in their childhood.[2]

One of the leading Christian psychologists has also connected adrenaline and sex as a cause for sexual addiction. He said,

> The risky, novel, or taboo action causes adrenaline to rush—just ask a bungee jumper, parachutist, hang glider, or other thrill-seeking person. When it comes to sex, some men [and women] try to get this adrenaline rush as intense as possible while having a sexual high. This produces a double excitement. The problem is, it only works for a short period of time. You get used to it, so that one particular type of thrill no longer excites you. You have to move on to something even riskier.[3]

This explains why some people constantly want to push the sexual edge into areas that are taboo, dangerous, risky, dirty, painful, and public. The combination of the adrenaline high and sexual pleasure should not be fed, but instead must be mitigated with contentment in normal marital sex and ceasing from all activities that bring an adrenaline rush to sex, meaning professional help may be needed.

Before we turn to what the Bible says about common sexual questions, one thing is important to note. Throughout this chapter, we are explaining what a married couple *may* do, not what they *must* do. The Bible often gives more freedom than our consciences can accept, and we then choose not to use all our freedoms. This is true of us (Mark and Grace); we do not do everything that is mentioned in this book or the ensuing chapters, although we are free in Christ to do so if our consciences should ever change. Those wanting more detailed analysis on the frequency of various sexual practices will find it in appendix V of the e-book and on our website www.pastormark.tv.

Admittedly, the remainder of this chapter has some technical data, but, we believe it is very important to show that we are not being gratuitous in answering certain questions but rather addressing what is reality for many people. The data shows the sexual generation gap and why many churches and Christian ministries are out of touch on sexual issues. It also reveals the effects porn has had on sexual behavior, particularly for younger people, and what is "common" behavior among the the "average" person. And, it provides pastors, ministry leaders, and counselors with solid data to assist them in helping others.

Masturbation

Both men and women of all ages masturbate, with men masturbating more than women, and younger people masturbating more than older people. The average age that individuals first begin masturbating also varies by gender. The average man first masturbates at 13.45 years and the average woman begins at 12.75 years, which roughly correlates with the same life stage as the onset of puberty.[4]

Men and Masturbation[5]

For men under the age of fifty-nine, more than 60 percent practiced solo masturbation in the past ninety days.[6] That number remained roughly 50 percent for men ages fifty-nine to sixty-nine.[7] Solo masturbation rates were highest among men between the ages of twenty-five to thirty-nine, with single men in a dating relationship reporting 95.5 percent, and 80 percent for all unmarried men in the past ninety days.[8] More than 30 percent of men ages forty-nine and under solo masturbated on average more than two times per week in the past year.[9] The lowest solo masturbation rate is among men more than seventy years of age, who reported nearly 27 percent in the past ninety days.[10] As compared to solo masturbation, masturbation with a sexual partner was less common in the past ninety days, with less than a 50 percent occurrence in all age groups.[11]

Women and Masturbation[12]

More than half of women ages eighteen to forty-nine reported solo masturbation during the previous ninety days, with rates being highest among those ages twenty-five to twenty-nine.[13] Relatively frequent solo masturbation (a few times each month or more) was reported by up to 48 percent of women ages eighteen to thirty-nine, but this frequency of masturbation was progressively less common in older age groups.[14] Solo masturbation rates for all women under the age of sixty were not affected by being in a dating or marital relationship, as masturbation rates were the same whether or not women were having regular sex.[15] Women ages sixty to sixty-nine in a dating or marital relationship were significantly less likely to be solo masturbating, and roughly one-third of all women ages sixty to sixty-nine reported recent solo masturbation.[16] Among women ages seventy or older, more than half not in a dating or marital relationship solo masturbated compared with only 12 percent of married women.[17]

Being masturbated by a partner was most common among women ages twenty-five to twenty-nine.[18] Across all age groups, women in a dating or marital relationship were far more likely to engage in partnered masturbation than nonpartnered women.[19] Partnered masturbation was most common among women ages twenty-five to twenty-nine and thirty to thirty-nine who were single and dating.[20]

Question 1: Is it lawful?

The Bible does not forbid masturbation. Some Christians wish that it did. Unable to find any verses that condemn masturbation, they have used the story of Onan in Genesis 38:6–10 as their proof text. But the story of Onan says nothing of masturbation. Instead, the story is about a man who died leaving his wife a childless widow. The dead man's brother was then expected to marry his widowed sister-in-law, have normal sexual relations with her, and enable her to have children. Although Onan was happy to have sex with his sister-in-law, he would pull out of her to ejaculate on the ground rather than obey God and become a father. His sin was not masturbation but wanting to have sex with a vulnerable sister-in-law without being in any way obligated or committed to her. So he practiced *coitus interruptus*, pulling out of Tamar at the moment of ejaculation in an effort not to impregnate her. Onan's sin was disobeying God and dishonoring Tamar by having sex without wanting to be obligated to her in any way or care for her, or, as Genesis 38:8 says, "raise up an heir to [his] brother."

The only possible mention of masturbation in the Bible is of a wife in Song of Songs 2:6, saying of her husband, "His left hand is under my head, and his right hand embraces me." One Bible commentary says of this verse,

"The Hebrew word translated 'embrace' is used in a sexual sense and may be rendered 'fondle.'"[21] Another says, "Most Hebrew scholars agree this means to 'stimulate sexually, or fondle.' . . . In the *Sumuzi Inanna* love romance we find the phrase, 'Your right hand you have placed on my vulva; your left, stroked my head.' The parallelism seems too direct to be coincidental."[22] In summary, the Bible does not forbid masturbation and in fact may on one occasion report it positively between a husband and wife.

Question 2: Is it helpful?

This is a very difficult and complex question. If a person is masturbating alone, without the knowledge of his or her spouse and includes pornography or lustful thoughts about anyone other than a spouse, then it is sinful. Since sex is given for such purposes as oneness,[a] intimate knowledge,[b] and comfort,[c] having sex with yourself seems to miss some of the significant biblical reasons for sexual intimacy, though that does not make it inherently sinful. At the very least, frequent solo masturbation is not ideal within a marriage.

According to a biophysicist who has studied the effects of sexual stimulation on the brain, "masturbation is playing with neurochemical fire. It affects one emotionally and neurologically. . . . You will be bound to something, because that is what it does neurologically—it associates the orgasm with something. The question to be asked is '*What* is it binding you to?'"[23] We can be bound to anything through repeated masturbation. In fact, Struthers explained that if a man had a baseball cap sitting on top of his computer and daily watched porn on his computer, after a month the man would have a physiological response of sexual arousal to a baseball cap. This is how fetishes end up as a requirement for some men to achieve sexual satisfaction.

Another common practice is masturbating oneself in the presence of and with the approval of a spouse, and it can be beneficial under a number of circumstances. Some spouses are very visual and enjoy seeing their partner do this before finishing their time together with sexual intercourse.

And there are parts of the body (for example, the wife's clitoris) that are

---

a Gen. 2:24.
b Gen. 4:1.
c 2 Sam. 12:24.

not engaged through normal intercourse, so for maximum pleasure to be achieved, it is helpful for the spouse to stimulate that part during intercourse. And we all learn by seeing, so an extra benefit is that by watching, each spouse can learn what pleases the other.

At times when a couple cannot be together because of such things as distance, sickness, injury, or the six or seven weeks of abstention a woman's body requires after the birth of a child, masturbation can be an acceptable and helpful form of relief until normal sexual relations can be resumed.

One question asked by the soldiers in our church is whether or not each spouse can masturbate while they are apart using images of their spouse's in their mind, in a photo, or even through seeing each other live through the Internet. The answer is yes, providing no one else is involved in any way, including viewing.

In watching a spouse masturbate, one can learn to do the same. For example, masturbating a husband is fairly easy for a wife to learn, as his genitalia are external. But the wife's genitalia are internal and more difficult to learn, so if the wife is willing to masturbate herself to orgasm while the husband watches, he can learn to do the same for her.

A third type of masturbation is masturbating one's spouse, which is often also called *manual stimulation*, and it can be a very enjoyable part of foreplay.

In seasons where normal intercourse is not possible, such as after the birth of a child, the lending of a helping hand to one's spouse can be greatly appreciated.

A woman's body most commonly achieves orgasm through the stimulation of her clitoris, which is not engaged during normal intercourse but can be through the hand of her husband.

Question 3: Is it enslaving?

There are a number of circumstances under which masturbation is not beneficial. If it is done out of laziness, then it is a sin. We should be giving to our spouses in the bedroom, making the effort to undress and be together, serving each other as an act of love.

If masturbation begins to be the normative sex act in your relationship and replaces regular intercourse, then it is becoming the center of the sexual relationship and therefore a problem. And if we are habituating our bodies to be most satisfied through masturbation rather than intercourse, we are setting in motion a host of problems, such as a man who cannot climax with his wife but instead has to finish with his own hand, which is devastating for a wife and symptomatic of a sexual addiction to masturbation.

Obviously this is an issue that will require a great deal of honest and gracious conversation between you and your spouse.

Oral Sex

Oral sex is using one's mouth and tongue to pleasure a partner's genitals. Culturally speaking, oral sex is increasingly more common and acceptable among both men and women in and outside marriage. Younger generations are increasingly likely not to consider it any more sexual than kissing, which is why it is imperative for parents not to simply teach their children to be abstinent, but also clearly define for them that oral sex is sex. No less than 61 percent of teenage girls have performed oral sex on a guy, and 62 percent of teenage girls have received oral sex from a guy.[24]

According to the most recent and comprehensive research, the following data provides an accurate summary of oral sex activity.[25] At least half of all women, single and married, ages eighteen to thirty-nine, gave or received oral sex in the past ninety days.[26] Women in dating or marital relationships were significantly more likely to report giving and receiving oral sex in the past ninety days.[27] Among men of all ages, men in their late twenties and thirties were most likely (80.7 percent) to receive oral sex from a woman, particularly if they were not married or living with a girlfriend.[28] The lowest rate of receiving oral sex in the past ninety days were men over age seventy who were not married but living with a partner (0.0 percent).[29] And men who reported receiving oral sex from a woman were also more likely in every age group to have also performed oral sex on a woman.

Question 1: Is it lawful?

Oral sex is lawful both culturally and biblically. Despite being three thousand years old and written in a highly conservative Eastern religious culture, the biblical book Song of Songs speaks of oral sex in a positive and poetic fashion.

In Song of Songs 2:3, the wife seemingly speaks of the delight she has in tasting his sweetness in her mouth as she performs oral sex (fellatio) on her husband, saying, "Like an apple tree among the trees of the woods, so is my beloved among the sons. I sat down in his shade with great delight, and his fruit was sweet to my taste." One Bible commentator said of this text, "In extra biblical literature, fruit is sometimes equated with the male genitals or with semen, so it is possible that here we have a faint and delicate reference to an oral genital caress."[30]

In Song of Songs 4:12–5:1 the husband likens his wife's unclothed body to a garden filled with delightful scents and flavors, including her moist vagina likened to a fresh spring. The wife then invites him to perform oral sex (cunnilingus) on her, saying, "Awake, O north wind, and come, O south! Blow upon my garden, that its spices may flow out. Let my beloved come to his garden and eat its pleasant fruits." After performing oral sex on his wife, the husband then says, "I have come to my garden, my sister, my spouse; I have gathered my myrrh with my spice; I have eaten my honeycomb with my honey; I have drunk my wine with my milk." Then, the only time in the entire book that God directly speaks, He celebrates the act, saying, "Eat, friends, and drink; drink your fill of love!" (5:1 NIV).

Various Bible commentators have seen the overt yet poetic meaning of these texts of Scripture. One scholar said that it is possible that "the 'garden' is a euphemism for the vulva."[31] Another said, "In the ancient Near East and elsewhere in the Bible (Prov. 5:15–20), these are highly erotic images. The images of fountain and garden probably are to be visualized together since a garden would need a water supply. The focus may well be on the ultimate place in the act of lovemaking, the woman's vagina."[32] Additionally, commenting on Song of Songs 7:2, a noted Old Testament scholar said, "this may be a subtle and tasteful allusion to the intimacies of [oral] sex."[33]

In summary, oral sex is permissible within the context of marriage. It is certainly not required, but it is permitted.

Question 2: Is it helpful?

Yes. Many husbands and wives enjoy oral sex.

For the husband, it is enjoyable foreplay, and most will find this to be a much-appreciated act of love by their wives.

For the wife, if the husband is patient and takes her counsel during the act on how to please her best, he can bring her to a heightened state of passion.

Question 3: Is it enslaving?

If oral sex becomes a frequent substitute for normal intercourse, then it is becoming a problem. So long as it is part of a couple's sexual life and not the primary sexual act, then it is a gift being stewarded well.

Anal Sex[34]

Likely due to the increase in pornography and sexualized nature of our culture, anal sex is increasingly more commonly discussed, accepted, and practiced by both men and women, single and married. This explains why most grand-mothers and grandfathers rarely, if ever, consider this act, which many of their granddaughters and grandsons are participating in.

More than 40 percent of all men ages twenty-five to fifty-nine have had anal sex with a woman at least once in their lifetime.[35] Among women, 10.3 percent to 14.4 percent of women ages eighteen to thirty-nine, both married and single, had anal sex in the past ninety days.[36] Among women eighteen to twenty-four years old, roughly one-fourth of those who were cohabitating and about one-fifth who were married reported having engaged in anal sex in the past ninety days.[37] Also women between eighteen and forty-nine years of age in a marital or cohabitating relationship were "significantly more likely to report having anal sex in the past ninety days."[38] Among both men and women of all ages, including both married and single, anal intercourse was significantly less frequent than vaginal intercourse.[39]

Younger people are far more likely to engage in anal sex, as those ages twenty-five to forty-nine are more than twice as likely to do so than those fifty and older.[40] Also, for men ages twenty-five to fifty-nine, those most likely to engage in anal sex were single or in a dating relationship; conversely, the least likely to engage in anal sex were married men.[41]

Question 1: Is it lawful?

Yes, legally and biblically anal sex is permissible for a married couple, as Scripture does not forbid it. This may surprise some people because they have heard anal sex referred to as sodomy. *Sodomy* is not a word that appears in the Bible, but is taken from an account in Genesis 19 about the city of Sodom. The two angels, appearing as men, whom the Lord had sent to investigate the sexual sin of Sodom and Gomorrah, were welcomed into Lot's home. As they rested there, the perverted men of the city surrounded the home, demanding that Lot's guests be sent out for homosexual sex and possibly even to be gang-raped by the crowd of men. God intervened and blinded the mob.

The two "men" then told Lot to get his family out of town before God reduced the hellish town to ashes. Lot and his family barely made it out of town in time as God rained down burning sulfur (burning asphalt) on Sodom and Gomorrah and killed all the people. The sin of Sodom was not anal sex between husband and wives, but rather homosexual sex between men, which the Bible repeatedly forbids.[a] Genesis 19:5 is also clear that the sin of Sodom was homosexual sex, saying, "They [the men of Sodom] called to Lot and said to him, 'Where are the men who came to you tonight? Bring them out to us that we may know them carnally [have sex with them].'" Therefore, anal sex within marriage is not sodomy, is not inherently sinful, and is permissible.

Question 2: Is it helpful?

This is a question that requires earnest consideration by a couple.

There is a difference between anal stimulation and penetration. More couples report some pleasure from anal stimulation with a lubricated finger than participate in fully penetrating anal sex.

For the husband, the male prostate can only be accessed through the anus. It is called by some the "male G-spot" as it is reportedly a source of great pleasure when stroked by such things as a wife's finger. For this reason, some couples choose to experiment on the husband.

For the wife, there are many factors to consider. Unlike the vagina, the anus has no natural lubrication, which means sufficient lubrication must be used. She must be relaxed, or she could suffer physical harm. Since the anus is much thinner than the vagina, it also tears more easily and can easily become infected if torn.

Some couples choose to use this method to prevent pregnancy. In conjunction with the rhythm method of birth control in which normal penis-vagina intercourse is suspended on a woman's days of fertility, it is possible to use anal sex as an option.

---

a Lev. 18:22; 20:13; Rom. 1:26–27; 1 Cor. 6:9–11; 1 Tim. 1:9–10; Jude 17.

Many Christian couples have decided that while anal sex is permissible, it is not beneficial, as they deem the risks too great. Some, however, have chosen to at least try it, for the variety. As a general rule, unless both the husband and wife want to attempt it and can do so without pain, shame, or harm, this should not be done. Unless both of you have a clear conscience about the matter, it is unwise to engage in this act.

Question 3: Is it enslaving?

If anal sex becomes an obsessive part of the marriage or begins to overtake other forms of marital sex, especially penis-vagina sex, then there may be a problem. And for men who have had gay sex, if it conjures up for them past fantasies and memories, then, while the act may not be sinful in general, it may be sinful in particular for them because of the associations made.

Menstrual Sex

Question 1: Is it lawful?

The Old Testament does forbid sex during a wife's menstrual cycle.[a] The question is whether or not that law is still binding on us today. To ascertain that requires a bit of theological consideration because it is only forbidden in the Old Testament and not in the New Testament.

When the Bible speaks of law, it usually refers to what human beings are commanded to do by God, such as the Ten Commandments. In particular, when speaking of the law, the Bible is often referencing the 613 laws in the first five books of the Old Testament.

One noted theologian on the law said, "Paul clearly teaches that Christians are no longer under the law covenant instituted under Moses."[42] This is why when the Bible speaks of the "old covenant" in comparison to the "new covenant,"[b] it is showing us that we are no longer under the law and obligated to it. He went on to explain, "Romans 10:4 asserts that Christ is the 'end of the law.' . . . Christ is the goal to which the law points; and when the goal is reached, the law also comes to an end."[43] The entire book of Hebrews is

---

a Lev. 15:19–33; 18:19; 20:18; 22:10.
b E.g., 2 Cor. 3:6–14.

in large part devoted to explaining how Jesus has brought an end to the old covenant law, which is why we do not need a high priest, temple, sacrificial system, and the like. Jesus is our High Priest, the presence of God, and the payment for sin.[44]

This fulfillment of the law explains why certain foods,[a] circumcision,[b] Passover,[c] animal sacrifices,[d] and the Sabbath[e] that were binding in the old covenant are not binding in the new covenant.[f] That new covenant believers no longer live under the old covenant ceremonial and civil law also explains why more obscure commands are no longer binding, such as requiring any male who ejaculates in his sleep to leave town for a season and bathe in a river,[g] making churches discipline people for eating shellfish,[h] or forbidding the wearing of clothing made of two kinds of fabric.[i]

However, there are some moral laws that are listed in both the Old Testament and New Testament. These include every one of the Ten Commandments[j]—with the exception of keeping the Sabbath—including not committing idolatry,[k] honoring parents,[l] not murdering,[m] not committing adultery,[n] not stealing,[o] not lying,[p] and not coveting.[q]

Determining which laws continue from the old covenant to the new covenant is admittedly difficult. One helpful distinction that can be traced back to the church father Tertullian (AD 160–222) is spoken of by Martin Luther (1483–1546) and is found in the Westminster Confession of Faith (1646).

---

a Lev. 11:1–44; Deut. 14:3–21; Acts 10:14; 11:8; Rom. 14:2.
b Rom. 4:9–12; Gal. 2:3–5; 5:2–4; Phil. 3:2–3; Col. 2:11–12.
c Rom. 14:5–6; Gal. 4:10; Col. 2:16–17.
d Rom. 3:25–26; 2 Cor. 5:21; Gal. 3:13.
e Ex. 2:8–11.
f Rom. 14:5; Col. 2:16–17.
g Lev. 15:16, 18, 32; 22:4; Deut. 23:10.
h Lev. 11:10–12.
i Lev. 19:19.
j Ex. 20.
k 1 Cor. 5:10–11, 6:9, 10:7; 2 Cor. 6:16; Gal. 5:20; Eph. 5:5.
l Rom. 1:30; Eph. 6:1–3; Col. 3:20.
m Rom. 1:29; 13:9; 1 Tim. 1:9.
n Rom. 2:22; 7:3; 13:9; 1 Cor. 6:9.
o Rom. 1:29–30; 1 Cor. 6:9–10; Eph. 4:28.
p Col. 3:9; 1 Tim. 1:10; 4:2; Titus 1:12.
q Rom. 1:29; 7:7–8; Eph. 5:3–5; Col. 3:5.

1. Ceremonial laws—referring to the priesthood, sacrifices, temple, cleanness, and so forth, are now fulfilled in Jesus. These laws are no longer binding on us because Jesus is our priest, temple, sacrifice, cleanser, and so forth.

2. Civil laws—referring to those pertaining to the governing of Israel as a nation ruled by God. Since we are no longer a theocracy, we believe these laws, while insightful, are not directly binding on us. Romans 13:1–7 says to obey even non-Christian governments because God will work through them too.

3. Moral laws—forbidding such things as rape, stealing, and murder. These laws are still binding upon us, even though Jesus fulfilled their requirements through His sinless life.

In summary, categories 1 and 2 are no longer binding. But category 3 is. Sex with one's wife during her menstrual cycle is a ceremonial law that fits in category 1. Therefore, it is no longer binding. This means it is not a sin and it is permissible for a man to have sexual intercourse with his wife during her menstrual cycle. This also permits us to engage in other aspects of the old covenant law that are fulfilled, not continued in the new covenant, and therefore no longer binding now that Jesus Christ has fulfilled the law for us.

Question 2: Is it helpful?

There are many reasons why menstrual sex may be beneficial. For couples who enjoy frequent sex, it allows them to do so without taking a break each month. Some women report increased pleasure from menstrual sex because their bodies have increased sensitivity. And because of the hormonal changes that accompany menstruation, some women report being more passionate during this time than normal.

There are also reasons why this may not be beneficial. Some women report increased pain and sensitivity that causes discomfort during their cycle, which means that abstaining for a few days or finding a sexual alternative they are comfortable with may be best. And for a husband, he may simply be turned off by this very natural but messy time of the month for his wife.

Question 3: Is it enslaving?

Because it is an occasional act, it is difficult to imagine this act becoming addictive. So long as both the husband and wife are okay with it, then there is little to worry about.

Role-Playing

Role-playing is when one or both spouses assume roles to act out in character as part of their flirtation and lovemaking. For some couples, this includes not only essentially functioning like an actor or actress playing a role, but also dressing up to heighten the sense of fantasy.

Question 1: Is it lawful?

Since the Bible does not speak directly to this issue, it is technically lawful, as neither biblical nor governmental law forbids it.

Question 2: Is it helpful?

There are some reasons role-playing could be helpful to some, though not all, couples. Some couples with good imaginations find it fun. For example, a couple we know has a background in theater, and this is the kind of thing they find mutually fun. If one or both spouses are shy but want to be adventurous, this kind of fun play can help. With the desire to stay faithful to each other for the entirety of their lives, admittedly things can get sexually predictable, and this kind of play can keep things interesting for a couple.

Role-playing can also be an unhelpful part of married sex. If either or both of you are fantasizing about anyone else during role-playing, then you are committing the sin of lust. This includes having your spouse dress up like someone else. Spouses who feel dirty or uncomfortable sexually because of sin they have committed or that has been committed against them sometimes disassociate. This means they mentally "check out" during sex with their spouses. For such people, role-playing could be a means by which they are neglecting working through their issues to have normal and healthy sexual relations with their spouses, and it is therefore sinful. It should never be used to avoid oneness with who you each truly are.

Question 3: Is it enslaving?

If role-playing becomes too frequent, a couple is likely in trouble. If they are more likely to connect sexually in a fantasy than in reality, they need to determine why. While this sort of thing may be an acceptable part of their relationship, if it becomes too frequent or the primary way they become sexually aroused, then this could be a sign of it becoming inordinately central to their sex life and therefore unhealthy.

Sex Toys

Question 1: Is it lawful?

Sex toys are legal, and they are also not forbidden in the Bible.

Question 2: Is it helpful?

Sex toys may be beneficial to a marriage. They can heighten the pleasure for one or both partners.

On the other hand, there are also many reasons why sex toys may not be beneficial to a marriage. If a toy is being used in secret without the presence or knowledge of the spouse, then oneness is not being practiced. If your spouse feels left out because his or her mate is more interested in the toy than in him or her, leaving your spouse to feel neglected, then there is a problem. Likewise if the toy becomes the center of sex and not an enhancement aid.

Question 3: Is it enslaving?

If the toy becomes more desirable and frequent than normal intercourse, then its use is unhealthy. Various toys do things that the human body simply cannot do. This means that, while they can be exciting and fun lovemaking accessories, the couple needs to also continually and honestly discuss if they are occupying an unhealthy and inordinate place in their sex life.

Note: In purchasing these kinds of toys, you may be best served to purchase them from one of the more discreet Web sites, including those overtly run by Christians, where there are not photos of nude people and pornography, as there are on most Web sites and in most retail stores.

Birth Control

Question 1: Is it lawful?

This is a very complicated question.[45] We differentiate between no birth control; contraception, which literally means "against (*contra*) conception" (such methods prevent conception, whereby a sperm fertilizes an egg); and abortion, which terminates the life of a fertilized egg. Following are five levels of birth control:

Level 1: No birth control. Some Christian couples determine to only use prayer in their family planning. As a result, they simply enjoy normal marital sexual relations and trust that if God desires for them to have a child, He will provide according to His timing. Family planning by simply praying and trusting that whatever happens is God's good will is acceptable.

However, when this form of family planning is dogmatically pushed as the only faithful Christian option, such foolish legalism can lead to both self-righteousness and harm.

Level 2: Natural birth control. Natural methods include any method of contraception where pregnancy is prevented by abstaining from vaginal sexual intercourse on days when the wife is likely to be fertile. The most popular natural method is the calendar–rhythm method, which has been replaced by more effective methods, such as the symptothermal method and the standard-days method. Fertility computers are a new development in contraceptive technology. They make these natural methods easier to use by telling a couple when sex will or won't result in pregnancy. The Roman Catholic Church approves the use of natural methods. Abstaining from normal sexual intercourse does not necessarily require abstaining from all sexual activity.

Natural birth control methods have many benefits. Unlike most forms of birth control, they involve the husband, are free, require no surgery, no chemicals, no devices, no drugs, have no side effects, are safe, reversible, and can also be used with other methods, such as a condom during fertile times. One of the potential difficulties is that they require discipline and planning, which not everyone is equally faithful to ensure. In conclusion, natural birth control is permissible for a Christian couple.

Level 3: Nonabortive birth control. Like the natural methods, nonabortive birth control methods also seek to influence the timing of conception but do so by taking either temporary or permanent additional measures.

Temporary nonabortive birth control methods are generally barrier methods and include all methods that permit intercourse but that prevent the sperm and egg from coming together. Perhaps the most common is the male condom. There is a reported 3 to 12 percent pregnancy rate per year with typical use.[46] Bringing the risk to 3 percent requires using the condom correctly every time.[47]

If the husband or wife is infected with a sexually transmitted disease, male condoms are the best method for preventing the transmission of it. Complaints about male condoms include the unromantic need to stop in the moment of passion to put one on, diminished pleasure sensation for the husband, and the physical barrier between a husband and wife in their moment of greatest intimacy.

Female barrier methods include the diaphragm, contraceptive sponge, cervical caps, and female condoms. Spermicides are also considered barrier methods because they kill sperm before they can reach a waiting egg, thus preventing fertilization.

There are many factors to consider with these methods. Sponges can be dangerous if left in too long, even causing infection or toxic shock. Female condoms are less effective than male condoms but can be inserted up to eight hours before intercourse, thereby enabling greater spontaneity than the male condom.[48] Most spermicides (including sponges with spermicides) use nonoxynol-9, which can create infection in some women but is helpful alongside other methods, such as a condom, by killing sperm. The use of spermicides, however, has been linked to a higher-than-normal incidence of severe birth defects—twice the rate of nonusers.[49] The cervical cap, or diaphragm, has been a favorite contraceptive method in Europe since the mid-1800s, and is considered 60 to 80 percent effective. It can be inserted more than a day before intercourse so as to allow greater spontaneity.[50] The reported failure rate of the diaphragm is anywhere from 2 to 20 percent.[51]

Permanent nonabortive birth control methods are those chosen by couples who have decided not to have any more children. This can be achieved either by female sterilization, also called tubal ligation, or vasectomy for men. Both of these methods require minor surgery and should be considered permanent, although it is theoretically possible, but difficult, to have a reversal.

To summarize, levels 1–3 are options for Christian couples to prayerfully consider without concern that they may terminate a fertilized egg and thereby take a human life. At the next level, we tread into murky waters that are more difficult to discern for Christian couples.

Level 4: Potentially abortive birth control. "The pill" is a categorical term for more than forty types of oral contraceptives, which are also referred to as "birth control pills" and sometimes "combination pills" because they contain a mixture of estrogen and progestin. These hormonal contraceptives are designed to override the female body's normal cycle and "trick" the brain into believing she's already pregnant, thus preventing the release of an egg from the ovaries. Today fifty to sixty million women worldwide take the pill each day, and it is the most widely prescribed drug in the world.[52]

Combined pills are generally very effective, as long as they are taken correctly: "With careful use, fewer than 1 woman in every 100 will get pregnant in a year. With less careful use, 3 or more women in every 100 will get pregnant in a year."[53] Hormonal methods of birth control tend to be more effective than others but also pose greater health risks. They include systems with estrogen and progestin, such as combination oral contraceptives, the vaginal ring, and the contraceptive patch, as well as estrogen-free methods such as the mini-pill (progestin-only pills), contraceptive injectables, and some intrauterine devices (IUDs). These are the same drugs used in emergency contraceptive pills. There are no hormonal methods available for men.

Generally speaking, hormonal birth control methods run the risk of causing an abortion. Because female hormones direct the process of ovulation, synthetic hormones can be used to keep an egg from being released so that sperm are not able to fertilize it. These same synthetic hormones can also prevent a fertilized egg from implanting in a woman's uterus and growing into a baby.

Author, pastor, and pro-life leader Randy Alcorn has written a great deal on this subject.[54] He said that there is not one but rather three purposes for birth control pills. First, the pill exists to inhibit ovulation, which is its primary means of birth control. Second, the pill thickens the cervical mucus with the effect that it becomes more difficult for sperm to travel to the egg. Third, the pill thins and shrivels the lining of the uterus so that it is unable or less able to facilitate the implantation of the newly fertilized egg. On this last point, Alcorn said, "Reproductive endocrinologists have demonstrated that Pill-induced changes cause the endometrium to appear 'hostile' or 'poorly receptive' to implantation."[55] Furthermore, "Magnetic Resonance Imaging (MRI) reveals that the endometrial lining of Pill users is consistently thinner than that of nonusers—up to 58 percent thinner."[56]

The first two purposes of birth control pills are contraceptive in nature and therefore acceptable for use by a Christian couple. The third function of birth control pills, however, is potentially abortive in that it seeks to disrupt the ongoing life of a fertilized egg. That potentiality is incredibly controversial; thus, faithful Christians who are staunchly pro-life and believe that life begins at conception are divided over the issue. Some Christian organizations have issued extensive reports after years of examining the issue, and those with further questions would be well served by reading their findings online.[57]

As Christian leaders who are admittedly not medically trained, we do not encourage members of our church to use the pill, but also would not discipline a member for sin if she did, as this is a complicated and unclear issue. Upon learning these things many years ago, we stopped using the birth control pill out of conscience.

Level 5: Abortive murder. Abortion is taking a human life, or murder, by killing a fertilized egg. Abortions include medical procedures of various kinds as well as RU-486, or the morning-after pill. Other items that cause abortion are the intrauterine device (IUD) and Norplant, which do not prevent conception but prevent implantation of an already fertilized ovum. The result is an abortion, the killing of a conceived person.[58]

Thomas W. Hilgers, MD, of the Mayo Graduate School of Medicine in Rochester, Minnesota, studied more than four hundred articles on the subject and concluded, "The primary action of the IUD must be classified as an abortifacient."[59]

Some will argue that there is a difference between a child in a mother's womb and one outside it. Scripture uses the same word (*brephos*) for Elizabeth's unborn child, John the Baptizer, in Luke 1:41, 44, as is used for the unborn baby Jesus in Mary's womb in Luke 2:12, and also for the children brought to Jesus in Luke 18:15.[60]

In summary, we would support couples practicing levels 1–3 of birth control, urge those considering level 4 to prayerfully and carefully reflect on their decision, and oppose any couple considering level 5, unless there were extremely weighty extenuating circumstances, such as a tragic situation in which both the mother and her unborn child cannot both live, and so a choice must be made.

Question 2: Is it helpful?

Birth control can be beneficial under a number of circumstances. It can work well for many, from a newly married couple waiting awhile to begin their family so they can finish their education, to a marriage that is suffering from such things as illness, injury, adultery, or dire poverty.

But birth control can also be compelled by sinful motivations. These can include putting lesser priorities like career above higher priorities like family or greedily wanting to make as much income as possible to the exclusion of everything else, and not incur the costs of child raising; being selfish and not wanting to have to care for a child; or immaturely not wanting to take on the responsibility that good parenting requires.

To answer this question, every couple needs to continually and honestly examine their hearts' motivations.

Question 3: Is it enslaving?

A couple who use birth control for too long can become so used to being without children that they never do actually seek to have children as God intends. And while using birth control for many years isn't enslaving, it's important to understand that waiting too long to start a family can decrease the odds of getting pregnant and having a healthy birth. Women are most fertile between the ages of eighteen and twenty-five. Fertility begins a slow decline at age twenty-five and speeds up dramatically at thirty-five.[61]

Cosmetic Surgery

Question 1: Is it lawful?

It is legal to have cosmetic surgery. Furthermore, it is not forbidden in Scripture, because it is a more recent medical invention.

Globally, most cosmetic surgeries are performed on women. In the United States, according to the American Society of Plastic Surgeons, the top five female cosmetic surgical procedures are: (1) breast augmentation, (2) nose reshaping, (3) liposuction, (4) eyelid surgery, and (5) tummy tuck. In the United States the top five male cosmetic surgical procedures are: (1) nose reshaping, (2) eyelid surgery, (3) liposuction, (4) breast reduction, and (5) hair transplantation.

For the last ten years, breast augmentation has been the most popular plastic surgery procedure internationally. The *ISAPS Global Survey* reveals a new trend, with liposuction representing 18.8 percent of all surgical procedures, followed by breast augmentation at 17 percent, and blepharoplasty (upper or lower eyelid lift) at 13.5 percent, rhinoplasty (nose reshaping) at 9.4 percent, and abdominoplasty ("tummy tuck") at 7.3 percent.

Opinion polls conducted across Europe point to a widening acceptance of cosmetic surgery as a part of normal life—particularly among the young. And the official Web site of the American Society of Plastic Surgeons[62] has as its largest segment of visitors eighteen to twenty-four-year-olds, accounting for 25 percent of Web traffic.[63]

Question 2: Is it helpful?

There are many reasons cosmetic surgery may be beneficial. It can make us more attractive to our spouses. And if our appearance is improved, we feel more comfortable being seen naked by our spouses, which can increase our freedom in lovemaking.

On the negative side, as with any medical procedure, there is the danger of death, injury, or disfigurement. There are also cost factors to consider, as good medical care can be expensive. If a spouse is getting the surgery to attract the attention of others, particularly sexual attention, then the motivation is sinful. And if your spouse wants you to look like another person because he or she is lusting after that person, then the motivation is sinful.

Question 3: Is it enslaving?

People who become obsessed with achieving some sort of ever-elusive perfect appearance can take cosmetic surgery too far. Actress Heidi Montag, for example, young and beautiful to begin with, underwent no fewer than ten such surgeries in one day. She has since gone on record with great regret, mourning her obsession with physical perfection and the toll it has taken on her body.[64]

In extreme cases, the clinical Body Dismorphic Disorder (BDD) is used to explain why some people think they look ugly or deformed when they in fact appear normal. Clinically "BDD is diagnosed in people who are 1) concerned about a minimal or nonexistent appearance flaw, 2) preoccupied with the perceived flaw (think about it for at least an hour a day), and 3) experience clinically significant distress or impaired functioning as a result of their concern."[65] For such people cosmetic surgery can become dangerously enslaving.

Cybersex

Question 1: Is it lawful?

Cybersex is when a couple communicates sexually through technology, including phone, photo, video, text, e-mail, chat, and video conferencing. Often included in cybersex is masturbation. Cybersex with anyone other than your spouse, and cybersex that includes seeing or discussing anyone other than your spouse sexually, is a sin of lust and heart adultery. But cybersex with one's spouse is permissible. If you choose to practice cybersex, you should use extreme caution that the images cannot become public in any way. Practically speaking, this can be nearly impossible.

Question 2: Is it helpful?

There are reasons that cybersex may be beneficial to your marriage. It allows a couple to remain in intimate contact throughout the course of a day when they are separated because of such things as work, or to continue some semblance of a sex life when they cannot be physically together, such as during a business trip or military deployment.

Question 3: Is it enslaving?

There are also reasons why cybersex may be too risky for some couples. If someone has a history of sinning sexually in this manner, he or she may be spiritually "weak" in this area and as a result be best served by simply abstaining, much like a former alcoholic choosing to abstain from all alcohol for safety reasons. And depending what technology is used, there is the risk that the event could be shared beyond the marriage.

Sexual Medication

Question 1: Is it lawful?

Living in a fallen world with a fallen body means that not everything will always work as God intended. So we use diet supplements and medications as needed in the pursuit of health and wellness. The Bible does not forbid this. In fact Luke, who wrote much of the New Testament, was a medical doctor. So medicine in general is lawful.

Question 2: Is it helpful?

When there are medically related sexual complications, medication can be helpful. For example, the man who struggles with impotence or premature ejaculation may find some help from his doctor conducting a physical and prescribing a medication. Similarly, a woman with such things as a hormone imbalance may also find help with a visit to a wise doctor. Obviously these kinds of situations can be very embarrassing. But out of love for one's spouse, it is good to be humble enough to seek wise medical help and resume normal sexual activity if at all possible.

Question 3: Is it enslaving?

As a general rule, sexual medication is not enslaving. Perhaps the only concern is that someone might want to push the human body beyond normal functions and frequencies with the use of sexual medication. Such a thing may suggest an underlying perversion or sinful sexual addiction.

Marital Sexual Assault

Question 1: Is it lawful?

The Bible repeatedly condemns sexual assault. This includes the horrendous account of the rape of women,[a] including one woman who is gang-raped to the point of death,[b] another who is raped by her brother,[c] and the sexual

---

a Gen. 34:1–5; 1 Sam. 13:1–15; Ezek. 22:11.
b Judg. 19:22–30.
c 2 Sam. 13:1–21.

assault of wives and virgins as the aftermath of a nation's being conquered.[a] The Bible condemns sexual assault and never excuses or diminishes its horror. In Deuteronomy 22:25–29, for example, we see great concerns for the violated woman and death by stoning for her male abuser.

"Researchers have estimated that sexual assault occurs in 10–14 percent of all marriages."[66] Men who sexually assault their wives commonly also abuse them in multiple other ways, including verbal, mental, emotional, and spiritual abuse, in addition to battering the women physically. These beatings and rapes have little, if anything, to do with sex. Instead, they are haunting degradations.

Under no circumstances is sexual assault of any sort acceptable in marriage. The Bible teaches husbands, "Love your wives, just as Christ loved the church,"[b] and "dwell with them with understanding, giving honor to the wife, as to the weaker vessel."[c] This biblical understanding explains why, in colonial Massachusetts from 1640 to 1680, the Puritans enacted the first laws anywhere in the world against wife beating. Family violence was considered sinful, and neighbors were expected to be watchful for abuse and intervene as needed to protect wives and children.[67] If there has been sexual assault in your marriage, you need professional and possibly even legal help for healing and protection.

Question 2: Is it helpful?

There is nothing beneficial from anyone, usually the wife, enduring assault or abuse of any kind, especially sexually. If you are a woman believing the lies that it is your fault because you make him angry, that you don't deserve to be treated any better, or that suffering a life of terror is better than the consequences of divorce, you are in danger. And unless he gets professional help and truly changes—which is rare—things will get worse. The studies on this issue confirm that such men can also become jealous of their own children and escalate violence against their pregnant wives, assault their own children, including molesting them, and even kill their wives.

---

a Isa. 13:16; Lam. 5:11; Zech. 14:2.
b Eph. 5:25.
c 1 Peter 3:7.

Question 3: Is it enslaving?

When someone is attacked, we call it assault. As horrible as that is, what is even worse is torment. Torment is when you're assaulted and you cannot escape, like prisoners of war and those who are held captive in slavery. For some women, their version of slavery and captivity in torment is called marriage.

Tragically, some women settle for this kind of life. Or perhaps even worse, they tell their church leadership, only to be told that when Paul said our bodies belongs to our spouses, it means the wife is basically a piece of property. Some tragic studies report that an assaulted wife who goes to her church instead of the police or a licensed counselor will be less likely to get ongoing emotional help and legal protection, but rather will return to the abuse in the name of submission—as if the abuse is what God had in mind for her.

Anytime a husband or church leader demands the wife obey the Bible without doing the same for the husband, he is sanctioning abuse. Any professing Christian man who assaults his wife is a heretic preaching a false gospel with his life. A man is to love his wife as Christ loves the church. Jesus' relationship with the church is not one of rape, violence, abuse, and degradation. There is no place for any assault—including sexual assault—in any marriage.

Conclusion

As you can see, there are many sexual acts that are technically acceptable according to God and our government. We are not saying that they are mandatory. Our aim is to open up the topic to married couples so they can lovingly, graciously, and prayerfully discuss what they would like to do and not do. We want to emphatically state that our intent is to inform heterosexual married couples of the full range of their sexual freedoms. But we do not want this information to be used in any way to force someone to act against his or her conscience.

Part 3

THE LAST DAY

11

REVERSE-ENGINEERING
YOUR LIFE AND MARRIAGE

The end of a thing is better than its beginning.
—Ecclesiastes 7:8

The most important day of your marriage is the last day.

Too many couples put their best energies into the first day. The cake, flowers, clothing, and photos have to be perfect. But while a wonderful first day of marriage is important, it's the last day that really counts.

Will the last day of your marriage come prematurely through divorce? Will the last day of your marriage be filled with regrets as you stand over the coffin of your spouse? Or by God's grace will the last day be a day to rejoice in a life lived together and remember the gift your spouse was to you while on earth?

To finish well on the last day of your marriage, it is not enough to simply have passion and principles. You also need a plan. Marriages start with passion and over the years accrue principles, but apart from a plan, the passion and principles are powerless. You must choose whether you will spend your time making plans or excuses.

This chapter will be a thorough homework assignment of sorts to make that plan. It comes out of the most painful season of our life and marriage. I (Mark) had been pushing myself hard for more than a decade since Mars Hill Church opened up, and I had overextended myself so much that I had worn out my adrenal glands and gotten an ulcer.

Some Sundays were brutal. I would sneak in a back door, avoiding any human contact because I simply did not have the emotional wherewithal to spend an entire day hearing of trauma in people's lives and arguing with religious types. At times I actually found myself nodding off on the side of the stage before one of the five services I preached live. So I foolishly started drinking energy drinks all day to power through Sundays. After preaching I would go home to sit in the dark and watch television, obviously depressed. Before long I was stressed each night at bedtime as the anxiety over whether or not I could sleep became constant. I felt like a car that could not turn off. I had multiple stress-related symptoms—heartburn, headaches, nervous eye twitch, aggressive driving, constant low-level anger, high blood pressure, and self-medicating with foods and drinks packed with fat, sugar, and simple carbohydrates, along with caffeine.

Perhaps a few months after things had reached this level, a godly friend in the church, named Jon, scheduled a meeting with me. God had laid it on his heart to speak some wisdom into my life. He did so with great humility, and in that meeting he gave me some insights that were life changing.

Jon had been taking notes on how he organized his life, things he had learned, and what he felt the Holy Spirit had asked him to tell me. His wisdom was a priceless gift. He called it "Reverse Engineering." The big idea is to anticipate life forward and live it backward.

In the ensuing months I sought to add to his wisdom as much insight as I could. For the church, I met with some of the pastors of the largest churches in America to see what I could learn about how we needed to reorganize. For my health, I found a doctor named John who was a naturopath and ordained pastor and started doing what he told me to do, which has changed my life. For my awareness, I started reading and studying material written by doctors and counselors on stress and adrenaline.[1] For my marriage, I started spending more energy than ever to connect with Grace and get our time together. I also met with a Bible-based counselor a few times to inquire what I needed to learn and how I could best serve Grace as her friend. I limped along through the winter and spring, making adjustments along the way.

That summer we took a family vacation in central Oregon with Grace's family. During the vacation, I kept a legal-size yellow pad handy and started writing out a lengthy homework assignment for Grace. I laid out the big ideas I had learned from Jon and others. And I listed pages of questions for her, leaving room for her to write out her answers.

I did not want to boss Grace around and tell her how our new life together would be. But I needed to help her by drawing out her thoughts, dreams, fears, and needs—or what Peter means when commanding husbands to be "understanding" with their wives.

After packing the kids and our stuff into the Suburban, everyone settled in for the roughly eight-hour drive home. Then I handed Grace the yellow legal pad of questions and kindly asked her to spend the time answering the questions and discussing with me anything she wanted to as she worked though them. I knew this would likely be my only chance to get my Martha-esque wife to sit down for eight hours doing planning. As her name would suggest, she was gracious and obliged.

One pastor said there are only four ways to live your life, and by choosing the last one on his list, we hoped to reverse-engineer our marriage.[2]

1. Reaction—passively dominated by urgencies and pushy people. This results in a life that is a frazzled mess, disorganized, without a sense of priorities, half-finished tasks, running late, and a frantic lifestyle.
2. Conformity—succumbing to the fear of man and just being and doing what everyone else wants, which is not necessarily following God's will for you and your family. This results in a boring life where everyone but God is pleased, and the person who is easily pushed around keeps busy and productive but is not passionate or free.
3. Independence—nonconforming rebellion in the name of freedom marked by doing only what you want and ignoring godly authority over you. This results in a life of defiance, independence, immaturity, self-reliance, and foolishness.
4. Intentionality—*reverse-engineering* your life and living it prayerfully and purposefully, journaling your thoughts throughout the day, and using silence and solitude to hear from God and organize your life. This results in a life that is purposeful and passionate to God's glory, people's good, and your joy.

I had been prone to living a life vacillating between reaction and independence. Grace was prone toward reaction and conformity. As always, we were opposites. In short, we were a mess. There was always a plan for the church, along with goals, timelines, and staff meetings to keep us on task.

But we had no such guiding wisdom for our marriage and family. My hope was to use the Reverse-Engineering wisdom to help us construct a framework document from which to guide our decision making. An edited version of what Grace filled out and what has guided our marriage, family, and ministry ever since is below. We have reworked portions of it over the years and found it to be an incredible benefit. We hope you and your spouse use it and do the following:

1. Honestly look back on the big moments of frustration, anger, disappointment, grief, and failure in your marriage. How much of what you experienced was the result of not preparing for the future and working toward it together? How many holidays, vacations, and other times that could have been wonderful ended up awful because you were both expecting the other person to take care of things the way you were hoping and felt disappointed when things did not come together? Rather than repeating your failures and frustrations, seek to put the trials and opportunities before you as something to work on together rather than between you to fight over. How could a wise plan that is acted upon help improve your future together? Turn your pains into plans.

2. Answer the questions prayerfully and carefully on your own. Accept that this will take time and work. But it is less costly to make a plan and work on it than it is to fail and be frustrated over and over.

3. Schedule an entire day together to share your answers and work through what the priorities and plans will look like for your family. Do not meet in a public place where you can be interrupted. Do not have your phones on or check the Internet, as you want to be fully present and not distracted. Ideally, this would be an overnight somewhere romantic and a nice place to dream of your future together and plan for it.

4. Redo the Reverse-Engineering questions as life changes, things happen, and adjustments need to be made.

5. Grow old together, stay married, remain one, be fruitful, and refuse to settle for distant parallel lives in a functional but cold, lonely marriage.

Reverse-Engineering

Reverse-Engineering Principles

Marriage affects and is affected by the rest of your life. One frequent problem with marriage books is that they focus solely on the marriage without considering the rest of life. This chapter is intended to help you work on your life—not just in it—by getting both your shoulder-to-shoulder and face-to-face time regularly. For this to happen, the following principles are helpful:

- You need a wise plan to do your work.
  "The plans of the diligent lead surely to plenty, but those of everyone who is hasty, surely to poverty" (Prov. 21:5).

- Your plan needs to include outside counsel.
  "Without counsel, plans go awry, but in the multitude of counselors they are established" (Prov. 15:22).

- Your plan must be biblical and prayerful.
  "Commit your works to the LORD, and your thoughts [plans] will be established" (Prov. 16:3).

- Your plan will change as God leads you.
  "A man's heart plans his way, but the LORD directs his steps" (Prov. 16:9).

Reverse-Engineering Plans

1. Your plan must be written down or typed up.
2. Consider the downside in all your planning. Be realistic, not unduly idealistic. What could go wrong? How could it fail? Where are the liabilities?
3. Include fun and margin for error. Any plan that does not have some intentional fun will lead to a boring life. Any plan that does not leave a margin for error in such things as time, money, and energy is destined to fail.
4. Account for your priorities. Work from conviction according to your priorities and not from guilt piled on you by Satan, other people, or your own faulty thinking.

5. Accept the size of your plate and fill it—some people have big plates; others have small plates. Be honest about what you can do and how much you can handle.

6. Take something off your plate whenever something is put on. Don't stack your plate until things fall off and your life is a mess.

7. Sync your plan with your family. The weekly sync meeting with your spouse is key. Imagine a company never meeting as a staff and how miserably they would fail.

8. Use simple systems and write everything in one place, like a notebook. Most systems are too complex. The key is to keep everything in one simple place together—prayer requests, grocery lists, to-do lists, and things God is teaching you.

9. Every night spend a few minutes organizing your priorities for the next day in your notebook. Do not simply have a long to-do list. Have a priority list and do the highest priority items first. You will never finish everything on your list, so don't worry about it. Do what is most important first and the rest as you are able.

10. Seek planning principles from wise people. Everyone has something to teach you if you are humble enough to learn. Learn from both the successes and failures of other people. Keep notes in your notebook of what you learn. As you meet people who are particularly skilled in such things as budgeting, investing, organizing their homes, and training their kids, ask if they would be willing to meet with you for a short meeting. If they agree, do not waste their time, but instead show up with a list of questions, thank them for meeting with you, ask your questions respectfully, listen carefully, don't talk too much, and take copious notes.

11. Cultivate personal mindfulness. Keep notes on what works and does not work in everything from holidays to vacations as well as in your weekly routine. This allows you to make changes and learn from your mistakes.

12. Get a life coach if you can. If you can afford a professional Christian life coach to help you get organized, that might be a great investment. I spent a few years being coached professionally, and Grace has also been coached for a year.

13. Work *on* your life, not just *in* it. Most people waste their whole lives working *in* them. If you take the time to work *on* your life, you will save time and increase your odds of living passionately, fruitfully, and joyfully. Life is to be more than just feeling overwhelmed every day with more work than can be done, which results in being exhausted and overwhelmed.

Reverse-Engineering Rhythms

- Daily—pray with and for each other, read the Bible and other good books; eat at least one meal together without the television on or other distractions, such as the phone; visit for at least twenty minutes each day getting your face-to-face time, checking in to see how each other is doing; and go to bed together.
- Weekly—have a date night, attend church together, attend a Christian small group or class together, and sabbath together with a purposeful and restful day off. To make all of this happen, schedule and keep a weekly sync meeting. This is a weekly calendar meeting on a time other than date night. This meeting is solely for you as a couple to go through your calendar and budget, getting and keeping your life unified as one. At this meeting you decide how to juggle your responsibilities, how to serve and pray for each other, who and what to say no to, how to get ready for the holidays, and how to plan out vacations and other events, well in advance.
- Quarterly—go for a romantic and fun overnight getaway together. Before you go, talk about your fears and expectations, and work together to make fun memories and connect.
- Annually—if finances allow, take a planned vacation that you are both excited about. Work together to get ready for the vacation, and while on vacation, do not allow other people and technology to rob you of time together. Guard this time and enjoy it. If you cannot afford it, consider inexpensive ways to take a vacation, including house swapping for a week or two with someone you know and trust.

Reverse-Engineering Questions

The following questions are ones we have used. You are free to add to them and delete them as needed.

Step 1: Write Out Priorities

Write out no more than seven priorities and place them in order of importance (for example, physical health, spiritual health, marital intimacy, parenting success). We have given you the first four that we always recommend be in this order. The truth is most people will have full plates doing these four, and even people with big plates cannot usually do more than seven things well. For you, this means that anything not on the list has to be cut, because it is prohibiting you from doing your God-given priorities. And by Christian, we mean reading your Bible, praying, attending church, being in a group or class, and so forth. Anything beyond that, such as church leadership in an unpaid position, should be in category 5 or lower.

1. Christian
2. Spouse
3. Parent
4. Worker (both paid and unpaid, such as being a stay-at-home mom)
5. Ministry volunteer
6.
7.

Step 2: Envision the Future

Pick a day for yourself, your family, and your ministry, sometime in the future (two years, five years, ten years), and envision that day. Pick a day that is far enough down the road that you have to work to get there, but is not so distant that you cannot see it. This has to be a reasonable look into a future date you can see. To do this, answer as many pertinent, specific questions about life on that day as you can reasonably generate. Following are some examples:

Spiritual
1. What church will you attend? Will it be a church with strong men leading so that the husband is motivated, engaged, and committed?
2. What criteria will determine what church you choose?
3. How will you serve in that church and be a blessing?
4. How many weeks of the year will you attend services?
5. What group or class will you be involved in to serve and grow?

6. How will you regularly teach your children about Jesus from the Bible?
7. How can you be vitally connected relationally in community with other people in the church, including older people you learn from, peers you walk with, and younger people you are mentoring?
8. What will evangelism and mission look like to your neighbors and community?
9. What will your spouse and children think about Jesus because of you?
10. Who in your spheres of family, friends, coworkers, and neighbors will you have shared the gospel with, seeking their salvation?
11. Husbands, how will you "wash her in the Word"?

Health

1. How much will you weigh?
2. How much will you exercise weekly?
3. What will have changed about your appearance?
4. How many hours of sleep will you average a night?
5. How many times a week will you nap?
6. On which day will you sabbath?
7. What will your diet be?

Employment

1. What will your job be?
2. How will your work be an act of worship unto God?
3. What can you do to become the best employee possible?
4. How will you need to guard your job from consuming your life and overtaking your other higher priorities?

Financial

1. What is your job? Will the wife be working?
2. Where do you work?
3. How much money do you make?
4. How is your money spent?
5. How is your money saved?
6. How is your money invested?

7. How is your money tithed?
8. What is your insurance, medical, and dental package?

Marriage

1. How often do you pray together?
2. When is your date night?
3. How do you take better care of each other?
4. Why has your love grown?
5. How has your home become a place for unplanned connecting?
6. What brings you together?

Sex

1. What have you and your spouse experimented with?
2. How often are you intimate?
3. What things are different?
4. How have you and your spouse changed physically and sexually?
5. What is different about your bedroom?

Family

1. How many children will you have?
2. How old will your children be?
3. How will they be educated at that time?
4. What special attention will each child need regarding his or her maturation up to that day?
5. Which family and friends are you closest with as a family?
6. What activities will you allow your children to participate in, and how will you manage all the time required for them?
7. Who will be the primary caregiver of your child(ren)?

Housing and Living

1. Where will you live?
2. How will the home be laid out (square feet, yard, deck, hot tub, bedrooms, bathrooms, garage, family room, dining space, kitchen, parking for guests, etc.)?

3. How will you use your home for your family, hospitality, and ministry?
4. How long is your commute?
5. How can you redeem your commute by making calls, listening to Bible teaching, etc.?
6. What vehicle will you drive?
7. What are the features of your home (parking for guests, square footage, size of yard, number of bedrooms, home study, hardwood floors, air conditioning)?
8. What furniture and appliances will you have gotten rid of or acquired?

Bedroom

1. What will your bedroom be like?
2. How will your bedroom be romantic and a private oasis to connect?
3. Will you have a TV in your bedroom? If you have a TV, keep it separate and not at the foot of your bed.
4. Will you have a private master bath?
5. Will you have a lock on your bedroom door for privacy if you have children?
6. Will you keep all your work (computers, projects, desk, etc.) out of your bedroom?

Technology

1. How will you use technology but not allow it to rule your life?
2. When will you agree to have the phone and computer off (dinnertime, while in your bedroom, on date night)?

Extended Family

1. Which close relatives are not living?
2. What is your relationship like with each close family member (for example, mom, dad, brother, sister, grandparent)?
3. How will you include or not include your extended family in vacations and holidays?
4. What has changed with your extended family?

Friends

1. How will you be better friends to each other?
2. Who are your closest friends?
3. Which people have you dropped as friends?
4. What things do you do with your friends?
5. Who no longer has your direct phone number or e-mail address?

Learning

1. What areas have you studied deeply?
2. How many books have you read by that date? What are some of the titles?
3. What other learning experiences have shaped you (such as, conferences, mentors, spiritual disciplines)?
4. How many minutes do you read each day?

Daily Habits

1. How will you pray alone and together each day?
2. How will you ensure that you eat at least one meal together nearly every day?
3. What will be your daily Bible reading?

Weekly Routine

1. What will your ideal week look like?
2. What will your weekly Sabbath day look like? What will you do to relax as a family and have fun together?
3. What weekly routines will provide anchors to your schedule (family movie night, family breakfast before school, etc.)?
4. What small group or class will you be in together at your church to grow and serve?

Weekly Date Night

1. What will your weekly date night look like? Where will you go? What will you do? How will you connect?

2. If you have kids, how will you get child care for date night (for example, co-op with other families where you rotate who takes the kids each week, finding a single woman in the church who wants to learn about marriage and kids who will volunteer, pay a babysitter, ask relatives)?

Quarterly Getaway

1. Will you go away together roughly once a quarter for at least one night? What will you do together?
2. What and where sounds fun and romantic to connect?

Step 3: Identify and Make Changes

Many people only change when crisis demands it. We go on a diet after our doctors say we are in danger, make a budget after we are in significant debt, and go to marriage counselors or pastors after the possibility of divorce has been put on the table. It is far wiser and more hopeful to make changes before crisis demands it.

Changes

1. What three things do you hope have changed with your spouse? Yourself? Your ministry? Your family? Your job?
2. What top three emotion-, time-, and energy-wasters do you need to drop immediately?
3. What three changes in your life would make the biggest difference?
4. What three things do you need the most (such as, different car, gym membership, computer, home office, cell phone, high-speed wi-fi at home)?
5. What obstacles are keeping you from living by your convictions (for example, a cluttered house, no budget, lack of prayer time)?

People

1. List the people who take but don't give toward a friendship, and determine if you are to continue serving them, back off your involvement in their lives, or simply make them take care of themselves.
2. Who do you need to distance yourself from because they are taking time, money, or energy away from your first priorities?

Handing Off

1. List all the things you can hand off to someone else (for example, ordering groceries online and having them delivered, mowing your lawn, doing your taxes, household projects, watching kids, running errands, outsourcing dry cleaning and ironing, scheduling appointments, answering your phone).

In closing, the rest of your marriage is really up to you and your spouse. Our hope is that you will take the principles and tools in this book to set in motion a great life together by God's grace and the Holy Spirit's power. We are praying that this book will be not merely information, but something God will use for your marital transformation. Jesus loves you, and so do we. The goal is progress, not perfection.

ACKNOWLEDGMENTS

We want to thank Jesus Christ for rising from death to give us the forgiveness of sins and power of the Holy Spirit to live new lives for the Father's glory and our joy.

We want to thank the elders of Mars Hill Church and their families for loving us well and seeking our good in Christ along with the rest of the people who call Mars Hill home.

We want to thank Mars Hill Executive Pastors Jamie Munson and Dave Bruskas and their families for being amazing to work with and for your friendship.

We want to thank the deacons, community group leaders, and Redemption Group leaders of Mars Hill Church who, along with various other leaders, make Mars Hill a very loving and special place.

We want to thank Pastor Mike Wilkerson and his wife, Trisha, for their work to help hurting people, including his book *Redemption*.

We want to thank Pastor Justin Holcomb and his wife, Lindsey, for their help to sexual assault victims, including their book *Rid of My Disgrace*. Justin's research for our book is also greatly appreciated.

We want to thank Mike Anderson for helping to get the message of this book out, along with Anthony Ianniciello and Jesse Bryan and Jordan Butcher as well as the other members of the Preaching and Theology, and Media and Communications branches of Mars Hill.

We want to thank Deacon Nathan Burke, who serves as a very faithful and wise assistant in everything.

We want to thank the Driscoll kids, aka "the fab 5," for being understanding while Mommy and Daddy were working on the book.

We want to thank the church planters and wives of Acts 29, who amaze us with their courage and fruitfulness.

We want to thank Grace's faithful female friends who prayed for, encouraged, and served her very specifically throughout the writing process, and who gave her helpful feedback on the early manuscript.

We want to thank Brian Hampton and our friends at Thomas Nelson who took a real risk publishing this book. They have been a real blessing to us every step of the way, and we are sincerely thankful for their partnership.

We want to thank Kristen Parrish for editing this book and making it much better through her gracious wisdom.

We want to thank our critics who help us continually serve Jesus better by the grace of God.

We want to thank anyone who helps us get the word out about this book because we do believe it can be used of God to help people, which is why we wrote it.

ABOUT THE AUTHORS

Pastor Mark Driscoll is the founding pastor of Mars Hill Church, which started in 1996 as a small Bible study led by him and his wife, Grace, at their home in Seattle, Washington—the least churched city in America at the time. Since then, Mars Hill has been recognized as the 54th largest, 30th fastest-growing, and 2nd most-innovative church in America by *Outreach* magazine and exploded with upwards of nineteen thousand people meeting across thirteen locations in four states.

Pastor Mark is one of the world's most downloaded and quoted pastors. He holds a B.A. in Speech Communication from Washington State University and a masters degree in Exegetical Theology from Western Seminary. He is the author of fifteen books and the co-founder of the Acts 29 Network, which has planted over 400 churches in the United States, in addition to thirteen other nations. He also founded the Resurgence, which is receives close to six million visits annually and services Christian leaders through books, blogs, conferences, and classes. Grace Driscoll delights in being a stay-at-home mom and helping raise the Driscoll's three sons and two daughters. She is also a graduate of the Edward R. Murrow School of Communication at Washington State University, where she earned a B.A. in Public Relations.

Find out more about Pastor Mark and Grace at PastorMark.tv

NOTES

Chapter 1

1. http://www.marshillchurch.org/search/results?q=peasant+princess.

Chapter 2

1. Those who would like to learn more about the life of Katharine von Bora Luther can read Dolina MacCuish, *Luther and His Katie* (Fearn, Tain, Ross-shire, Scotland: Christian Focus, 1983); and William Henry Lazareth, *Luther on the Christian Home: An Application of the Social Ethics of the Reformation* (Philadelphia: Muhlenberg Press, 1960). Perhaps the best and most concise treatment of Katharine's life comes from Kirsi Stjerna's *Women and the Reformation* (Malden, MA: Blackwell, 2009).
2. Lazareth, *Luther on the Christian Home*, 19.
3. Ibid.
4. Ibid., 22–23.
5. Ibid., 25.
6. Ibid., 30.
7. John Piper and Justin Taylor, *Sex and the Supremacy of Christ* (Wheaton, IL: Crossway Books, 2005), 228.
8. Lazareth, *Luther on the Christian Home*, 32.
9. Ibid.
10. Ibid., 32.
11. Ibid., 74.
12. Saint Aelred of Rievaulx, *Spiritual Friendship* (Collegeville, MN: Cistercian Publications, 2005).
13. Alan Loy McGinnis, *The Friendship Factor: How to Get Closer to the People You Care For* (Minneapolis: Augsburg Fortress, 2004).
14. Dee Brestin, *The Friendships of Women: The Beauty and Power of God's Plan for Us* (Colorado Springs: David C. Cook, 2008).
15. John Gottman and Nan Silver, *The Seven Principles for Making Marriage Work* (New York: Three Rivers Press, 1999), 17.
16. Ibid., 19–20.
17. Augustine, *Confessions* 2.5.10.

18. Augustine, *Confessions* 4.8.13.

19. This concept (as well as some other big ideas in this chapter) is adopted from Steve Wilkins, *Face to Face: Meditations on Friendship and Hospitality* (Moscow, ID: Canon Press, 2002).

20. Charles Ray, *Mrs. C. H. Spurgeon (A Biography of Susannah Spurgeon)* (Pasadena, TX: Pilgrim Publications, 1905), 51–52.

21. Dietrich Bonhoeffer, *Letters and Papers from Prison* (New York: Simon and Schuster, 1997), 42–43.

22. The concept of shoulder-to-shoulder and face-to-face marriages came up in a conversation I had with pastor and author Douglas Wilson.

23. Alan Loy McGinnis, "When Tears Are a Gift from God," in *The Friendship Factor: How to Get Closer to the People You Care For* (Minneapolis: Augsburg Fortress, 2004), 122–30.

24. C. S. Lewis, *The Four Loves* (Orlando: Harcourt Brace, 1988), 71.

25. Gary Thomas, *Sacred Marriage: What If God Designed Marriage to Make Us Holy More Than to Make Us Happy?* (Grand Rapids: Zondervan, 2000), 13.

Chapter 3

1. Gary Chapman, *The Five Love Languages: How to Express Heartfelt Commitment to Your Mate* (Chicago: Moody Press, 1995).

2. W. Bradford Wilcox and Steven L. Nock, "What's Love Got to Do with It? Equality, Equity, Commitment, and Women's Marital Quality," *Social Forces* 84, no. 3 (March 2006): 1321–45.

3. W. Bradford Wilcox, "Five Myths on Fathers and Families," *National Review*, June 19, 2009, http://www.nationalreview.com/articles/227738/five-myths-fathers-and-family-w-bradford-wilcox.

4. Ibid.

5. Sally Lloyd-Jones, *The Jesus Storybook Bible: Every Story Whispers His Name* (Grand Rapids: Zondervan, 2007), 200.

6. "New Marriage and Divorce Statistics Released," The Barna Group, March 31, 2008, http://www.barna.org/barna-update/article/15-familykids/42-new-marriage-and-divorce-statistics-released.

7. W. Bradford Wilcox is director of the National Marriage Project and associate professor of sociology at the University of Virginia. Professor Wilcox is also a member of the James Madison Society at Princeton University. Wilcox's research focuses on marriage and cohabitation, and on the ways religion, gender, and children influence the quality and stability of American family life.

He has published articles on marriage, cohabitation, parenting, and fatherhood in the *American Sociological Review, Social Forces*, the *Journal of Marriage and Family*, and the *Journal for the Scientific Study of Religion*. His first book, *Soft Patriarchs, New Men: How Christianity Shapes Fathers and Husbands* (Univ. of Chicago Press, 2004), examines the ways the religious beliefs and practices of American Protestant men influence their approach to parenting, household labor, and marriage. Professor Wilcox has received the following two awards from the American Sociological Association Religion Section for his research: the Best Graduate Paper Award and the Best Article Award (with Brian Steensland et al.). His research has also been featured in the *New York Times*, the *Wall Street Journal*, the *Washington Post, USA Today*, the *Boston Globe*, the *Los Angeles Times*, NBC's *Today Show*, CBS News, and many NPR stations.

8. W. Bradford Wilcox, *Soft Patriarchs, New Men: How Christianity Shapes Fathers and Husbands* (Chicago: University of Chicago Press, 2004), 158.

9. Ibid., 162–63.

10. Ibid., 162–63.

11. Ibid., 199–200.

12. W. Bradford Wilcox, "Religion and the Domestication of Men." *Contexts: Understanding People in Their Social Worlds* 5 (2006): 42–46.

13. Wilcox, *Soft Patriarchs*, 182.

14. Ibid., 195.

15. Ibid., 196; "Religion and the Domestication of Men," 42–46; Nicholas H. Wolfinger and W. Bradford Wilcox, "Happily Ever After? Religion, Marital Status, Gender, and Relationship Quality in Urban Families," *Social Forces* 86 (2008): 1311–37, http://www.fcs.utah.edu/~wolfinger/SFfinal.pdf.

16. Wolfinger and Wilcox, "Happily Ever After? 1311–37.

17. Ibid.

18. Wilcox, *Soft Patriarchs*, 178.

19. Edward O. Laumann et al., *The Social Organization of Sexuality: Sexual Practices in the United States* (Chicago: University of Chicago Press, 1994), 501.

20. Vaughn R. A. Call and Tim B. Heaton, "Religious Influence on Marital Stability," *Journal for the Scientific Study of Religion* 36, no. 3 (September 1997): 386–87, http://www.jstor.org/stable/1387856.

21. Wolfinger and Wilcox, "Happily Ever After? 1311–37.

22. Tim B. Heaton and Edith L. Pratt, "The Effects of Religious Homogamy on Marital Satisfaction and Stability," *Journal of Family Issues* 11, no. 2 (June 1990): 191–207, doi: 10.1177/019251390011002005.

23. Call and Heaton, "Religious Influence on Marital Stability," 382–92.

24. Laumann et al., 502.

25. Wilcox and Nock, "What's Love Got to Do with It? 1321–45.

26. Ibid.

27. Ibid.

28. Christopher G. Ellison, Amy M. Burdette, and W. Bradford Wilcox, "The Couple That Prays Together: Race and Ethnicity, Religion, and Relationship Quality Among Working-Age Adults," *Journal of Marriage and Family* 72 (August 2010): 963–75.

29. Schools like Reformed Theological Seminary and Covenant Theological Seminary have many of their very expensive graduate-level classes online for free to download. Also, all of my [Mark's] sermons are free in audio and video format at www.MarsHill.com.

Chapter 4

1. For further reading on the theological underpinnings of these doctrines, please read John Piper and Wayne Grudem, *Recovering Biblical Manhood and Womanhood* (Wheaton, IL: Crossway, 2006; it is also available for free online at http://www.cbmw.org/rbmw/); Andreas J. Kostenberger and David W. Jones, *God, Marriage, and Family* (Wheaton, IL: Crossway, 2010); and Wayne Grudem, *Evangelical Feminism and Biblical Truth: An Analysis of More Than 100 Disputed Questions* (Sisters, OR: Multnomah, 2004).

2. Wendy Virgo, *Influential Women* (Grand Rapids: Kregel Publications, 2009), 201.

3. Paul David Tripp, *War of Words* (Phillipsburg, NJ: P&R Publishing, 2000), 71.

4. Edward T. Welch, *When People Are Big and God Is Small: Overcoming Peer Pressure, Codependency, and the Fear of Man* (Phillipsburg, NJ: P & R Publishing, 1997), 14.

5. For more on this issue, *Running Scared* by Edward T. Welch (Greensboro, NC: New Growth Press, 2007) is very helpful, and we borrow many ideas from him in this portion of the chapter.

6. Raymond C. Ortlund Jr., "Male-Female Equality and Male Headship," in *Recovering Biblical Manhood and Womanhood: A Response to Evangelical Feminism*, eds. John Piper and Wayne Grudem (Wheaton, IL: Crossway Books, 2006), 95.

7. Ibid., 105.

8. John 5:19.

9. John 5:30.

10. Patrick Erwin, "Seven Signs You Have a Work Spouse," *CNN Living*, November 10, 2008, http://www.cnn.com/2008/LIVING/worklife/11/10/cb.seven.signs .work.spouse/index.html. Accessed January 16, 2012.

11. "Will an Office 'Romance' Make You More Successful?" *CNNMoney .com*, January 27, 2006, http://money.cnn.com/2006/01/27/news/funny/ office_marriage/index.htm?cnn=yes; Irene S. Levine, "The Work Spouse: Indispensable Friend or Playing with Fire?" *Psychology Today*, December 16, 2010, http://www.psychologytoday.com/blog/the-friendship-doctor/201012/ the-work-spouse-indispensable-friend-or-playing-fire.

Chapter 5

1. John Gottman and Nan Silver, *The Seven Principles for Making Marriage Work* (New York: Three Rivers Press, 1999), 2.

2. Ibid., 26–47.

3. Gary Thomas, *Sacred Marriage: What If God Designed Marriage to Make Us Holy More Than to Make Us Happy?* (Grand Rapids: Zondervan, 2000), 96.

4. See Martin H. Manser, et al., *Zondervan Dictionary of Bible Themes: The Accessible and Comprehensive Tool for Topical Studies* (Grand Rapids: Zondervan, 1999). Manser identifies various examples and causes of Jesus Christ's anger, including petty legalism in religious observance (Matt. 15:3; 23:1–4; Mark 3:4–5); attempts to prevent access to Him (Mark 10:14); and people leading others into sin (Matt. 18:6–7; Mark 9:42; Luke 17:1–2). Jesus demonstrated His anger when He purged the temple (Matt. 21:12–13; Mark 11:15–17; Luke 19:45–46; John 2:14–16) and when He cursed the fig tree (Mark 11:14; Matt. 21:19). Jesus also spoke words in anger against demons (Matt. 17:18; Mark 9:25; Luke 9:42; see also Mark 1:25–26; Luke 4:35), against His disciples (Luke 9:55–56; see also Matt. 16:23; Mark 8:33), against Pharisees (Matt. 23:13; see also Matt. 12:34; 15:7–9, cf. Mark 7:6–8; Matt. 23:15–16, 23–33; Luke 11:42–44; 13:15; John 8:44), against unbelief (Matt. 17:17; Mark 9:19; Luke 9:41; see also Matt. 12:39–45, cf. Luke 11:29–32; Mark 8:38; Luke 11:50–51), against false prophets (Matt. 7:15), against the rich (Luke 6:24–26), and against unrepentant cities (Matt. 11:20; see also Matt. 11:21–24; Luke 10:13–15). Jesus expresses the anger of God the Father (John 3:36; see also Matt. 5:21–22, 29; 22:7, 13; 25:30, 46; Luke 21:23). We also read of the anger of the glorified Christ against the unbelieving world (Rev. 6:16) and against the wayward church (Rev. 2:16; see also Rev. 2:5, 22–23; 3:3, 16).

5. *Yours Affectionately, John Wesley: The Rev John Wesley and His Correspondents* (Museum of Methodism, Wesleys Chapel, 49 City Road, London EC1Y 1AU, March 2003), 16.

6. Ibid., 21.

7. Doreen Moore, *Good Christians Good Husbands? Leaving a Legacy in Marriage and Ministry* (Geanies House, Fearn Scotland: Christian Focus Publications, 2004), 57.

Chapter 6

1. Jerry Ropelato, "Internet Pornography Statistics," Top Ten Reviews, 2008, http://www.internet-filter-review.toptenreviews.com/internet-pornography-statistics.html.

2. "Porn Profits: Corporate America's Secret," *ABC News*, May 27, 2004, http://abcnews.go.com/Primetime/story?id=132370&page=1; or "American Porn: Corporate America Is Profiting from Porn—Quietly," *ABC News*, January 28, 2003, http://www.freerepublic.com/focus/f-news/832158/posts.

3. Ropelato, "Internet Pornography Statistics."

4. Ibid.

5. Ibid.

6. Ibid.

7. Ibid.

8. Ibid.

9. Jane D. Brown, et al., "Sexy Media Matter: Exposure to Sexual Content in Music, Movies, Television, and Magazines Predicts Black and White Adolescents' Sexual Behavior," *Pediatrics* 117, no. 4 (April 2006): 1018–27, http://pediatrics.aappublications.org/cgi/content/abstract/117/4/1018.

10. Elizabeth Terry-Humen, et al., "Trends and Recent Estimates: Sexual Activity Among U.S. Teens," *Child Trends Research Brief 2006–2008* (Washington, DC, 2006): 2.

11. John C. LaRue Jr., "Churches and Pastors Rate Sexual Issues," *Your Church* 51, no. 1 (January/February 2005): 88, http://www.christianitytoday.com/yc/2005/001/13.88.html.

12. Ropelato, "Internet Pornography Statistics."

13. For example, see Debra Boyer and Susan Breault, "Danger for Prostitutes Increasing, Most Starting Younger," *Beacon Journal* (September 21, 1997); Melissa Farley, Howard Barkan, et al., "Prostitution, Violence Against Women, and Posttraumatic Stress Disorder," *Women & Health* 27, no. 3 (1988): 37–49; David Finkelhor and Angela Browne, "The Traumatic Impact of Child Sexual

Abuse," *American Journal of Orthopsychiatry* 55, no. 4 (1985): 530–41; and Mimi H. Silbert, "Compounding Factors in the Rape of Street Prostitutes," in *Rape and Sexual Assault*, vol. 2, ed. A. W. Burgess (New York: Garland, 1988), 77.

14. Phyllis Chesler, "A Woman's Right to Self-Defense: The Case of Aileen Carol Wuornos," in *Patriarchy: Notes of an Expert Witness* (Monroe, ME: Common Courage Press, 1994).

15. Simon P. Wood, trans., "The Fathers of the Church," *Clement of Alexandria* (New York: Fathers of the Church, 1954), xxxiii, 175.

16. H. Wayne House, "Should Christians Use Birth Control?" *Christian Research Institute*, http://www.equip.org/articles/should-christians-use-birth-control. Accessed January 16, 2012. *Ocellus Lucanus*, text and commentary by Richard Harder (Berlin, 1926).

17. William G. Cole, *Sex in Christianity and Psychoanalysis* (New York: Oxford University Press, 1966).

18. Vern L. Bullough, *Sexual Variance in Society and History* (New York: Wiley Interscience, 1976).

19. Thomas Aquinas, *Summa Theologica*, trans. Fathers of the English Dominican Province (New York: Benziger Brothers, 1948), III, qu. 41, art. 4, http://www.newadvent.org/summa/5041.htm.

20. Belden C. Lane, "Two Schools of Desire: Nature and Marriage in Seventeenth-Century Puritanism," *Church History* 69 (2000): 372–402.

21. Stephanie Coontz, *Marriage, a History: How Love Conquered Marriage* (New York: Penguin, 2006), 86; Pierre Guichard and Jean-Pierre Cuviller, "Barbarian Europe," in *A History of the Family, Volume I: Distant Worlds, Ancient Worlds*, eds. Andre Burguiere et al., (Cambridge, MA: Belknap Press, 1996), 331.

22. Charles Lewis, "Avoid 'Misuse of Sex' in Marriage, Canadian Bishops Warn," *National Post*, January 28, 2011, http://life.nationalpost.com/2011/01/28/canadian-bishops-warn-against-%e2%80%98misuse-of-sex%e2%80%99-in-marriage/. Accessed January 16, 2012.

23. Mary Pride, *The Way Home: Beyond Feminism, Back to Reality* (Wheaton, IL: Crossway Books, 1985), 27.

24. William Whately, *A Bride-Bush, or a Direction for Married Persons* (London, 1616), 18–20; and William Gouge, *Of Domestical Duties* (London: J. Haviland, 1622), 221. Quoted in Lane, "Two Schools of Desire," 372–402.

25. "How Sexual Experiences Become Addictions," http://www.new-life.net/sex2.htm. Accessed February 2011.

Chapter 7

1. Justin S. and Lindsey A. Holcomb, *Rid of My Disgrace* (Wheaton, IL: Crossway, 2011), 33–34.

2. Ibid.

3. Miroslav Volf, *The End of Memory: Remembering Rightly in a Violent World* (Grand Rapids, MI: Wm. B. Eerdmans, 2006), 75.

4. Holcomb and Holcomb, *Rid of My Disgrace*, 28–29. Their definition of rape, and different types of rape, is helpful as well:

   The definition of rape is straightforward in nature. As defined in the *American Journal of Psychiatry*, rape is. . . "forced sexual intercourse that may be heterosexual or homosexual which involves insertion of an erect penis or an inanimate object into the female vagina or the male anus; in both sexes, rape may also include forced oral or anal penetration" (C. Faravelli, A. Glugni, S. Salvatori, V. Ricca, "Psychopathology After Rape," *American Journal of Psychiatry* 61, no. 8 [2004]: 1483–1485). The definition of rape then proceeds to be broken down into varying categories based on the relationship between the victim and the perpetrator. Acquaintance rape is rape in which the victim knows the offender but has had no dating relationship with him or her. Date rape is rape in which the victim knows the perpetrator through some level of social interaction. Statutory rape is rape in which intercourse may be a consensual event but the act between the two individuals violates the age-of-consent law. Spousal rape is rape in which the victim and perpetrator are married or participating in a *de facto* living situation (Alan Wertheimer, *Consent to Sexual Relations*, Cambridge Studies in Philosophy and Law [Cambridge: Cambridge University Press, 2003], 74–77). 213n5.

5. Ibid., 15.

6. Martin Luther, "The Seven Penitential Psalms" (1517) in *Day by Day We Magnify Thee: Daily Readings for the Entire Year* (Minneapolis: Fortress, 1982), 321.

7. See Mike Wilkerson, "Introduction" in *Redemption: Freed by Jesus from the Idols We Worship and the Wounds We Carry* (Wheaton, IL: Crossway, 2011), 21–40.

8. A. W. Tozer, *The Knowledge of the Holy* (New York: Harper, 1978).

9. Such as Linda Dillow and Lorraine Pintus, *Intimate Issues* (Colorado Springs, CO: Waterbrook Press, 1999); Edward T. Welch, *When People Are Big and God Is Small* (Phillipsburg, NJ: P&R Publishing, 1997); C. J. Mahaney, *Humility: True Greatness* (Sisters, OR: Multnomah Publishers, 2005);

Timothy S. Lane and Paul David Tripp, *How People Change* (Greensboro, NC: New Growth Press, 2006); David Powlison, *Seeing with New Eyes* (Phillipsburg, NJ: P&R Publishing, 2003); Jani Ortlund, *Fearlessly Feminine* (Sisters, OR: Multnomah Publishers, 2000); and Carolyn Mahaney, *Feminine Appeal* (Wheaton, IL: Crossway, 2004).

10. See http://www.ccef.org.

11. Holcomb and Holcomb, *Rid of My Disgrace*, 63.

12. www.kidsneedtoknow.com.

Chapter 8

1. William M. Struthers, *Wired for Intimacy: How Pornography Hijacks the Male Brain* (Downers Grove, IL: InterVarsity Press, 2009), 85.

2. Ibid., 95.

3. Ibid., 96.

4. Ibid., 97.

5. Ibid., 98–99.

6. Ibid., 105.

7. Ibid., 67.

8. David Leafe, "Playboy mansion? More like a squalid prison: Former Playmates tell of 'grubby' world inside Hugh Hefner's empire," Daily Mail, December 31, 2010, http://www.dailymail.co.uk/femail/article-1342643/Hugh-Hefners-Playboy -mansion-like-squalid-prison-say-Playmates.html. Accessed January 16, 2012.

9. E.g., *The Girls Next Door, Gene Simmons* [of Kiss] *Family Jewels, Married to Rock*, and *Rock of Love with Bret Michaels*.

10. "Laurence Fishburne's Daughter: How I Got Started Making Porn," *UsMagazine.com*, August, 10, 2010, http://www.usmagazine.com/moviestvmusic/ news/laurence-fishburnes-daughter-how-i-got-started-making-porn--2010108.

11. Drew Pinsky and S. Mark Young, *The Mirror Effect: How Celebrity Narcissism Is Endangering Our Families—and How to Save Them* (New York: Harper, 2010).

12. Ibid., 201–6.

13. Robert Jensen, "Cruel to Be Hard: Men and Pornography," *Sexual Assault Report* (January/February 2004), 33–48.

14. Ted Bundy, interview by James Dobson, "Fatal Addiction: Ted Bundy's Final Interview," January 23, 1989, http://www.pureintimacy.org/piArticles/ A000000433.cfm.

15. William M. Struthers, *Wired for Intimacy: How Pornography Hijacks the Male Brain* (Downers Grove, IL: InterVarsity Press, 2009), 37–38.

16. Naomi Wolf, "The Porn Myth," *New York Magazine*, 2003, http://nymag.com/nymetro/news/trends/n_9437/.

17. Struthers, *Wired for Intimacy*, 20.

18. Robert Grove and Blaise Zerega, "The Lolita Problem," *Red Herring*, January 2, 2002, 47–53.

19. Gail Dines, *Pornland: How Porn Has Hijacked Our Sexuality* (Boston, MA: Beacon Press, 2010), 142.

20. Ibid., 94.

21. Struthers, *Wired for Intimacy*, 106.

22. In addition to the resources cited in this chapter, the following may be helpful. For the spouse who has been cheated on with porn: Vicki Tiede, interview by Tim Challies, "Spiritual Healing in the Midst of a Husband's Addiction to Pornography," January 12, 2011, http://www.challies.com/interviews/spiritual-healing-in-the-midst-of-a-husbands-addiction-to-pornography (this is a woman's gospel-centered insights to healing from a husband's pornography addiction); Debra Laaser, *Shattered Vows: Hope and Healing for Women Who Have Been Sexually Betrayed* (Grand Rapids: Zondervan, 2008); Linda Dillow and Lorraine Pintus, *Intimate Issues* (Colorado Springs: Waterbrook Press, 1999) (which includes a chapter addressing what to do when the husband is failing in the area of pornography); Laurie Hall, *An Affair of the Mind* (Colorado Springs: Focus on the Family Publishing, 1998); Fred and Brenda Stoeker and Mike Yorkey, *Every Heart Restored: A Wife's Guide to Healing in the Wake of a Husband's Sexual Sin* (Colorado Springs, CO: Waterbrook Press, 2010). Additional resources: www.pureintimacy.org (this is a Focus on the Family and Dr. James Dobson website, which has a great deal of information about intimacy, sexual addiction, and sexuality in general); http://xxxchurch.com/ (which has a ton of resources and recommendations, including accountability software); Stephen Arterburn, Fred Stoeker, and Mike Yorkey, *Every Man's Battle: Winning the War on Sexual Temptation One Victory at a Time* (Colorado Springs, CO: Waterbrook Press, 2000); Douglas Wilson, *Fidelity: What It Means To Be a One-Woman Man* (Moscow, ID: Canon Press, 1999); Mark Driscoll, *Porn-Again Christian: A Frank Discussion on Pornography and Masturbation*, http://relit.org/porn_again_christian/ (a free e-book for men); Mark Driscoll, "Sexual Sin" in Religion Saves sermon series (Mars Hill Church, Seattle, WA, February 3, 2008), http://www.marshillchurch.org/media/religionsaves/sexual-sin (a sermon available in audio, video, and transcript form on overcoming sexual sin); and http://www.covenanteyes.com/ (online accountability software).

Chapter 9

1. This idea is borrowed from Joseph and Linda Dillow, Peter and Lorraine Pintus, *Intimacy Ignited* (Colorado Springs: NavPress, 2004).

2. C. J. Mahaney, *Humility: True Greatness* (Sisters, OR: Multnomah, 2005), 13.

3. John Gottman and Nan Silver, *The Seven Principles for Making Marriage Work* (New York: Three Rivers Press, 1999), 4.

4. According to author Gary Thomas, during a lecture he gave at a retreat for Mars Hill Church elders and elders' wives.

5. William Henry Lazareth, *Luther on the Christian Home: An Application of the Social Ethics of the Reformation* (Philadelphia: Muhlenberg Press, 1960), 226n82.

6. Ted L. Huston and Anita L. Vangelisti, "Socioemotional behavior and satisfaction in marital relationships: A longitudinal study," *Journal of Personality and Social Psychology* 61, no. 5 (1991): 721–33.

7. This was calculated based on which group had the highest percentage in the "weekly" through "four times a week or more" categories. The findings reported here were calculated by a Docent researcher using publicly available data from the 2008 General Social Survey (GSS), accessible online here: http://www.norc.org/GSS+Website. Data were weighted appropriately.

8. See Edward O. Laumann et al., *The Social Organization of Sexuality: Sexual Practices in the United States* (Chicago: University of Chicago Press, 1994); and Edward O. Laumann, Robert T. Michael, and Gina Kolata, *Sex in America: A Definitive Survey* (New York: Warner Books, 1994).

9. Vaughn Call, Susan Sprecher, and Pepper Schwartz, "The Incidence and Frequency of Marital Sex in a National Sample," *Journal of Marriage and the Family* 57, no. 3 (August 1995): 639–52, http://www.jstor.org/stable/353919.

10. Tara Parker-Pope, "When Sex Leaves the Marriage," *New York Times*, June 3, 2009, http://well.blogs.nytimes.com/2009/06/03/when-sex-leaves-the-marriage/.

11. Ibid.

12. Ibid.

13. Kathleen Deveny, "We're Not In the Mood," *Newsweek*, June 30, 2003, http://www.newsweek.com/2003/06/29/we-re-not-in-the-mood.html.

14. Edmund S. Morgan, "The Puritans and Sex," *The New England Quarterly* 15, no. 4 (December 1942): 593, http://classjump.com/Sateren/documents/6016350500.pdf.

15. Archibald D. Hart, *Unmasking Male Depression* (Nashville: Thomas Nelson, 2001).

16. Ibid., 38–41.

17. Ibid., 39–40.

18. Linda Carroll, "Men sleep better beside mate; women worse," MSNBC.com, October 10, 2007, http://www.msnbc.msn.com/id/21091112/.

19. Not all of these are by Christians, and we do not agree with everything that these resources teach, but they are helpful when read with discernment: Douglas E. Rosenau, *A Celebration of Sex* (Nashville: Thomas Nelson, 2002); Lou Paget, *How to Be a Great Lover* (New York: Broadway Books, 1999); Lou Paget, *Orgasms* (New York: Broadway Books, 2004); Lou Paget, *How to Give Her Absolute Pleasure* (New York: Broadway Books, 2000); Ian Kerner, *She Comes First* (New York: HarperCollins, 2004); Kevin Leman, *Sheet Music* (Carol Stream, IL: Tyndale, 2003); http://christiannymphos.org/; and http://www.sexualpositionsfree.com/.

20. Shaunti Feldhahn, *For Women Only* (Sisters, OR: Multnomah, 2004).

21. Shaunti Feldhahn, "Keeper of the Visual Rolodex," in *For Women Only*, 109–35.

22. Daniel Akin, *God on Sex* (Nashville: Broadman and Holman, 2003), 213.

23. Joseph C. Dillow, *Solomon on Sex* (Nashville: Thomas Nelson, 1977), 133.

24. John G. Snaith, *The New Century Bible Commentary: The Song of Songs* (Grand Rapids: Wm. B. Eerdmans, 1993), 101.

25. Joseph and Linda Dillow, Peter and Lorraine Pintus, *Intimacy Ignited* (Colorado Springs: NavPress, 2004), 221.

26. Akin, *God on Sex*, 215.

27. Tremper Longman III, *Song of Songs: The New International Commentary on the Old Testament* (Grand Rapids: Wm. B. Eerdmans Publishing Co., 2001), 195.

Chapter 10

1. See Patrick Carnes, *Don't Call It Love* (MN: Gentle Press, 1991), 38ff.

2. Eric Griffin-Shelley, *Sex and Love: Addiction, Treatment, and Recovery* (Westport, CT: Praeger Publishers, 1997), 52.

3. Archibald D. Hart, *The Sexual Man* (Nashville: Thomas Nelson, 1994), 48–49.

4. Harold Leitenberg, Mark J. Detzer, and Debra Srebnik, "Gender Differences in Masturbation and the Relation of Masturbation Experience in Preadolescence and/or Early Adolescence to Sexual Behavior and Sexual Adjustment in Young Adulthood," *Archives of Sexual Behavior* 22 (April 1993): 87–98. Sample was 280 respondents from two "Introduction to Psychology" classes.

5. See Debby Herbenick et al., "Sexual Behavior in the United States: Results

from a National Probability Sample of Men and Women Ages 14–94," *Journal of Sexual Medicine* 7, suppl. 5 (October 2010): 255–65, doi: 10.1111/j.1743-6109.2010.02012.x.

6. Michael Reece et al., "Sexual Behaviors, Relationships, and Perceived Health Among Adult Men in the United States: Results from a National Probability Sample," *Journal of Sexual Medicine* 7, suppl. 5 (October 2010): 291–304, doi: 10.1111/j.1743-6109.2010.02009.x.

7. Ibid.

8. Ibid.

9. Ibid.

10. Ibid.

11. Ibid.

12. See Herbenick et al., "Sexual Behaviors, Relationships, and Perceived Health Among Adult Women in the United States," 277-900.

13. Ibid.

14. Ibid.

15. Ibid.

16. Ibid.

17. Ibid.

18. Ibid.

19. Ibid.

20. Ibid.

21. Robert B. Hughes and J. Carl Laney, *Tyndale Concise Bible Commentary* (Wheaton, IL: Tyndale House Publishers, 2001), 250.

22. Joseph C. Dillow, *Solomon on Sex* (Nashville: Thomas Nelson, 1977), 27.

23. William M. Struthers, *Wired for Intimacy: How Pornography Hijacks the Male Brain* (Downers Grove, IL: InterVarsity Press, 2009), 172.

24. Herbenick et al., "Sexual Behavior in the United States," 255–65.

25. Ibid.

26. Herbenick et al., "Sexual Behaviors, Relationships, and Perceived Health Among Adult Women in the United States," 277–90.

27. Ibid.

28. Reece et al., "Sexual Behaviors, Relationships, and Perceived Health Among Adult Men in the United States," 291–304.

29. Ibid.

30. Dillow, *Solomon on Sex,* 27.

31. Marvin H. Pope, *Song of Songs* (New Haven, London: Yale University Press,

2008), 499. For more on the garden, see Shalom M. Paul ("A Lover's Garden of Verse: Literal and Metaphorical Imagery in Ancient Near Eastern Love Poetry," in *Tehillah le-Moshe: Biblical and Judaic Studies in Honor of Moshe Greenberg*, ed. Mordechai Cogan et al. [Winona Lake, IN: Eisenbrauns, 1997], 99–110), who comments that the garden "functions not only as a favorite assignation (with its esthetic and sensual delights and hideaways) for lovers' trysts and *afresco amour,* but may simultaneously allude to female sexuality and fertility in general and to the pudenda in particular," with examples from Sumerian, Akkadian, and Egyptian love poetry (100).

32. Tremper Longman III, *Song of Songs: The New International Commentary on the Old Testament* (Grand Rapids: Wm. B. Eerdmans Publishing Co., 2001), 155.

33. Ibid., 195

34. Herbenick et al., "Sexual Behavior in the United States." 255–65.

35. Ibid.

36. Ibid.

37. Herbenick et al., "Sexual Behaviors, Relationships, and Perceived Health Among Adult Women in the United States," 277–90.

38. Ibid.

39. Reece et al., "Sexual Behaviors, Relationships, and Perceived Health Among Adult Men in the United States," 291–304.

40. Ibid.

41. Ibid.

42. Thomas R. Schreiner, *Forty Questions About Christians and Biblical Law* (Grand Rapids, MI: Kregel, 2010), 67.

43. Ibid., 69.

44. Ibid., 67.

45. I have previously explored the topic of birth control in the sermon series Religion Saves (http://www.marshillchurch.org/media/religionsaves/birth-control) as well as in chapter 1 of my book based on that series, "Birth Control" in *Religion Saves: And Nine Other Misconceptions* (Wheaton, IL: Crossway, 2009), 15–44.

46. William R. Cutrer and Sandra L. Glahn, *The Contraception Guidebook: Options, Risks, and Answers for Christian Couples* (Grand Rapids: Zondervan, 2005), 74.

47. Ibid., 75.

48. Ibid., 77.

49. John Jefferson Davis, *Evangelical Ethics: Issues Facing the Church Today*, 3rd ed. (Phillipsburg, NJ: P & R Publishing Co., 2004), 35.

50. Cutrer and Glahn, *The Contraception Guidebook: Options, Risks, and Answers for Christian Couples* (Grand Rapids: Zondervan, 2005), 82–83.

51. Davis, *Evangelical Ethics,* 35.

52. Ibid.

53. Health Service Executive, "Your Sexual Health: Methods of Contraception," http://www.healthpromotion.ie/sexual_health/contraception/. Also see Planned Parenthood, "Birth Control Pill – How Effective Are Birth Control Pills," February 9, 2008, http://www.plannedparenthood.org/health-topics/ birth-control/birth-control-pill-4228.htm.

54. One of his great works on the subject is his book *Does the Birth Control Pill Cause Abortions?* You can download the entire book or read condensations of the book for free here: http://www.epm.org/books/does_the_birth_ control_pill_cause_abortionsDetail.php. In addition, articles on abortion, birth control, and related issues can be found here: http://www.epm.org/ resources-prolife_abortion.html.

55. H. I. Abdalla et al., "Endometrial Thickness: A Predictor of Implantation in Ovum Recipients?" *Human Reproduction* 9, no. 2 (1994): 363–65, quoted in Randy Alcorn, "Does the Birth Control Pill Cause Abortions: A Short Condensation," Eternal Perspective Ministries, http://www.cpm.org/ resources/2010/Feb/17/short-condensation-does-birth-control-pill-cause-a/. Accessed January 16, 2012.

56. J. M. Bartoli et al., "The Normal Uterus on Magnetic Resonance Imaging and Variations Associated with the Hormonal State," *Surgical and Radiologic Anatomy* 13 (1991): 213–20; B. E. Demas, H. Hricak, and R. B. Jaffe, "Uterine MR Imaging: Effects of Hormonal Stimulation," *Radiology* 159 (1986): 123–26; S. McCarthy, C. Tauber, and J. Gore, "Female Pelvic Anatomy: MR Assessment of Variations during the Menstrual Cycle and with Use of Oral Contraceptives," *Radiology* 160 (1986): 119–23; and H. K. Brown et al., "Uterine Junctional Zone: Correlation Between Histologic Findings and MR Imaging," *Radiology* 179 (1991): 409–13. Quoted in Alcorn, "A Short Condensation of Does the Birth Control Pill Cause Abortions?"

57. See Focus on the Family, "Position Statement: Birth Control Pills and Other Hormonal Contraception," http://www.focusonlinecommunities.com/servlet/ JiveServlet/download/74132-1459/Position_Statement-Birth_Control_Pills_ and_Other_Hormonal_Contraception.pdf;jsessionid=B66C9D89FEA819C5 0EE8E33BA39AE436.node0. Accessed January 16, 2012; and Trustees of the Christian Medical and Dental Associations, "Possible Post-Fertilization Effects

of Hormonal Birth Control," Hormonal Birth Control, September 1998, http://www.cmda.org/wcm/CMDA/Issues2/Beginning_of_Life1/Abortion1/Ethics_Statements2/Hormonal_Birth_Contr.aspx.

58. Randy Alcorn, *Prolife Answers to ProChoice Arguments* (Sisters, OR: Multnomah Publishers, 1994), 118.

59. Thomas W. Hilgers, "The Intrauterine Device: Contraceptive or Abortifacient?" *Minnesota Medicine* (June 1974): 493–501.

60. Charles H. H. Scobie, *Ways of Our God: An Approach to Biblical Theology* (Grand Rapids: Eerdmans, 2003), 834.

61. For example, see A. Toth, *The Fertility Solution: A Revolutionary Approach to Reversing Infertility* (New York: Atlantic Monthly Press, 1991), 9, http://www.fertilitysolution.com/Fertility-Solution-Book/; Patricia Mendell, "The American Fertility Association's Top Ten Fertility Myths," American Fertility Association, http://www.theafa.org/library/article/the_american_fertility_associations_top_ten_fertility_myths/; and "Infertility Risk Assessment," American Fertility Association, http://www.theafa.org/library/article/infertility_risk_assessment/.

62. www.plasticsurgery.org.

63. Bill Tancer, "The Young and Plastic Surgery Hungry," *Time*, May 7, 2008, http://www.time.com/time/business/article/0,8599,1738111,00.html.

64. Roxanna Sherwood, "Heidi Montag: 'I Wish I Could Go Back to the Original Heidi,'" *ABC News*, November 22, 2010, http://abcnews.go.com/Nightline/video/heidi-montags-plastic-surgery-regrets-12240693.

65. Katharine A. Phillips, "Body Dysmorphic Disorder: Recognizing and Treating Imagined Ugliness," *World Psychiatry Journal* 3, no. 1 (February 2004): 12–17, http://www.ncbi.nlm.nih.gov/pmc/articles/PMC1414653/.

66. Justin S. and Lindsey A. Holcomb, *Rid of My Disgrace* (Wheaton, IL: Crossway, 2011), 32. See R. K. Bergen, *Wife Rape: Understanding the Response of Survivors and Service Providers* (Thousand Oaks, CA: Sage, 1996); D. Finkelhor and K. Yllo, *License to Rape: Sexual Abuse of Wives* (New York: Holt, Rinehart, and Winston, 1985); D. E. H. Russell, *Rape in Marriage* (Indianapolis: Indiana University Press, 1990); and P. Mahoney and L. Williams, "Sexual Assault in Marriage: Prevalence, Consequences and Treatment for Wife Rape," in *Partner Violence: A Comprehensive Review of Twenty Years of Research*, eds. J. Jasinski and L. M. Williams (Thousand Oaks, CA: Sage, 1998).

67. Ibid., 246.

Chapter 11

1. Wayne Cordeiro, *Leading on Empty* (Minneapolis: Bethany House, 2009); Archibald D. Hart, *Adrenaline and Stress* (Nashville: Thomas Nelson, 1995); and Archibald D. Hart, *Unmasking Male Depression* (Nashville: Thomas Nelson, 2001).

2. Cordeiro, *Leading on Empty*.

INDEX

You've read the book.
Now reap the benefits.

Whether a pastor, christian counselor, ministry leader, small group leader, or someone who wants to dig deeper into the message of Real Marriage with your spouse, the Real Marriage curriculum is an invaluable resource.

Developed specifically for couples and small groups by Pastor Brad House of Mars Hill Church, this 11-week curriculum takes the lessons learned in the book and applies them practically to help you transform your marriage—and help others do the same.

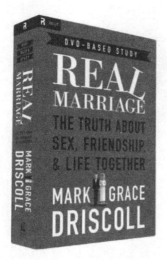

Included in the curriculum:

- A study guide taking you through 11-weeks worth of discussion, insight, and application
- DVDs featuring messages from Pastor Mark and Grace to supplement the book and study guide
- And, for leaders, numerous free materials to help you plan and implement a full campaign around the book in your ministry, including extensive research on sex and marriage and message preparation help

Don't wait another day to begin working on your real marriage—and help others do the same.

For more information, and everything related to Mark and Grace Driscoll, visit PastorMark.tv/realmarriage

 RE:LIT

 Thomas Nelson
Since 1798

RESURGENCE

Over two million leaders served every year

Our mission is to serve leaders, and to help equip you for your God-given mission. How can we serve you?

Each year, millions of leaders trust Resurgence for:

Timely articles: As the highest visited Christian leadership blog, we feature articles from prominent Evangelical leaders addressing the challenges of ministry in a post-Christian society.

Books: Re:lit has published dozens of books to equip leaders on theology and practical ministry.

Events: Resurgence conferences bring together some of the world's top speakers and preachers to transform hearts and minds for ministry action.

Teaching: Podcast and vodcasts feature select talks and lectures from Resurgence events.

Training: Re:train is a master's-level theology center with some of the best professors in the world, as well as practical training for day-to-day ministry from some of the most well-known and respected pastors today.

For more information about Resurgence, visit theResurgence.com

 RESURGENCE

HAVE QUESTIONS?

Pastor Mark has answers.

Pastormark.tv: Culture. Theology. Practice.

Whether you have questions on deep theological issues like the Trinity or practical ministry issues like how to build a winning team—and how to build a great marriage—*pastormark.tv has the answers your looking for.*

Join the millions of visitors who trust Pastor Mark Driscoll for practical and biblical insight on cultural issues, theology and application, leadership and ministry, marriage, and more.

Visit Pastormark.tv today.